Christian Theology after Christendom

Praise for *Christian Theology after Christendom: Engaging the Thought of Douglas John Hall*

"This gathering, of insights and commitments, is an appropriate tribute to one of the most remarkable thinkers in North America today. The chapters in *Christian Theology after Christendom: Engaging the Thought of Douglas John Hall* lay down the markers for the way beyond post Christendom." —**Mary Jo Leddy**, Regis College, Toronto

"With vulnerability, passion, and a keen awareness of our time, the authors in this edited collection strive to understand where we have come from while discerning the ways forward for the Christian movement, especially in North America. Meditating on and inspired by the groundbreaking work of contextual theologian Douglas John Hall, this book traces fresh lines on the rutted ground of theological discourse. Those, like myself, who are within the ministry of the church, will find here compass points which take seriously our own place on the front lines of being church in a time of disestablishment." —**Nicholas Athanasiadis**, minister in the Presbyterian Church (PCC) who has served in several congregations across Canada

Christian Theology after Christendom

Engaging the Thought of Douglas John Hall

Edited by
Patricia G. Kirkpatrick
and Pamela R. McCarroll

Foreword by
Walter Brueggemann

Afterword by
Douglas John Hall

LEXINGTON BOOKS/FORTRESS ACADEMIC
Lanham • Boulder • New York • London

Published by Lexington Books/Fortress Academic
An imprint of The Rowman & Littlefield Publishing Group, Inc.
4501 Forbes Boulevard, Suite 200, Lanham, Maryland 20706
www.rowman.com

6 Tinworth Street, London SE11 5AL, United Kingdom

Copyright © 2021 The Rowman & Littlefield Publishing Group, Inc.

All rights reserved. No part of this book may be reproduced in any form or by any electronic or mechanical means, including information storage and retrieval systems, without written permission from the publisher, except by a reviewer who may quote passages in a review.

British Library Cataloguing in Publication Information Available

Library of Congress Cataloging-in-Publication Data

Names: Kirkpatrick, Patricia G., editor. | McCarroll, Pamela (Pamela R.), editor.
Title: Christian theology after Christendom : engaging the thought of Douglas John Hall / edited by Patricia G. Kirkpatrick, and Pamela R. McCarroll ; foreword by Walter Brueggemann ; afterword by Douglas John Hall.
Description: Lanham : Lexington Books/Fortress Academic, [2020] | Includes bibliographical references and index. | Summary: "Christian Theology after Christendom brings together contemporary thinkers to engage and build upon Douglas John Hall's work-and to take up his challenge to reclaim a contextual and de-colonizing theology of the cross as a means to speak of the realities of life and faith today"—Provided by publisher.
Identifiers: LCCN 2020038412 (print) | LCCN 2020038413 (ebook) | ISBN 9781978706965 (cloth) | ISBN 9781978706989 (pbk) | ISBN 9781978706972 (epub)
Subjects: LCSH: Hall, Douglas John, 1928- | Theology—History. | Theology of the cross.
Classification: LCC BX4827.H244 C47 2020 (print) | LCC BX4827.H244 (ebook) | DDC 232/.4—dc23
LC record available at https://lccn.loc.gov/2020038412
LC ebook record available at https://lccn.loc.gov/2020038413

Contents

Foreword ix
Walter Brueggemann

Introduction and Acknowledgments xiii
Patricia G. Kirkpatrick and Pamela R. McCarroll

1 The Art of Theology: Five Approaches to Curating the Work
   and Thought of Douglas John Hall 1
   David B. Lott

2 Illusion and Hope 15
   Michael Bourgeois

3 Faith and Fragilization: Douglas John Hall and Charles Taylor
   in Dialogue 29
   Andrew Root

4 Contextual Theology in Canada: Between Covenant and Treaty 45
   Allen G. Jorgenson

5 Indian Residential Schools and the Churches: An Exercise in the
   Theology of the Cross 57
   Brian Thorpe

6 Hall's Eco-Theology of the Cross in a Climate-Changed World 69
   Harold Wells

7 What Are People For? Reimaging Theo-anthropology in the
   Anthropocene 85
   Pamela R. McCarroll

8	God and the Church after Christendom: Rethinking "Power" through Douglas Hall's *Theologia Crucis* *Harris Athanasiadis*	101
9	The Relevance of the Theology of Douglas John Hall for the Cuban Context *Adolfo Ham*	117
10	ReWilding the Gospel: Douglas John Hall and Post-Christendom Religious Dialogue *Gary A. Gaudin*	131
11	The Memory of Divine Pathos: Heschel, Hall, and the Hebrew Bible *Patricia G. Kirkpatrick*	143
12	The Gospel of Irresolution: Thinking along with Douglas John Hall About Cross Theology, Illness, and Not Yet Resurrection *Deanna A. Thompson*	153

Afterword: Christian Theology after Christendom—Three Essentials   165
Douglas John Hall

Bibliography   179

Index   187

About the Contributors   193

Douglas John Hall at the November 2019 Symposium in His Honor. *Source*: Photo by Neal McPherson.

Foreword

I am glad to join in this salute to Doug Hall, who by his faith and by his work merits and evokes all of the celebrative commendation that we can muster. The writers of this collection of essays have been thinking well, something Hall himself for a very long time has done exquisitely and faithfully. He is, I am glad to say, my friend and my ongoing tutor. My first sighting of Doug Hall was while we were graduate students together at Union Seminary in the late 1950s. As I recall, I do not think I ever had a conversation with him then. But for all of us graduate students he was the "adult" in the room whom we all admired and wanted to emulate. He was personally well connected to the all-stars on the seminary faculty as we wanted to be. And already then, he exuded a somberness that is sometimes mistaken for melancholy, though his capacity for shrewd discernment has left ample ground for melancholy as well.

My first instruction from him came when I read his book, *Lighten Our Darkness* (1976), which I consider to be his best and most important book. He inducted me into the theology of the cross in a way that awakened me from my dogmatic slumbers. I recently went back to see what I had underlined in his book in my early reading of it. My underlining included his exposition of Luther's theology of the cross and the faithful capacity to "call the thing what it actually is." Of this theme Hall wrote:

> The cross of the world and of man remains after all the Easter sermons have been preached and all the Hallelujahs sung. "Vietnam" has not disappeared. Nor have our own deepest personal involvements in the night. We cannot indulge in expectations of release which are only credible to those who are prepared "to call evil good." The test of expectation is whether it articulates itself from the cross, from the grave, from hell—and knows it! (121)

And then Hall went on to the "Theology of Beggars" and the "Theology of Limits." It turns out that this "Theology of the Cross" is at the center of his intellectual life as the most urgent and most demanding dimension of our faith. This signature accent is now exactly on point for our society, which has lost its way in a theology of glory. I have since then read through Hall book by book as he has taught us how that theology of the cross pertains definitionally to the life of the church and to the life of our society. He has done so with consistent honesty, courage, and gravitas in a way that has made Hall among our most important teachers. I am grateful that he is to this day my teacher.

My friendship with Doug and Rhoda got seriously underway in 2000 when we came together on my campus, Columbia Theological Seminary, for a semester-long seminary with eight leaders of the world church. I was the titular leader of the seminar, but Doug embodied courage, sensibility, good humor, and steadfastness that made our common work generative. The seminar eventuated in our shared book, *Hope for the World: Mission in a Global Context* (2001). The book includes a consensus paper, "Hope from Old Sources for a New Century," that is, primarily Doug's work. He was able to lead us to that consensus because he listened well to the rest of us and evoked from members of the seminar our best thinking and our theological courage. That paper urged the "development of a prophetic consciousness" that can be an antidote to the despair of the world that issues in fear, greed, and violence. It concludes, not surprisingly, with reference to Luther: "The only enduring 'mark of the true church' is the presence in it of the holy cross" (22).

Doug's own essay in that volume is entitled "The Canadian Context." In the essay he identifies four "important differences" in Canada that distinguish it from the United States and qualify the more generic "North American" lumping together. These important differences include "unusual hospitality to diversity," a "strong social consciousness," "a certain typical skepticism," and "an international awareness." It is for good reason that Doug Hall, the Canadian, is an important teacher for the U.S. church! He concludes his essay (with reference to Canadians),

> At least the Christians among us, together with others of (international) good will, ought to do everything in our power to help our country become what it—potentially—is. (38)

A happy by-product of our seminar is that for a season I could engage with Doug and Rhoda in meals, coffee, worship, and much talk.

I have no doubt that when the history of North American theology of this generation is written, Doug Hall will be featured as a major definitive player because of his courage, honesty, and gravitas thoughtfulness coupled with his great learning. I am glad to join his many students, colleagues, and friends in celebrating him for his well-lived as yet unfinished vocation as a transformative educator in the church. Our shared debt to him is very great. Beyond that, we may be grateful to him, and more grateful to God for his great gifts and the wise, generous, generative use he has made of his gifts. And beyond that I am glad to count him as a friend as we both age beyond our working capacity. May he and Rhoda be blessed as they have blessed us! My great love to them!

Walter Brueggemann
Columbia Theological Seminary

Introduction and Acknowledgments
Patricia G. Kirkpatrick and Pamela R. McCarroll

The following pages bring together contemporary thinkers to engage and build upon Douglas John Hall's work—and to take up his challenge to reclaim a contextual and decolonizing theology of the cross as a means to speak of the realities of life and faith today. With a focus on contemporary issues, this collection of essays critically analyzes and deconstructs the centuries-old colonial triumphalism of Christian theology and the church in the West. The volume seeks to frame the present-day crises in ways that honor a deeply rooted *theologia crucis* that does not colonize the "other." It explores constructive decolonizing possibilities for Christian theology at the end of Christendom.

Many "signs of the times" appear to point to the necessity for a radically altered Christian witness. It is not that the theological moorings that are rooted in solid foundations of biblical and theological interpretation are no longer needed. Rather, in each generation, these must come into dialogue with a new set of conversation partners. The Christian witness that can serve this age is one that is sensitive to the immense damage inflicted by Christian colonial triumphalism, and one that is sufficiently profound to uncover the spiritual malaise of our era. It is also a Christian witness capable of engaging with other faith traditions similarly committed to the future of global stability and human civilization. Surely, we are in a time when diverse faith traditions no longer compete for dominance in destructive attempts to define a singular Truth. Rather, we are now positioned to create a vision that can accommodate many and varied particularities. In other words, we are now positioned to find a language sufficient for our multiplicity, and able, by adopting a "fractal view of religious diversity," as Perry Schmidt-Leukel suggests, to speak compellingly to different contexts, different particularities (Gifford Lectures, 2017). Whatever the future might hold, it is clear that the thinking of the church must alter if it is to serve the world and the communities it represents in ways that steward and honor life in all its fullness and diversity.

Christianity, in its dominant Western forms, has conceived of its mission and theology in inherently imperialistic and colonizing terms, sometimes explicitly, sometimes modified by the rhetoric of worldly concern. This colonizing Christianity, manifested in various expressions of Christendom, has been called the "theology of glory" by Martin Luther. Some, including Douglas John Hall, have argued persuasively that the theology of glory is behind all Western paradigms of domination that have colonized peoples, lands, and thought considered to be outside a Western patriarchal norm. The construction of divine power embedded within this theology has justified the domination of the church over all other faiths, institutions, and cultures outside the Western world. Not only does such theology justify oppressive relations over others; it also minimizes and ignores the humiliation, suffering, and rejection of Jesus, while also undermining the witness of the scriptures. This witness in fact points to a powerless, marginalized, and persecuted church—a church challenged to embody power and express its hope in ways that counter the colonizing domination of empire; a church that stands in solidarity with those who are powerless, marginalized, and oppressed.

The demise of Christendom offers Christians a chance to assess this centuries-old colonial triumphalism critically, and to open themselves to radically different possibilities for being church and thinking the faith through the theology of the cross. Though coined by Luther, the theology of the cross was not Luther's invention but the recovery of a theme recurrent throughout the scriptures. It is a theological lens and way of being that is evident as early as the prophetic books, and that is present in monastic, mystical, and other theological alternatives to colonizing Christendom. As a "key signature" (as Hall would say), or approach, the theology of the cross offers profound resources for inspiring renewed understandings of theology and life upon which the church might base its hope for a future *beyond Christendom.*

Douglas John Hall has been one of the most influential Protestant theologians in North America through the latter half of the twentieth and into the twenty-first century. His writings on the contextual theology of the cross, the post-Christendom church, stewardship, and ecology, and his incisive analyses of North American contexts have opened up new trajectories of thought and practice in theology and the church. We believe that his holistic integration of *theologia crucis* into the contextualization of theology offers a profound challenge and invitation for theology after Christendom. In this volume, we build upon his work as we consider together what decolonizing theology and faith through a theology of the cross might offer for the living of these days.

This collection of essays draws together Christian theologians and scholars from North America and beyond to think together through the lens of the *theologia crucis* about life, the earth, being human, and being church today in a precarious and complicated world. It presents the theology of the cross as a decolonizing approach that opens up space to reorient Christian thought in life-giving and generative ways. These essays recontextualize the theology of the cross to address contemporary concerns. The essays focus on a range of issues of pressing concern, including injustice against indigenous peoples, the climate crisis, politics, secularity, issues of power and vulnerability, the decline of the church, suffering, and spirituality. While some essays focus on deconstructing the colonial theologies of glory that lead to systemic injustice, all essays include constructive moves to reimagine possibilities for theology today in a post-Christendom world. This collection is for anyone interested in a contextual theology of the cross and in ways faith seeks understanding in contexts where nothing seems inevitable and where the church faces drastic decline. We believe this collection makes an essential contribution to theology for the church today as it explores the implications of post-Christendom decolonizing thought and practice today in North American contexts.

The gathering of voices represented in this volume reflects the concerns of contextual theologians of the cross for today. Each seeks to speak to the church, to the academy, and to the larger public caught in the intellectual, spiritual, and organizational structures of Christendom. We are delighted to include a foreword by Walter Brueggemann, Old Testament scholar, public intellectual, and dear friend of Douglas Hall. The collection concludes with a substantial afterword, written by Hall, which provides his own reflections on theology over the last several decades.

The chapters within this book focus on one or more themes that run through Hall's work and explore how Hall's insights may be brought to bear on theology and church today. David's Lott's essay along with that of Michael Bourgeois provide the reader with substantial insights into the many and varied themes Hall has broached throughout his work. Andrew Root, Allen Jorgenson and Brian Thorpe focus specifically on various Canadian contexts—the latter two focusing on the church's involvement in the cultural genocide of indigenous peoples. Harold Wells and Pamela McCarroll engage dimensions of the environmental crisis and explore pathways forward through theology and practice. Harris Athanasiadis, Adolfo Ham and Gary Gaudin write poignantly on the post-Christendom church through the lens and influence of Hall's theology. Patricia Kirkpatrick brings Hall's interfaith engagement to the fore in a discussion of Abraham Joshua Heschel's understanding of God's divine Pathos and its influence on Hall's theological perspective. Finally, in a powerful essay Deanna Thompson, a theologian living with incurable cancer, in dialogue with Hall delves into the meaning of the cross and resurrection, offering a gospel of irresolution—a gospel sorely needed in the face of the uncertainty and fragility of being.

We are grateful to have engaged with most of the authors as they presented their papers at a Colloquium in honor of Douglas John Hall, held at McGill University, November 1–3, 2019. This event was generously cosponsored by McGill University, Emmanuel College, and Victoria University. The Colloquium was an inspiring event on all counts and we are grateful for substantial, thoughtful engagement in "theology that matters," as one person described it. We are indebted to the United Theological College and its interim principal Maylanne Maybee for their hospitality and leadership in worship and to Amanda Rosini for her organizational prowess. Also, our sincere gratitude is extended to Professor D. R. Runnalls, dean of the former faculty of Religious Studies at McGill, for her generous contribution toward the running costs of the Colloquium.

We gratefully acknowledge the substantial support we have received for this book project from many institutions and individuals. First, we are grateful to our institutions, Emmanuel College of Victoria University and McGill University, and particularly to Principal Michelle Voss Roberts and Director Garth Green who have supported this project throughout. We are grateful for the generous financial support from Emmanuel College through the Academic Initiatives Research Grant fund that enabled the volume to be completed in a timely manner. We are enormously grateful to Rev. Dr. Kay Diviney for her insightful, and gracious, editorial engagement in preparing the volume for submission. Also, we are grateful to the United Church of Canada and Anglican Church of Canada for their ongoing encouragement and support for the project. Finally, we are grateful to all the authors who so enthusiastically have offered the work of their hearts, minds, and hands to this project, and who have been a delight to work with and to get to know.

Chapter 1

The Art of Theology

Five Approaches to Curating the Work and Thought of Douglas John Hall

David B. Lott

One of the joys and privileges of living on Capitol Hill in Washington, DC, is the easy access it provides me to the city's world-class museums and art galleries. When I step out my front door, within a half hour I can walk to the National Gallery of Art or to many of the Smithsonian museums on the National Mall. Because of this, over the past twenty years I have gotten to take in countless priceless artifacts and artistic masterpieces—all for free!—and develop my knowledge of the world of art. Part of this learning has to do with observing how the curators of these exhibitions do their behind-the-scenes work. Curators don't simply gather a group of artworks from a single artist, genre, or time period, and then arrange them randomly. Rather, at their best, they help viewers to see what is before them by designing exhibitions that reveal something that might otherwise remain hidden to the untrained eye, without being obvious or manipulative in their efforts. How curators arrange these artworks relative to one another, in order to show unexpected qualities and affinities, can shape or change one's perspective on what they are viewing. In so doing, curators attempt to tell stories, illustrate themes, and reveal the times within which the artists lived, and perhaps tell us something about our time as well.

Consider two recent examples from the National Gallery in Washington. The first ever North American retrospective of the Venetian Renaissance master painter Jacopo Tintoretto[1] was in many ways a textbook example of a single-artist survey, in that it took viewers on a more or less biographical journey through the artist's lifeworks. Entering the exhibition, one was immediately met by Tintoretto's self-portrait, in which he depicted himself as a bright youth on the cusp of a brilliant career of artistic discovery.[2] Just before leaving the exhibition, one encountered another self-portrait, this one a sage-like old man not long from death.[3] Such framing allowed viewers to appreciate how Tintoretto's talents had deepened and darkened over time. By contrast, a delightful exhibition on "The Life of Animals in Japanese Art" covered over seventeen centuries of art pieces focused on a single topic, expressed through a variety of genres and forms.[4] By placing the ninth-century folding screens depicting, say, foxes, alongside sixteenth-century paintings and twentieth-century sculptural representations of the same animal, the curators demonstrated the persistence of animals in the Japanese imagination, even as the context of time and genre changed. The contrasting import of these two exhibitions suggests that any exhibition, whether of art or artifacts, is never strictly objective in its presentation. Each offers its curator's vision.

Studying the art of the museum curator can change our ideas of what it means to present an overview of any individual with a tangible lifework, whether that be composed of art, of music, of books, or even of theology. There is no single best way to do that, though some ways work better than others, depending on what one wishes to convey through that overview. Anyone who has ever attempted to assemble a collection of essays by one or multiple authors knows that editors often function as curators. The difference between a collection that is simply an uneven hodgepodge of articles tossed together and one that has been actually *curated*—that is, assembled with care for flow, quality, and adherence to a theme—is palpable to the reader. So, to present an overview of the work of Douglas John Hall, I want to exercise my prerogative as his one-time editor by suggesting and critiquing five approaches that one might take to "curating" his thought as presented in his two dozen books. In so doing, I hope to provide a taxonomy for examining his lifework that allows insights one might not get simply by taking a single approach—and that also provides a springboard for reflecting further on his oeuvre and main theological concerns.

CHRONOLOGICAL APPROACHES

The most common approach taken in an overview of any subject is based in their biography or history, what one might call a *chronological approach*. Starting from the beginning of or from a defined point in a person's life or career, one follows the subject's work and development up to another, later point—possibly even beyond death, if there is posthumous work or if one wants to examine the individual's reputation. This was the approach of the Tintoretto exhibition. A chronological approach that considers a full lifespan does more than present a life-in-full. It can also assure that vital context is provided throughout. Focusing on a single moment or period in a person's lifework, without taking into account of what brought them to that stage of development or achievement, may distort the meaning or significance of their work. On the other hand, the advantage of examining a well-defined, limited period within a person's life or career is that it may render a more finely honed picture of how an individual affected, and was affected by, salient events.

Hall has given us some of that necessary context in his lovely retrospective volume *Bound and Free: A Theologian's Journey* (2005),[5] which is an invaluable document for addressing my question "What would it mean to do a chronological overview of the work of Douglas John Hall?" Strictly speaking, it would mean starting with 1971's *Hope against Hope*[6] and working through his two dozen books up to his final masterpiece, 2013's *What Christianity Is* Not.[7] However, a chronological analysis of Hall's work assumes that the development of his thought is easily traced, that A leads to B, which leads to C, and so on. I would argue that this type of chronological sequencing of theological development is not easily discernible in Hall's work. As I wrote in the introduction to the *Collected Readings*:

> Although one does not detect great shifts in his thought over the years, his books do demonstrate how his key concerns adapt specifically to the events, movements, and cultural circumstances contemporaneous with the time of their writing. For instance, in *Lighten Our Darkness*, written in the mid-1970s, he examines the theology of the cross in the light of Watergate, Vietnam, nuclear threats, and the communist bloc. Later, in *The Cross in Our Context* (2003), Hall analyzes the theology of the cross in light of the 9/11 terrorist attacks, the Iraq and Afghanistan wars, American imperialism, the collapse of the communist state, and the climate crisis. Both books offer a common understanding of the cruciform nature of Christian existence, but one refracted through a changing context.[8]

I do not mean to imply that his work is somehow static, but rather that the Douglas John Hall that we meet in his early books was remarkably fully formed in his thinking. In his *Christian Century* article from 2010, "Cross and Context: How My Mind Has Changed," we see that much of the change he chronicles occurred largely before his publishing career began in earnest.[9] Because his theological method is grounded so strongly in context, the major changes that one can see in his work over the years have to do more with that very difference in context. Over time, Hall becomes an increasingly *better* contextual theologian. His voice grows stronger in its passion and clarity, but the underlying thought remains very consistent and increasingly accessible. I think that—unlike someone like Jürgen Moltmann, who has a distinct progression in his volumes of systematic thought[10]—moving chronologically through Hall's catalog does not produce any striking revelations or particular insight into his work.

A second problem with this chronological approach is that some of Hall's early books do not hold up well for contemporary audiences, precisely because of that contextual method. Yes, the theology of the cross presented in *Lighten Our Darkness* is as prescient and clear as it was when first published in 1976.[11] It abides as a core statement not only for all of Hall's work but for all of the literature on this "never much loved" and "thin tradition." Hall writes in his preface to the 2001 revised edition, "*Lighten Our Darkness* has been the programmatic statement of every subsequent theological work of mine, as anyone will easily recognize who peruses it in light of my trilogy, the three books on the theology of stewardship, the various studies of Christendom and the Christian future, *God and Human Suffering*, and so forth."[12] But even in this updated and gender-inclusive edition, the book as a whole feels like a bit of an artifact, not fully suited to the hic et nunc. The once-familiar social commentators he references, like Karl Menninger, Kurt Vonnegut, and Lynn White, hold limited meaning for those who did not live through the 1970s. Indeed, they underscore how the observations of white males dominated this period when the "Death of God" was still a hot topic in public theology, and when being a public theologian still seemed possible. But like his reflections on technology, race, political divides, and other cultural references, now such discussion frankly feels quaint and dated. In short, *Lighten Our Darkness* is perhaps not the best place for new readers to start a Douglas John Hall inquiry, as they may well feel bogged down in what now seem like cultural anachronisms.

I would suggest that one might instead take a more or less *reverse chronological approach* to reading through Hall's oeuvre. Start with *What Christianity Is Not*, which Professor Hall told me personally, more than any of his books, says exactly what he wants it to say. Then I would read the essays in *Waiting for Gospel*,[13] which lay out many of his major theological concerns in terms and contexts that are accessible to the twenty-first-century readers. Next, tackle *The Cross in Our Context*[14] for a strong summation of how the theology of the cross informs the major themes of Christian theology, then work your way through the *Christian Theology in a North American Context* trilogy from beginning to end.[15] Move on to *God and Human Suffering*, which explores the theology of the cross relative to a timeless theme of theodicy.[16] From there, I think that *Lighten Our Darkness* becomes a far more meaningful work, and one can see more clearly my sense that the development of Hall's work over time is much more about the context in which it appears than about evolutionary or fundamental changes in thinking.

EVALUATIVE APPROACHES

A second way to "curate" a person's lifework is what I label the *evaluative approach*. Here, the curator determines what should be regarded as the best, or most important, or most influential works. Of course, in so doing, other works are implicitly deemed less significant or worthy of attention. In popular music, this might take the form of the "Best of" or "Greatest Hits" collection. This sort of approach is irresistible in Internet culture on websites such as Buzzfeed, which feature opinionated rankings of the best work of musicians, actors, filmmakers, and sports stars. Who is the greatest of all time? What work is overrated? This often takes the form of what has been given the neologism of "listicle"—an article that is essentially a ranked list, with a title that is "click bait," designed to whet your interest so you will "click" on it. So, on Buzzfeed you might see a link to a piece titled "We Rank All of Douglas John Hall's Books, and You Won't Believe What's Number 1!!!" (You know you'd click on that, and then argue with it ferociously.)

It's more likely, however, that the serious curator would try to identify a core canon in the person's lifework—a set of works that they assume would find common agreement among most experts. So, let me suggest eight of Hall's books that might form his core canon: *Lighten Our Darkness*; *The Steward*;[17] *God and Human Suffering*; the *Christian Theology in a North American Context* trilogy; *The Cross in Our Context*; and *What Christianity Is Not*. Surely some reading this are thinking, "But what about . . . ?" or "Why'd you include *that*?" Some might want to add or subtract from this list, or create a list of additional titles that comprise an important sub-canon. But certainly, we could all agree that those eight books would be a formidable core canon for any theologian.

The work of the curator must always have an evaluative dimension. But when one adheres too closely to the evaluative approach, focusing on what is essential or best known, other, not insignificant, questions are slighted or omitted. In my list, for instance, you don't see any book specifically focused on Hall's work on disestablishment, a major omission.

THEMATIC APPROACHES

This brings me to a third method: the *thematic approach*. "The Life of Animals in Japanese Art" at the National Gallery of Art is an example of a thematically designed exhibition. As I noted, much of its power came from covering nearly seventeen centuries and a variety of art forms. One can easily imagine a more focused show, concentrating on, say, Japanese animal art of the Edo period, or on tigers in the Japanese artistic imagination, or on animal-oriented Japanese folding screens and tapestries. Any of those might be valid curatorial approaches that could concentrate the viewers' understanding, but they would lack the imaginative breadth of this more expansive show.

In the writings of Douglas John Hall, one can identify three core themes: (1) the theology of the cross, (2) stewardship, and (3) Christian disestablishment and the future of the church. Yes, there are other themes, but most of them overlap in one way or another with one or more of these three. Roughly half of his books could be directly categorized under at least one of these three core concerns. The problem here, again, is what gets left out when thematic categories are too strictly adhered to or treated as definitive. Any number of Hall's books, such as his more biographical volumes,[18] don't easily fit under any one of these themes. The *Christian Theology in North America* trilogy seems to occupy a category unto itself as well, even though it addresses all of these core concerns.

Focusing exclusively on any one of those themes is a valid and important option in accessing particular dimensions of Hall's lifework. But what if one category comes to overshadow the others? Surely Hall's books on stewardship[19] are important to our understanding of his lifework, but I think few would place them at his legacy's center, or privilege them over his work on the theology of the cross or the future of the church. Another problem you may see here, and in the chronological and evaluative approaches, is that they do not account at all for Hall's many uncollected essays, lectures, interviews, and other archival materials; they privilege only his published books. As a result, much valuable material goes missing from our perspectives. The thematic approach is essential for exploring either the breadth of a person's work or for examining one aspect in depth, but it rarely does both well. Like the evaluative approach, its pitfalls suggest that it be used carefully if we wish to get a better sense of Hall's work.

DECONTEXTUAL APPROACHES

Let me suggest two other approaches to Hall's work that I think hold more promise in considering his legacy and how it might be carried into the future. The first I call, somewhat ironically, the *decontextual approach*. This is more or less the tack I took in the *Collected Readings* volume. When Fortress Press commissioned me to compile that collection, they restricted me to drawing only from the ten Hall books for which the publishing house held copyright, which put fourteen titles off-limits.[20] As the "core canon" I proposed above suggests, any compendium of Hall's work that does not include anything from *Lighten Our Darkness*, *The Steward*, or *What Christianity Is Not* can hardly be considered comprehensive, much less definitive. But the Fortress books nevertheless constitute a solid core of his work from which to gather an authoritative collection. My question then became, How to do that? How to be the curator of this work?

First, I read through nearly all of his books, not just the Fortress titles, in order to familiarize myself with the whole of his thought—the *biographical approach*. Then I selected about two dozen excerpts from the Fortress books that I felt were representative of his work and that, with some introductory context added, stood well enough on their own—the *evaluative approach*. From there, however, it was clear that I could not simply put the selections in chronological order and call it a manuscript; doing so would make a hash of Hall's thought. So, I read and sorted the pieces many times over, culling them to sixteen excerpts that I felt illustrated the contextual method that Hall expounds upon at length in *Thinking the Faith*—the *thematic approach*. I created a thesis in which I argue that his contextual method is his most distinctive contribution to contemporary theology and used those selections to demonstrate how that method has undergirded his writings on the theology of the cross and Christian disestablishment. I asserted that while the theology of the cross is certainly the hermeneutic that informs all his work from the very beginning, *Thinking the Faith* is the true pivotal book in his oeuvre for how it illustrates the contextual method underlying his other works.[21] The method and themes are inseparable; one can't discuss his work on theology of the cross or stewardship with any authority without engaging his contextual method.

The *Collected Readings* volume serves not necessarily as an exemplar but as one example of how scholars might curate Hall's work going forward, especially if it is to be kept alive in the classrooms and churches. Acting as curators to *de*contextualize and *re*contextualize the work of this contextual theologian, we may find new internal affinities within his oeuvre. Certain individual volumes will surely have longer lives in print than others or have shifting valuations according to changing contexts. But the fates of individual volumes should not be our main concern or stop us from digging deep into his work to decontextualize pieces from those books that can stand well on their own, set them in a new order, and relate them to changing contexts and other voices. This, I think, represents the best chance for Hall's work to live on in the ecosystem of church, academy, and print media.

For instance, a section from *Confessing the Faith*, "The Ethic of Resistance and the Ethic of Responsibility," is a vital theological resource for Christians calling one another to resistance since the 2016 U.S. presidential election.[22] Of resistance, Hall writes, "Protestantism is not only a protest against doctrine put forward as final truth, it is also a protest against power masquerading as ultimate. In the name of the Ultimate, Protestantism resists the contingent, finite, and penultimate that pretends to ultimacy."[23] Yet he also reminds us that we dare not neglect "the worldly responsibility that discipleship of the Christ entails."[24] This could hardly be a more perfect call to faithfully confront the devastation that is occurring even now in our world. Surely there are many other pieces of Hall's work that could be assembled to be a wholly relevant volume of political, ethical theology in the age of Trump. His broader work on stewardship, not just from those three 1980s volumes, deserves to be rediscovered and recontextualized to address the climate crisis and the role Christians have as "stewards of the mysteries of God" (1 Cor. 4:1, RSV).[25] A hardy soul might attempt to condense parts of the trilogy into a concise systematics. The materials are there before us—not just in his books but also in those many articles, lectures, and archival papers. Who will take up the challenge of re-presenting and recontextualizing them for current and future generations?

CONVERSATIONAL APPROACHES

For my final approach, let me take you back to the National Gallery of Art. November 9, 2016. The city of Washington was in a gloomy haze, not just because of the cold drizzle and mist that had shrouded the city, but also because of the unwelcome shock of Donald Trump's election to the U.S. presidency. In my own fog of bewilderment, I decided to walk down to the National Gallery of Art, hoping that taking in some objects of beauty might help counter the ugliness of this man's persona and politics that would surely mark the next four years and which had already unmade social and political norms. Every car and person I passed appeared to be moving a bit more slowly; the streets were markedly quieter than on a usual weekday. The few conversations I heard felt like unwelcome disruptions in a city alone in its thoughts and apprehensions.

The first room I entered features a group of around a dozen paintings by the abstract expressionist Mark Rothko.[26] His classic works after 1949 feature unevenly painted blocks of color set above and below, or within, one another, expressing inchoate emotions that the painter does not define for the viewer, but surely represent the unsettled state of his mind, with which he lived until his suicide in 1970. Being and nonbeing sit alongside one another in his paintings. They never settle into any one, certain thing.

Adjoining the Rothko room is a collection of fourteen abstract paintings called "The Stations of the Cross" by Rothko's contemporary in abstract expressionism, Barnett Newman.[27] These are not representational art. In none of them does a cross or any human form appear, nor were they originally conceived under this rubric of the stations. Instead, most of them are raw canvases covered with off-white paint, with irregularly placed bars or gash-like lines of black or gray extending from top to bottom. Newman, who was Jewish, was reaching here for a new kind of spirituality in art that was not specifically religious. You won't find a glittering Christ of glory here, or the premonition of a triumphant resurrection, or even a transubstantiation. They simply invite our contemplation.

Crossing a rooftop plaza, one finds a room filled with a collection of mobiles and stabiles by Alexander Calder.[28] As much as these sculptural works can delight and uplift the viewer in their physical forms, just as compelling are the shadows produced by these pieces as the mobiles move and the light hits them from different angles. The eye is directed to look not just at what is physically before it, but at those elusive shadows, that which disappears when the light is removed. In all of these, we see the very ideas that Hall is trying to convey in *Lighten Our Darkness* and many other works. The theology of the cross may be grounded in Christian history, but it is not exclusively a Christian possession. It is made possible by the very fact that it is in the world, in the same way that humans are also subject to change and finitude, sometimes in the most painful of ways.

Such works of art are not just a tonic in our current Trumpian world of artificial, tacky, gilded glory. They are among the many cultural genres and forms I believe we must engage in relation to Hall's work, and to the work of other theologians, in order to know the theology of the cross as indigenous not just to North America but to the world. One criticism that some have addressed to Hall is that the voices of too-often silenced peoples—North American women, persons of color, and others—though hardly absent from his published work, lack prominence. On the one hand, this reticence reflects a genuine and admirable modesty on Hall's part: he refuses to co-opt the voices of these others or substitute his words for theirs. On the other hand, the center of theological preoccupation has shifted: Hall's early struggle with the dominant power of Christian Protestant neoorthodoxy, while not entirely absent from our time, is not the primary struggle of twenty-first-century theologians. We are increasingly called to recognize and even privilege those other voices, both here in North America and globally. Our conversations are more and more pluralistic in terms of gender, sexuality, race, ethnicity, and religion. This is why I call for a *conversational approach* to his work, one in which we seek out and attune ourselves to its external affinities that are abundant and embodied in the world, if we will only look for and hear and see them. We must not be the sorts of curators who talk only to or among ourselves. Rather, we must be willing to go out and find those places where the theology of the cross is being embodied in our world, not just by those who name themselves Christian or by certain types of Christians.

The U.S. philosopher and theologian John Caputo, in his brilliant new book *Cross and Cosmos: A Theology of Difficult Glory*, has created what I believe is the most bracing account of the theology of the cross we have seen from anyone since, well, Douglas John Hall.[29] Caputo, perhaps more than anyone to date, pushes the theology of the cross to its most radical edges, showing it to be, at heart, a primary exemplar of the "weak theology" that he has advocated in his many books. While taking the work of Martin Luther and other historical figures utterly seriously, he pushes the reader outside the too-easy confines of traditional Christianity, not least in its ecclesial forms and into the world. Even more important, he engages the work of African American theologians Delores Williams and James Cone to broaden the conversation about the theology of the cross to include the too-often excluded voices. Caputo's book energizes our discussion of the theology of the cross in ways few recent works have. It is thrilling, difficult, and essential work.

Yet it is not just visual artists and theological interlocutors that we must engage to advance our understanding of the theology of the cross in our current context. We can also look to filmmakers, musicians, novelists, and others engaged in cultural endeavors to find its echoes in our midst. The so-called film archaeologist Bill Morrison, in such films as *Dawson City: Open Time* and *The Great Flood*, draws on archival materials and found footage, often severely damaged by time, water, and other elements, to create bracing, avant-garde documentaries.[30] His films press the viewer to stare directly at that very damage which others would dismiss, to recognize both its own singular beauty and the fleeting glimpses of the world the original makers were trying to capture before those images were lost to nature and neglect.

One can hear echoes of the theology of the cross in the works of such contemporary musicians as Leonard Cohen, Nick Cave, Rosanne Cash, and Kendrick Lamar, all of whom invite listeners to ponder and embrace themes of loss, finitude, and a search for, well, a light in the darkness. Even a TV sitcom like NBC's "The Good Place" engages classic philosophical ideas within a quasi-afterlife to explore what it means to be human, and the elusive goal of being "good." All these remind us of how the darkness is not just outside ourselves, but also within.

And we may turn to fiction as well, in works from diverse writers like Colson Whitehead, Louise Erdrich, Esi Edugyan, and Valeria Lusielli, who call us to find solidarity with the broken and oppressed, to help them claim the power too often denied them in the real world. Viet Thanh Nguyen, in his Pulitzer-Prize-winning novel, *The Sympathizer*, explores how human beings are capable simultaneously of great good and great evil, embodying Luther's notion of *simul iustus et peccator*. I conclude with the final words of his novel, spoken in the voice of a Vietnamese political prisoner who, after a harrowing journey between the United States and his native land, finds himself at sea with a group of boat people, which capture well the "difficult glory" that both Hall and Caputo describe:

> But we are not primitives, and we are not to be pitied. If and when we reach safe harbor, it will hardly be a surprise if we, in turn, turn our backs on the unwanted, human nature being what we know of it. Yet we are not cynical. Despite it all—yes, despite everything, in the face of *nothing*—we still consider ourselves revolutionary. We remain that most hopeful of creatures, a revolutionary in search of a revolution, although we will not dispute being called a dreamer duped by an illusion. Soon enough we see the scarlet sunrise on that horizon where the East is always red, but for now our view through our window is a dark alley, the pavement barren, the curtains closed. Surely we cannot be the only ones awake, even if we are the only ones with a single lamp lit. No, we cannot be alone! Thousands more must be staring into the darkness like us, gripped by scandalous thoughts, extravagant hopes, and forbidden plots. We lie in wait for the right moment and the just cause, which, at this moment, is simply wanting to live. And even as we write this final sentence, the sentence that will not be revised, we confess to being certain of one and only one thing—we swear to keep, on penalty of death, this one promise:
> *We will live!*[31]

NOTES

1. For examples of Tintoretto's work, go to https://www.nga.gov/exhibitions/2019/tintoretto-the-artist-of-venice-at-500.html.

2. https://collections.vam.ac.uk/item/O80701/self-portrait-as-a-young-oil-painting-tintoretto-jacopo/.

3. https://www.nga.gov/exhibitions/2019/tintoretto-the-artist-of-venice-at-500.html.

4. Samples from this exhibition may be found at https://www.nga.gov/exhibitions/2019/life-of-animals-in-japanese-art.html.

5. Douglas John Hall, *Bound and Free: A Theologian's Journey* (Minneapolis, MN: Fortress Press, 2005).

6. Douglas John Hall, *Hope against Hope: Towards an Indigenous Theology of the Cross* (Tokyo: World Student Christian Federation, 1971).

7. Douglas John Hall, *What Christianity Is Not: An Exercise in "Negative" Theology* (Eugene, OR: Cascade Books, 2013). This linear approach is more or less what I took in writing my introduction to David B. Lott, ed., *Douglas John Hall: Collected Readings* (Minneapolis, MN: Fortress Press, 2013).

8. David B. Lott, "Introduction," in *Douglas John Hall: Collected Readings*, ed. Lott.

9. Douglas John Hall, "Cross and Context: How My Mind Has Changed," *The Christian Century* 127, no. 18 (September 7, 2010), https://www.christiancentury.org/article/2010-08/cross-and-context.

10. See, for example, Margaret Kohl, ed., *Jürgen Moltmann: Collected Readings* (Minneapolis, MN: Fortress Press, 2014). In compiling David B. Lott, ed., *Sallie McFague: Collected Readings* (Minneapolis, MN: Fortress Press, 2013), I took a somewhat modified chronological approach.

11. Douglas John Hall, *Lighten Our Darkness: Towards an Indigenous Theology of the Cross* (Philadelphia, PA: Westminster, 1976).

12. Douglas John Hall, "Preface to the Revised Edition," in *Lighten Our Darkness: Towards an Indigenous Theology of the Cross*, xix, revised edition, revised and with a foreword by David J. Monge (Lima, OH: Academic Renewal Press, 2001).

13. Douglas John Hall, *Waiting for Gospel: An Appeal to the Dispirited Remnants of Protestant Establishment* (Eugene, OR: Cascade Books, 2012).

14. Douglas John Hall, *The Cross in Our Context: Jesus and the Suffering World* (Minneapolis, MN: Fortress Press, 2003).

15. Douglas John Hall, *Thinking the Faith: Christian Theology in a North American Context* (Minneapolis, MN: Augsburg, 1989; paperback reprint: Minneapolis: Fortress Press, 1991); *Professing the Faith: Christian Theology in a North American Context* (Minneapolis, MN: Fortress Press, 1993); and *Confessing the Faith: Christian Theology in a North American Context* (Minneapolis, MN: Fortress Press, 1996).

16. Douglas John Hall, *God and Human Suffering: An Exercise in the Theology of the Cross* (Minneapolis, MN: Augsburg, 1986).

17. Douglas John Hall, *The Steward: A Biblical Symbol Come of Age* (New York: Friendship Press, 1982; revised edition, Grand Rapids, MI: Eerdmans; New York: Friendship Press, 1990; rpt., Eugene, OR: Wipf & Stock, 2004).

18. For instance, Douglas John Hall, *Bound and Free: A Theologian's Journey*; and *The Messenger: Friendship, Faith, and Finding One's Way* (Eugene, OR: Cascade Books, 2011).

19. In addition to *The Steward*, these include *The Stewardship of Life in the Kingdom of Death* (New York: Friendship Press, 1985; revised edition, Grand Rapids, MI: Eerdmans, 1986) and *Imaging God: Dominion as Stewardship* (Grand Rapids, MI: Eerdmans; New York: Friendship Press, 1986; reprint, Eugene, OR: Wipf & Stock, 2004).

20. This list includes eight books originally published by either Augsburg Books or Fortress Press, and two titles for which Fortress Press acquired the rights and republished.

21. Hall frequently quotes Jürgen Moltmann in calling the theology of the cross as the "key signature" of all Christian theology. See David B. Lott, "Introduction," in *Douglas John Hall: Collected Readings*, ed., Lott, 1–9, esp. p. 5.

22. Douglas John Hall, "The Ethic of Resistance and the Ethic of Responsibility," in *Confessing the Faith*, 332–40; see also chapter 15 in David B. Lott, ed., *Douglas John Hall: Collected Readings*, 227–36.

23. Douglas John Hall, "The Ethic of Resistance and the Ethic of Responsibility," in *Confessing the Faith*, 333; see also chapter 15 in David B. Lott, editor, *Douglas John Hall: Collected Readings*, 229.

24. Douglas John Hall, "The Ethic of Resistance and the Ethic of Responsibility," in *Confessing the Faith*, 336; see also chapter 15 in David B. Lott, ed., *Douglas John Hall: Collected Readings*, 232.

25. Hall uses this phrase frequently in his work, including as the title of chapter 3 of *Bound and Free: A Theologian's Journey*, 106–21; see also chapter 16 in David B. Lott, ed., *Douglas John Hall: Collected Readings*, 237–51.

26. For examples of Rothko's classic work cited here, go to https://www.nga.gov/features/mark-rothko/mark-rothko-classic-paintings.html.

27. The paintings in Newman's "Stations of the Cross" exhibition may be viewed here: https://www.nga.gov/collection/locationview.69377.html?room=ET-615-B&ngaObjectId=69377&sortOrder=LOCATIONVIEW_DEFAULT&pageNumber=1.

28. Examples of Calder's work in this gallery may be viewed at https://www.nga.gov/features/tower-2-alexander-calder.html.

29. John D. Caputo, *Cross and Cosmos: A Theology of Difficult Glory*, Indiana Series in the Philosophy of Religion, ed. Merold Westphal (Bloomington, IN: Indiana University Press, 2019).

30. For more information on the films of Bill Morrison, go to https://billmorrisonfilm.com/.

31. Viet Thanh Nguyen, *The Sympathizer* (New York: Grove Atlantic, 2015), 382.

WORKS CITED

Caputo, John D. *Cross and Cosmos: A Theology of Difficult Glory*. Indiana Series in the Philosophy of Religion. Ed. Merold Westphal. Bloomington, IN: Indiana University Press, 2019.

Hall, Douglas John. *Bound and Free: A Theologian's Journey*. Minneapolis, MN: Fortress Press, 2005.

———. *Confessing the Faith: Christian Theology in a North American Context*. Minneapolis, MN: Fortress Press, 1996.

———. "Cross and Context: How My Mind Has Changed." *The Christian Century* 127, no. 18 (September 7, 2010). https://www.christiancentury.org/article/2010-08/cross-and-context.

———. *The Cross in Our Context: Jesus and the Suffering World*. Minneapolis, MN: Fortress Press, 2003.

———. "The Ethic of Resistance and the Ethic of Responsibility." In *Confessing the Faith: Christian Theology in a North American Context*, 332–40. Minneapolis, MN: Fortress Press, 1996. Reprinted in *Douglas John Hall: Collected Readings*, ed. David B. Lott, chap. 15. Minneapolis, MN: Fortress Press, 2013.

———. *God and Human Suffering: An Exercise in the Theology of the Cross*. Minneapolis, MN: Augsburg, 1986.

———. *Hope against Hope: Towards an Indigenous Theology of the Cross*. Tokyo: World Student Christian Federation, 1971.

———. *Imaging God: Dominion as Stewardship*. Grand Rapids, MI: Eerdmans; New York: Friendship Press, 1986. Reprint: Eugene, OR: Wipf and Stock, 2004.

———. *Lighten Our Darkness: Towards an Indigenous Theology of the Cross*. Philadelphia, PA: Westminster, 1976. Revised edition, foreword by David J. Monge, ed. Lima, OH: Academic Renewal Press, 2001.

———. *The Messenger: Friendship, Faith, and Finding One's Way*. Eugene, OR: Cascade Books, 2011.

———. *Professing the Faith: Christian Theology in a North American Context*. Minneapolis, MN: Fortress Press, 1993.

———. *The Steward: A Biblical Symbol Come of Age*. New York: Friendship Press, 1982. Revised edition, Grand Rapids, MI: Eerdmans; New York: Friendship Press, 1990. Reprint, Eugene, OR: Wipf and Stock, 2004.

———. *The Stewardship of Life in the Kingdom of Death*. New York: Friendship Press, 1985. Revised edition, Grand Rapids, MI: Eerdmans, 1986.

———. *Thinking the Faith: Christian Theology in a North American Context*. Minneapolis, MN: Augsburg, 1989; paperback reprint: Minneapolis, MN: Fortress Press, 1991.

———. *Waiting for Gospel: An Appeal to the Dispirited Remnants of Protestant Establishment*. Eugene, OR: Cascade Books, 2012.

———. *What Christianity Is Not: An Exercise in "Negative" Theology*. Eugene, OR: Cascade Books, 2013.

Kohl, Margaret, ed. *Jürgen Moltmann: Collected Readings*. Minneapolis, MN: Fortress Press, 2014.

Lott, David B. "Introduction." In Lott, ed., *Douglas John Hall: Collected Readings*, 1–9. Minneapolis, MN: Fortress Press, 2013.

———, ed. *Douglas John Hall: Collected Readings*. Minneapolis, MN: Fortress Press, 2013.

———, ed. *Sallie McFague: Collected Readings*. Minneapolis, MN: Fortress Press, 2013.

Nguyen, Viet Thanh. *The Sympathizer*. New York: Grove Atlantic, 2015.

Chapter 2

Illusion and Hope

Michael Bourgeois

LOSE YOUR ILLUSIONS

In October 2018, Canadian Broadcasting Corporation (CBC) journalist Neil Macdonald published an opinion piece entitled "Lose Your Illusions. It's an Ugly, Dystopian World." Macdonald's stark judgment was provoked by two events: the confirmation of Brett Kavanaugh to the U.S. Supreme Court and what it revealed about Americans' attitudes about sexual assault; and the brutal murder of dissident Saudi journalist Jamal Khashoggi in the Saudi Arabian consulate in Istanbul by, as was then already becoming clear, Saudi agents acting under orders from Crown Prince Mohammed bin Salman. Alluding to U.S. President Donald Trump's connection with both events, Macdonald concluded: "People my age grew up believing the world, led by the West, was becoming ever more progressive. It wasn't, and it isn't. All it took was one ambitious real estate huckster to dispel the illusion."[1]

Macdonald's call for people his age to lose their illusions about the state of the world in the wake of the Kavanaugh confirmation and the Khashoggi killing echoes Douglas John Hall's characterization, in a 1999 essay, of Western culture in the wake of World War I.

> World War I was the shock that it was . . . because the violence and viciousness that it revealed lying just beneath the urbane surface of the West's high culture had been so successfully repressed by that culture. If at the end of the war "disillusion" was "the one dominant result transcending all others," it was because so much of what had come to be by the end of the nineteenth century was sheer illusion: the illusion of unimpeded progress, of the moral neutrality of science and technology, of the essential goodness of the human spirit, of humanity's rightful mastery over nature, of the victory of rationality over ignorance and

superstition, of the socially beneficial character of individual pursuit of wealth and power, and so on. So unconditionally positive were the expectations of the leading classes of European and North American societies that the experience of negation—and especially of a negation as bloody as "the Great War" proved to be—could only overwhelm.[2]

In this chapter, I will engage Douglas John Hall's contextual theology to explore illusions about the Global North today and suggest some grounds for hope in the wake of disillusionment. First, I will briefly summarize elements of Hall's theology that are especially relevant for this task. Second, I will revise and update two of the central components of the North American context Hall identified thirty years ago, namely, economic injustice and the environmental crisis. In conclusion, I will suggest some directions for a disillusioned but hopeful engagement with the world today.

ELEMENTS OF HALL'S CONTEXTUAL THEOLOGY

A fundamental contention of Hall's theology, expressed variously but consistently throughout his work, is

> that the God of the Jews and the Christians intends to mend the world; that redemption must mean the redemption of creation, not its destruction or replacement but fulfillment; that the resurrection of Jesus Christ must not be turned into a *Deus ex machina* type of escape from history but is rather the source of Christian courage to enter all the more boldly into the process of history, time being something like the moving edge of the eternal.[3]

This contention provides the underlying theological rationale for a specifically *contextual* theological method, one that takes seriously the material conditions of the world so that we might express and participate in God's love for the world by undertaking meaningful work toward its mending. Hall has briefly defined contextual theology this way:

> [I]n that mode of reflection which we call Christian theology, there is a meeting between two realities: on the one hand the Christian tradition, namely, the accumulation of past articulations of Christians concerning their belief, with special emphasis upon the biblical testimony; and on the other hand, the explicit circumstances, obvious or hidden, external and internal, physical and spiritual, of the historical moment in which the Christian community finds itself. . . . [T]he latter reality ("the context"), far from being the passive partner in the dialogue, constitutes for the theological community the most decisive *formative*

element—the confronting question to which the tradition must address itself if it is to become something beyond mere tradition, if it is to become *Gospel*.⁴

Because our understanding of the circumstances of our historical moment is formative for contextual method, the veracity of accounts of those circumstances on which we rely is crucial. Hall noted that "the pioneers in this methodological transformation" in theology have been "Blacks, women, the oppressed of the third world" and others throughout the world "shaken by the threat of thermonuclear war, world hunger, environmental and technological crises, economic inequality, *etc*." As a result, "[t]hey are persons for whom the 'old, old story,' as told and retold within the dominant conventions of Christendom, no longer functions as 'Gospel' but is felt to be part of the machinery of oppression, the ideology of the dominant culture by which minorities are kept in their places and the *status quo* maintained."⁵ As we describe the significant features of our contexts, then, we must learn from those who suffer from and who have thereby become disillusioned about rose-tinted depictions of the world. As Hall noted elsewhere, "Hope worth its salt has to emerge from an ongoing dialogue with the data of despair."⁶

Hall explained that contextual theology is in one sense "merely an extension of the long apologetic tradition" of communicating the Gospel in terms comprehensible to and meaningful for a specific culture. He also argued, however, that in another sense contextual theology adds something new to theological method, what he called "the *sense of place*." For Hall, attention to the sense of place is essential in part to enable Canadians and other Christians to break the hold of the "long European *locus* of the faith." The assumed normative status of Europe as the defining "place" for Christian theology has led in North America, for example, to "ignoring and suppressing the indigenous peoples, their climate, their politics, their values, and above all their religious traditions."⁷ This sense of place has led Hall to explore in many of his publications what a specifically *Canadian* contextual theology would look like, distinct not only from European but also from U.S. American theologies, while also noting relevant similarities with our continental neighbors. Hall's sense of place, further, entails not only a geographical sense but also a broader, metaphorical sense: "It refers to explicit conditions which set one apart from others." While "persons share a great many things in common . . . in spite of their particularities" nevertheless "there are 'spaces' within the general time-frame . . . whose characteristics are such that they represent specific conditions with high theological significance."⁸

Hall offered his own account of the specific conditions of the broader North American space near the end of the twentieth century in his 1991 *Thinking the Faith*, the first volume of his *Christian Theology in a North American Context* trilogy. Hall named "the *underlying* crisis in our culture as the breakdown of the modern worldview which is our foundational *mythos*" and judged any effort to characterize the crisis "in less stark and encompassing terms" as "an exercise in reductionism." Nevertheless, he acknowledged that this crisis "expresses itself in, and is complicated by, a great variety of more specific and tangible problems."[9] He offered, then, his "far from exhaustive" description of seven "critical components of our context": the end of the Constantinian era for Christianity; the reality of religious pluralism; the implications of the Holocaust for Christian theology; the challenge from Marxism; "the rebellion of nature"; the threat of nuclear war; and the rise of apocalypticism and "religious simplism."[10] Much of Hall's analysis remains valid thirty years later. For example, while expressed differently in various countries, and in regions within countries, the disestablishment of Christianity and the spread of religious pluralism continue to shape the North American context. One implication of the post-Christendom location for a Canadian contextual theology is that Christians must engage the work of mending the world in conversation and cooperation with people of other faiths and of no faith. As Hall argued forty years ago in *The Canada Crisis: A Christian Perspective*: "The search for a *Christian* rationale for the care of nation does not take place in isolation from others who are also searching for reasons for their hope. There can be no thought of 'going it alone.' Christians who behave as if going it alone were desirable, or even possible, have not yet awakened to the fact that Christendom is over."[11]

As Hall acknowledged, however, other components could and should be added to his description. For example, any account of the North American context requires attention to colonialism, white racism, and Christianity's complicity in them. In Canada, that account must include the churches' participation in the Indian Residential Schools and the associated family separation, attempted cultural genocide, and physical and sexual abuse of Indigenous children.[12] It must also examine the intersection of colonialism, racism, and misogyny evidenced by the epidemic of missing and murdered Indigenous women and girls.[13] Further, significant changes in the North American context since Hall's 1991 account warrant attention today. The end of the Cold War, marked by the fall of the Berlin Wall in 1989 and the dissolution of the Soviet Union in 1991, was a main cause of these changes. One important consequence has been the dramatic reduction in the threat of nuclear war. I will focus, however, on revising two other components of Hall's account because of their pervasive influence, not only in North America but also globally. First, his account of the challenge posed by Marxism requires revision in the wake of the end of the Cold War and the ensuing dominance of neoliberal capitalism in the Global North. Second, Hall's description of "the rebellion of nature" requires amplification in view of current expectations of the imminence and severity of the global climate crisis and neoliberal capitalism's relationship to it.Both components of our context are implicated in illusions about the world prevalent today.

ILLUSIONS IN THE POST-COLD WAR GLOBAL NORTH

Neil Macdonald's appeal to people his age of course raises questions about who has and does not have such illusions about prospects for the world "led by the West." His criticism of what the Kavanaugh confirmation hearings revealed about attitudes toward sexual assault goes some way toward addressing why women should have few, if any, illusions about the world's progressiveness, but Macdonald's assessment ignores the fact that most poor people and people of color—of his and other ages—know that their world is not getting more progressive, and also know that the idea that it is getting more progressive masks the ways in which it has not gotten and is not likely to get more progressive for most of the world's people. It also ignores the fact that younger people facing a likely climate catastrophe in their lifetimes are typically less sanguine about their chances for a secure, comfortable future. Indeed, writing in *Hope for the World* at the start of the twenty-first century, Hall and the other Campbell Seminar scholars had already assessed the "prevailing mood of humankind" as "*despair*."[14]

With such assessments of prospects for the world becoming more progressive under the West's leadership, who then remains disillusioned? In light of Macdonald's work as a journalist, his call to "lose your illusions" may be less a personal confession and more an appeal to people of his age (and, perhaps, his race, gender, and class) to see the world as it really is for most of the rest of the world.[15] As Hall and the other Campbell Seminar scholars observed:

> The modern vision, the rhetoric of which still informs much of the public life of the world's possessing peoples, has failed visibly. Although its failure is cushioned by the present (and likely temporary) economic and technological successes of the so-called developed world, the condition of the dispossessed peoples of the planet is worsened by the incapacity of the possessing peoples for either self-knowledge or planetary responsibility.[16]

Macdonald's injunction to "lose your illusions" is important to address, then, because versions of the idea that "the world, led by the West, [is] becoming ever more progressive" remain common, maintained and perpetuated by the world's "possessing peoples." Such illusions distort our view of the world and inhibit our ability to engage the "data of despair" and "enter all the more boldly into the process of history" for the mending of the world.[17]

One of the most telling expressions of the cultural optimism of the West since the late twentieth century is Francis Fukuyama's 1989 essay, "The End of History?" Published shortly before the fall of the Berlin Wall when signs of the Cold War's end were already at hand, Fukuyama proclaimed that "the century that began full of self-confidence in the ultimate triumph of Western liberal democracy seems at its close to be returning full circle to where it started: not to an 'end of ideology' or a convergence between capitalism and socialism, as earlier predicted, but to an unabashed victory of economic and political liberalism."[18] Fukuyama, who at the time worked for the U.S. State Department, did not mean the "end of history" in the sense of the "end of time" or "end of the world" sometimes associated with Christian and other religious eschatologies. Rather, he meant "end of history" as the ultimate point—both in time and in value—of human political evolution. "What we may be witnessing," he wrote, "is not just the end of the Cold War, or the passing of a particular period of postwar history, but the end of history as such: that is, the end point of mankind's [sic] ideological evolution and the universalization of Western liberal democracy as the final form of human government."[19] Despite subsequent world events that seem to have invalidated his argument—for example, the 1992–1995 Bosnian War, the 1994 Rwandan genocide, the rise of Al-Qaeda and the 2003 Iraq War, the 2008 global financial crisis, and the continuing Syrian Civil War, begun in 2011, and rise of the Islamic State—as recently as 2014 Fukuyama continued to affirm that his central thesis would be borne out in the long run. "Even as we raise questions about how soon everyone will get there, we should have no doubt as to what kind of society lies at the end of History."[20]

Versions of Fukuyama's thesis continue to have their advocates, at least but not only among the world's "possessing peoples." While these advocates resist seeing "the data of despair" that cast doubt on their view of the goodness and finality of liberal democracy and neoliberal capitalism, others have been more willing to question their present goodness and inevitable ultimacy. One of those is Jennifer Welsh, whose 2016 Massey Lectures, *The Return of History: Conflict, Migration, and Geopolitics in the Twenty-First Century*, explicitly argues against Fukuyama's thesis. She maintains instead that "[t]he negative political and economic trends we are experiencing a quarter century after the end of the Cold War are starting to feel less like 'transitions' on the path toward a post-historical world, and more like the return of history."[21]

Welsh's catalogue of the elements of history's return includes four main areas: the return of barbarism by both governments and nongovernment forces; the return of mass migration of peoples and western governments' inadequate and inhumane responses to it; the return of the Cold War in the geopolitics of Russian president Vladimir Putin; and the return of increased economic inequality in Western liberal democracies and its threat to their economic and political stability. While the "data of despair" she reports for each element are essential for any complete account of our current context, I will focus only on economic equality because the glowing portrait of neoliberal capitalism is central to Fukuyama's thesis and other post-Cold War versions of the illusion of Western cultural triumphalism.

Citing the research of contemporary economists and data from organizations such as the World Bank and the International Monetary Fund, Welsh describes in detail how "[i]nequality in liberal democracies such as the United States is back at levels it was around the time of the First World War, and in some cases is getting worse."[22] She notes further that "trends in Canada may not be quite as pronounced . . . but they are similarly worrying. Whereas in the 1980s and early 1990s government policies of redistribution significantly reduced income gaps, from the mid-1990s onward inequality has been on the rise. Canadian public policy scholars Keith Banting and John Myles refer to this trend as 'redistributive fade' and Canada's was among the most dramatic among OECD [Organization for Economic Cooperation and Development] countries."[23] Welsh's attention to the recent growth of extreme economic inequality in Western liberal democracies arises not simply from a concern for the injustice of such inequality itself, but also from a concern about the corrosive effects of that inequality on those societies. She enumerates three such effects: first, economic inequality undermines the growth, efficiency, and stability of an economy; second, inequality of income and assets runs the risk of becoming entrenched inequality of opportunity; and third, economic advantage can leverage political advantage, which in turn reinforces economic inequality.[24] Little wonder, then, that while the world's possessing peoples proclaim the glory of neoliberal capitalism, its dispossessed peoples despair.

As thorough as Welsh's catalogue of the "data of despair" is, a component that she neglects is the imminent climate crisis. Welsh's focus on international relations makes this omission understandable, but the climate crisis must be included in any adequate account of our context that updates Hall's description of the "rebellion of nature." Further, despite widespread scientific consensus on and public attention to the threat of climate change, damaging illusions persist. As Swedish climate activist Greta Thunberg noted in her September 2019 address to the UN Climate Action summit: "People are suffering. People are dying. Entire ecosystems are collapsing. We are in the beginning of a mass extinction. And all you can talk about is money and fairytales of eternal economic growth."[25]

Climate science showing that increased levels of atmospheric carbon dioxide due to human activity would lead to global warming began in the late nineteenth century and was sufficiently established by 1965 that U.S.

president Lyndon Johnson's Science Advisory Committee submitted a report on it to him. Concern about anthropogenic global warming became widespread by 1988, as seen in that year's World Conference on the Changing Atmosphere and the first meeting of the United Nations' Intergovernmental Panel on Climate Change (IPCC).[26] During the subsequent thirty years, climate scientists continued to refine their analyses and projections of the rate of greenhouse gas emissions and the likely results. In various reports they warned that unchecked global warming would cause significant, even catastrophic environmental and social effects during the twenty-first century, and recommended strategies for action by governments and others to reduce greenhouse gas emissions. Despite widespread scientific consensus on causes, effects, and possible solutions, however, action to slow anthropogenic climate change has been inadequate. In 2019, the Emissions Gap Report from the United Nations Environmental Program (UNEP) concluded that while some positive steps have been taken, "[t]here is no sign of GHG [greenhouse gas] emissions peaking in the next few years" and that, as a result, more ambitious action will be required to avoid the expected severe consequences of the current rate of global warming.[27]

Signaling the relationship of climate change to social, political, and economic concerns, the 2019 UNEP report also argued that "[c]limate protection and adaptation investments will become a precondition for peace and stability, and will require unprecedented efforts to transform societies, economies, infrastructures, and governance institutions."[28] In *This Changes Everything: Capitalism vs. the Climate*, Naomi Klein addresses the relationship between economics and climate change more directly and deepens Welsh's critique of post-Cold War capitalism by describing how neoliberal economic policies have undermined government's efforts to implement measures to decrease carbon emissions to slow global warming. Global consensus on the need for action on climate science was building concurrently with the global rise of neoliberal economics to remove restrictions on free trade. On the one hand, in 1992 the first United Nations Earth Summit met in Rio de Janeiro, Brazil, and in 1997 the Kyoto Protocol was adopted as part of the United Nations Framework Convention on Climate Change; on the other hand, also in 1992, Canada, Mexico, and the United States signed the North American Free Trade Agreement, and in 1995 the World Trade Organization began operations. The subsequent dominance of the ideology of free trade has resulted in a "habit of willfully erasing the climate crisis from trade agreements."[29] Further, recognition of the large-scale structural changes required to address the climate crisis adequately has informed and motivated climate change denial. Neoliberal capitalism has, in effect, manufactured climate change denial as part of the strategy to thwart environmental regulation of economic activity.[30]

A DIS-ILLUSIONED HOPE

Hall argued in 1991 that "Christian and other forms of liberalism, combined with certain gleanings from 19th-century social evolutionary thought, has conditioned bourgeois society to assume that, whatever disquieting events may be occurring on the surface of history, the great subterranean movements of time are always 'pro-life.' This highly positive doctrine helps to insulate us against many dangerous realities present in our contemporary society, including the nuclear menace."[31] As Hall himself would certainly argue, the North American context has changed in some significant ways in the last thirty years, including in the decreased threat of nuclear war. As a whole, those changes have increased the breadth and depth of disillusionment among most people and of despair among many. Nevertheless, some illusions persist, especially the related illusions of the benevolence of the alliance of capitalism and liberal democracy and of the stability of earth's climate despite unchecked anthropogenic carbon emissions. Jennifer Welsh and Naomi Klein help to dispel these illusions, but they also provide realistic grounds for hope.

One issue in various forms of Christian eschatology is the extent to which human action contributes to the establishment of the reign of God: for some, human action contributes little or nothing, while for others it is crucial. Hall emphasizes divine sovereignty in the coming of God's reign, but his insistence that "the resurrection of Jesus Christ must not be turned into a *Deus ex machina* type of escape from history but is rather the source of Christian courage to enter all the more boldly into the process of history" affirms that human action matters.[32] Our hope ultimately rests in God, but that hope inspires action for the world's mending. Post-Constantinian Christians seeking opportunities for collaboration with others for the mending of the world can, then, work with all who find hope in such action.

Welsh argues that while the triumph of Western liberal democracy is not guaranteed, neither is the continued expansion of barbarism, mass flight, international conflict, and economic inequality. Recent history tends to falsify the "end of history" thesis, but should also "prompt us to revisit the courageous struggles of the past that helped to establish our own liberal democracies, and the decisions and compromises that were made—both nationally and internationally—to ensure that inequality would be contained and managed, difference would be respected, wars would be limited, and power put in the service of collective rather than narrow objectives."[33] She maintains that extreme inequality is not an inevitable feature of liberal democracy, but is rather the result of conscious policy choices by governments.[34] Further, she argues that the current crises of Western liberal democracies can be addressed if governments consciously choose different policies that reverse current levels of economic inequality. "[T]he return of history should encourage us all to remember that our own liberal democratic society was not inevitable—that it required sacrifice, compromise, and leadership—and that we must all, as individuals, take a more active role in its preservation and growth."[35]

Like Welsh, Klein strikes a note of hope without inevitability of success, but where Welsh places her hope in individuals, Klein places hers in collective action, a mass social movement "deeply rooted in specific geographies but networked globally as never before."[36] After having critiqued "magical thinking" responses to the climate crisis such as alternative technologies and climate engineering, Klein describes social movements that offer hope for meaningful responses to the climate crisis, including local resistance to resource extraction projects, student-led movements for divestment from fossil fuel companies, and the assertion of land and treaty rights by Indigenous peoples. As she observes with reference to Indigenous rights, "the outcome of this power struggle is by no means certain. As always, it depends on what kind of movement rallies behind these human rights and moral claims."[37] Despite the obstacles and the uncertainty of the outcome, Klein finds hope for these movements in earlier social movements such as the abolition of slavery "that have succeeded in challenging entrenched wealth in ways that are comparable to what today's movements must provoke if we are to avert climate catastrophe."[38]

Welsh's and Klein's rejection of both optimistic and fatalistic forms of historical inevitability, then, creates space for meaningful human choices and actions. Their work, and the work of others,[39] can therefore help post-Christendom Christians dispel the pernicious illusions of our time by discerning "the explicit circumstances, obvious or hidden, external and internal, physical and spiritual, of the historical moment in which the Christian community finds itself."[40] Thus facing "the data of despair," we and others who share God's love for the world may be encouraged to "enter all the more boldly into the process of history" to mend it.

NOTES

1. Neil Macdonald, "Lose Your Illusions. It's an Ugly, Dystopian World," *CBC News: Opinion* (October 16, 2018), accessed September 23, 2019, https://www.cbc.ca/news/opinion/khashoggi-column-1.4863809. Born in 1957, Macdonald is currently an opinion columnist for CBC News and senior correspondent for *The National*.

2. Douglas John Hall, "'The Great War' and the Theologians," in Gregory Baum, ed., *The Twentieth Century: A Theological Overview* (Ottawa, ON: Novalis, 1999), 6–7. Hall quotes Barbara Tuchman, *The Guns of August* (New York: Dell, 1962), 489.

3. Douglas John Hall, *Confessing the Faith: Christian Theology in a North American Context* (Minneapolis, MN: Fortress Press, 1996), 455. Cf. his *This World Must Not Be Abandoned: Stewardship, Its Worldly Meaning* (Toronto, ON: Church World Development & Relief, 1981).

4. Douglas John Hall, "On Contextuality in Christian Theology," *Toronto Journal of Theology* 1, no. 1 (Spring 1985), 3–4. For Hall's more extensive discussion of contextual method, see *Thinking the Faith: Christian Theology in a North American Context* (Minneapolis, MN: Augsburg, 1989; paperback reprint: Minneapolis, MN: Fortress Press, 1991), 69–145.

5. Hall, "On Contextuality in Christian Theology," 7.

6. Douglas John Hall, *The Canada Crisis: A Christian Perspective* (Toronto, ON: Anglican Book Centre, 1980), 15.

7. Hall, "On Contextuality in Christian Theology," 9–10.

8. Hall, "On Contextuality in Christian Theology," 11.

9. Hall, *Thinking the Faith*, 197–99.

10. Hall, *Thinking the Faith*, 200–35.

11. Hall, *The Canada Crisis*, 26.

12. Truth and Reconciliation Commission of Canada, *Canada's Residential Schools: The Final Report of the Truth and Reconciliation Commission of Canada* (Montreal, QC and Kingston, ON: McGill-Queen's University Press, 2016). For more on Indigenous peoples and the churches in Canada, see the chapters by Allen Jorgenson and Brian Thorpe in this book.

13. National Inquiry into Missing and Murdered Indigenous Women and Girls, *Reclaiming Power and Place: The Final Report of the National Inquiry into Missing and Murdered Indigenous Women and Girls* (Gatineau, QC: National Inquiry into Missing and Murdered Indigenous Women and Girls, 2019).

14. "Hope from Old Sources for a New Century," in Walter Brueggemann, ed., *Hope for the World: Mission in a Global Context*, 16. In a letter sent on the occasion of the November 2019 conference "Christian Theology after Christendom: Engaging the Thought of Douglas John Hall," Brueggemann indicated that Hall had substantially written this Campbell Seminar consensus paper.

15. For example, in November 2010, while working as CBC's Washington correspondent, Macdonald investigated the United Nations' inquiry into the February 2005 assassination of former prime minister of Lebanon Rafik Hariri. Macdonald reported that the UN inquiry had received credible evidence that Hezbollah, Lebanon's "Party of God," was responsible for Hariri's death, but that the inquiry had failed to act on the evidence due to "timidity, bureaucratic inertia and incompetence bordering on gross negligence." The inquiry's inaction led in part to the subsequent assassination of the Lebanese police investigator who had uncovered the evidence. Neil Macdonald, "CBC Investigation: Who Killed Lebanon's Rafik Hariri?" *CBC News* (November 21, 2010), accessed September 23, 2019, https://www.cbc.ca/news/world/cbc-investigation-who-killed-lebanon-s-rafik-hariri-1.874820.

16. "Hope from Old Sources for a New Century" in Walter Brueggemann, ed., *Hope for the World*, 16.

17. Hall, *Confessing the Faith*, 455.

18. Francis Fukuyama, "The End of History?" *The National Interest* 16 (Summer 1989): 3. Fukuyama expanded his argument in his book *The End of History and the Last Man* (New York: Harper Collins, 2002).

19. Fukuyama, "The End of History?," 4.

20. Francis Fukuyama, "At the 'End of History' Still Stands Democracy," *Wall Street Journal* (June 6, 2014), accessed November 1, 2019, https://search-proquest-com.myaccess.library.utoronto.ca/docview/1533237942/fulltext/6729CE6030534A47PQ/1?accountid=14771.

21. Jennifer Welsh, *The Return of History: Conflict, Migration, and Geopolitics in the Twenty-First Century*, The 2016 Massey Lectures (Toronto, ON: House of Anansi, 2016). In 2017, Welsh published an updated edition with a new afterword that more explicitly addressed the events of 2016 and concluded: "The 1989 victory of Western liberal democracy is starting to look more and more like ancient history."

22. Welsh, *The Return of History*, 258.

23. Welsh, *The Return of History*, 261, citing Keith Banting and John Myles, eds., *Inequality and the Fading of Redistributive Politics* (Vancouver, BC: University of British Columbia Press, 2013).

24. Welsh, *The Return of History*, 267–75.

25. Greta Thunberg, "If World Leaders Choose to Fail Us, My Generation Will Never Forgive Them," *The Guardian* (September 23, 2019), accessed September 23, 2019, https://www.theguardian.com/commentisfree/2019/sep/23/world-leaders-generation-climate-breakdown-greta-thunberg. For more on global warming and eco-theology, see the chapter by Harold Wells in this book.

26. Naomi Klein, *This Changes Everything: Capitalism vs. the Climate* (Toronto, ON: Alfred A. Knopf Canada, 2014), 73.

27. United Nations Environment Program, "Executive Summary," *Emissions Gap Report 2019* (Nairobi: United Nations Environment Program, 2019), 5.

28. United Nations Environment Program, "Executive Summary," 10.

29. Klein, *This Changes Everything*, 64–95, 75–80.

30. Klein, *This Changes Everything*, 31–63.

31. Hall, *Thinking the Faith*, 226.

32. Hall, *Confessing the Faith*, 455.

33. Welsh, *The Return of History*, 36.

34. Welsh, *The Return of History*, 310.

35. Welsh, *The Return of History*, 42.

36. Klein, *This Changes Everything*, 290.

37. Klein, *This Changes Everything*, 366.

38. Klein, *This Changes Everything*, 455.

39. For example, Rebecca Solnit, *Hope in the Dark: Untold Histories, Wild Possibilities*, 3rd ed. (Chicago, IL: Haymarket Books, 2016).

40. Hall, "On Contextuality in Christian Theology," 3.

WORKS CITED

Brueggemann, Walter, ed. *Hope for the World: Mission in a Global Context*. Louisville, KY: Westminster John Knox, 2001.

Fukuyama, Francis. "At the 'End of History' Still Stands Democracy." *Wall Street Journal* (June 6, 2014). Accessed November 1, 2019. https://search-proquest-com.myaccess.library.utoronto.ca/docview/1533237942/fulltext/6729CE6030534A47PQ/1?accountid=14771.

Fukuyama, Francis. "The End of History?" *The National Interest* 16 (Summer 1989): 3–18.

Fukuyama, Francis. *The End of History and the Last Man*. Toronto, ON: Maxwell Macmillan Canada, 1992.

Hall, Douglas John. *The Canada Crisis: A Christian Perspective*. Toronto, ON: Anglican Book Centre, 1980.

——— "The Canadian Context." In Walter Brueggemann, ed., *Hope for the World: Mission in a Global Context*, 35–38.

——— *Confessing the Faith: Christian Theology in a North American Context*. Minneapolis, MN: Fortress Press, 1996.

——— *The Cross in Our Context: Jesus and the Suffering World*. Minneapolis, MN: Fortress Press, 2003.

——— "Despair as a Pervasive Element." In Walter Brueggemann, ed., *Hope for the World: Mission in a Global Context*, 83–94.

——— "'The Great War' and the Theologians." In Gregory Baum, ed. *The Twentieth Century: A Theological Overview*, 3–13. Maryknoll, NY, London, and Ottawa: Orbis Books, Geoffrey Chapman, and Novalis, 1999.

——— "On Contextuality in Christian Theology." *Toronto Journal of Theology* 1, no. 1 (Spring 1985): 3–16.

——— *This World Must Not Be Abandoned: Stewardship, Its Worldly Meaning*. Toronto, ON: Church World Development & Relief, 1981.

——— *Thinking the Faith: Christian Theology in a North American Context*. Minneapolis, MN: Augsburg, 1989; paperback reprint: Minneapolis, MN: Fortress Press, 1991.

Klein, Naomi. *This Changes Everything: Capitalism vs. the Climate*. Toronto, ON: Alfred A. Knopf Canada, 2014.

MacDonald, Neil. "CBC Investigation: Who Killed Lebanon's Rafik Hariri?" *CBC News* (November 21, 2010). Accessed September 23, 2019. https://www.cbc.ca/news/world/cbc-investigation-who-killed-lebanon-s-rafik-hariri-1.874820.

———. "Lose Your Illusions. It's an Ugly, Dystopian World." *CBC News: Opinion* (October 16, 2018). Accessed September 23, 2019. https://www.cbc.ca/news/opinion/khashoggi-column-1.4863809.

Muliro, Arthur. "Clinging to Hope: An Urgent Call to Rejuvenate and Revitalize Institutions of Liberal Democracy: An Interview with Jennifer Welsh." *Development* 60 (2017): 149–56.

National Inquiry into Missing and Murdered Indigenous Women and Girls. *Reclaiming Power and Place: The Final Report of the National Inquiry into Missing and Murdered Indigenous Women and Girls*. Gatineau, QC: National Inquiry into Missing and Murdered Indigenous Women and Girls, 2019.

Solnit, Rebecca. *Hope in the Dark: Untold Histories, Wild Possibilities*. 3rd ed. Chicago, IL: Haymarket Books, 2016.

Thunberg, Greta. "If World Leaders Choose to Fail Us, My Generation Will Never Forgive Them." *The Guardian* (September 23, 2019). Accessed September 23, 2019. https:// www.theguardian.com/commentisfree/2019/sep/23/world-leaders-generation-climate-breakdown-greta-thunberg.

Truth and Reconciliation Commission of Canada. *Canada's Residential Schools: The Final Report of the Truth and Reconciliation Commission of Canada.* Montreal, QC and Kingston, ON: McGill-Queen's University Press, 2016.

United Nations Environment Programme. "Executive Summary." *Emissions Gap Report 2019.* Nairobi: United Nations Environment Programme, 2019.

Welsh, Jennifer. *The Return of History: Conflict, Migration, and Geopolitics in the Twenty-First Century.* The 2016 Massey Lectures. Toronto, ON: House of Anansi, 2017.

Chapter 3

Faith and Fragilization

Douglas John Hall and Charles Taylor in Dialogue

Andrew Root

There was a tangible energy in the air. There always is in Princeton. The little historic oasis town in New Jersey always has a palpable feel to it. It must be the anxious energy of students driving as hard as they can not to be spotted as imposters. Or maybe that anxious energy is coming from the professors and grad students. But for these three days it seemed blunted. There was still a buzz but the desperation seemed to be dialed down. I figured it was the weather. These were stunning spring days, the sun shining so welcomingly around the colonial houses, spilling over the old academic brick buildings and through the newly leafed trees as if they were stained glass.

It was against this backdrop that each morning, for the three days of a conference, Douglas John Hall and I walked from Princeton Seminary to Nassau Street for a cup of coffee. We always took the long way to have more time to talk. Having completed my PhD work to take up a faculty position at Luther Seminary in St. Paul, Minnesota, I had just recently left Princeton Seminary. I was a lowly assistant professor, still trying to find my way. Professor Hall was winding down a career of traveling and presenting, the McGill professor completing another chapter of a stellar career. Professor Hall informed me on one of those walks that this would be one of his last trips across the border. I was right at the beginning of my career, presenting at one of my first conferences; Professor Hall was presenting at one of his last.

Those three mornings set a trajectory for the first decade of my career. Professor Hall's wisdom and friendship, as well as his work, formed me as a scholar. My forthcoming writing projects were filled with footnotes on his work, my students read book after book with his name on it. Those three mornings started a dialogue that's lasted many years. Professor Hall's trilogy and my worn highlighter have taken the place of the Princeton streets and a cup of mediocre coffee.

A little less than a decade into my career, I received an email inviting me to review a philosophy book for a theological journal. The book had been receiving a good amount of acclaim across a number of disciples. The journal's book editor explained in an email, "Your work with Hall and his contextual theology, I believe, makes you a good person to review this book." I agreed to write the review. I didn't realize until the book arrived that it was 770 pages long, landing on my desk with an intimidating thud.

To my surprise this book too came from McGill. The writer of the tome was the philosopher Charles Taylor, and the book was *A Secular Age*. I'd hoped it would take me just a week to closely read the book and another two days to write my 800-word review. Now, as I find myself in the middle of the second decade of my career, I'm still reading Taylor's tome, and my 800 words have turned into over a 1,000 pages across multiple books (and counting). And yet, my syllabi are still filled with Hall texts, my footnotes still keeping the dialogue going that began over fifteen years ago in Princeton.

So on this honored occasion of celebrating and engaging Professor Hall's work, I'd like to place into dialogue these two McGill giants who have so deeply affected my career. I'll contend that Hall is just the kind of theologian needed to respond to the secular age that Taylor sketches out. Working independently of each other (though both have told me they know each other: Taylor's daughter even did a degree under Hall), they have yet produced work that overlaps in some interesting and informative ways.

BIOGRAPHICAL CONNECTIONS

Their overlaps begin with their biographies. Hall and Taylor are both native and devoted Canadians of the same generation. While they spent most of their careers at McGill, the reach of both transcends Canada's borders. Both men have significant connections (and made indelible impact) on the continent, in the United Kingdom, and in the United States. But even so, for both, Montreal is always close to their hearts.

Both men carry British names. Hall grew up in an Ontario village with deep British roots. Although Taylor too has a British-style name, as well as a British-Canadian father, he is Quebecois from head to toe (his mother's side is filled with significant people in Quebec society).[1] Both are deeply invested in the French ethos of Montreal and Quebec. Though Hall is a Protestant and Taylor is a Catholic, their work is inextricably bound to the experience of Canada, and particularly Quebec, over their lifetimes. Hall writes with the merger and then decline of the United Church in his mind; the secularization of Canada over his lifetime is central to his theological construction. For Taylor, Quebec itself serves as a microcosm of his whole secularity project. In *A Secular Age*, Taylor seeks to name for the whole of the West what happened in miniature in his home province. Taylor explores how religion, which was once so central and interconnected (Taylor calls this "embedded") within so many elements of Quebec society, so quickly was cut loose, and for many, pushed to the margins.

While both men are Quebec-located Canadians with connections to the United Kingdom and an eye on America, their central dialogue partners are German. And they're not just any Germans; they're German heroes who, at different periods, led the backwater Germanic nations into new times. For Hall, this dialogue partner is of course Martin Luther. For Taylor, it's Johann Gottfried Herder.[2] A tangential connection worth naming is Herder's link to Luther. Though Taylor is undeniably Catholic, his philosophical direction unmistakably leans toward the romantic over the rationalist: the romantic response to the French Enlightenment is a central lens in Taylor's understanding of the West. Like his Oxford teacher, Isaiah Berlin, Taylor finds counter-Enlightenment voices like Hamann and Herder fundamental to the formation of our present cultural imagination—and an inspiration for his own outlook.[3] It was Lutheran pietism, and Luther himself, that inspired Johann Hamann, who was the teacher of Johann Herder. So while Taylor never wavers from his Catholic location, nor Hall from his Protestant roots, a particular trace (a trace for Taylor; it's much more than that in Hall) of Luther is found in both thinkers.[4]

As this comparison shows (and we'll see more below), both scholars hold that some sense of reappropriation is necessary. Hall is forceful in pushing theology to concern itself with the context before it, for theology to live by giving attention to the contemporary moment. While leaning in the philosophical romantic direction, Taylor too is no hater of the modern project: he refuses to long for a past world. Yet, nevertheless, both believe discourse with the past (Hall calls this the "tradition"' Taylor embodies it in his philosophical genealogies) will move us forward. Both believe the resources of the past are necessary for living fully into the future. The objective is the world in front of us, but never cut off from (or ignorant of) what came before us. This is so because both Hall and Taylor admit that they're coming to faith as those who are "believing again."

Taylor references Roger Lundin's *Believing Again: Doubt and Faith in a Secular Age*[5] as both his own story and a necessary disposition for belief in a secular age. Hall also points to a kind of believing again, in his case after reading Luther for the first time as young man in the company of his local pastor. Hall "believes again" after reading Luther; Taylor after reading Yves Congar and the other *Nouvelle Theologies*.[6]

The theme of "believing again" invites us to move beyond consideration of overlapping biographies and intellectual traditions into a direction conversation with their thinking. In order to "converse" with both, I'll honor Hall by loosely following the lead of his teacher Paul Tillich. Playfully using Tillich's correlational method, I'll allow Taylor the philosopher to raise the questions through his descriptive cultural philosophy. I'll then let Hall the theologian answer by way of his constructive theology. In the end, as I said above, I hope to show that Douglas John Hall is just the kind of theologian that the secular age described by Charles Taylor needs.

THE THREE SECULARITIES

Taylor is helpful in sketching out the silhouette of our secular age. He shows us the lines that give shape to the secular, revealing that the secular is multivalent. This leads him to assert that the secular has at least three forms—the "three seculars" (to which I'll add a pre-secular form to help us see how the secular takes shape). When we assert that we're in a secular age, or state that the church must respond to the secular, we need to be clear on which of the three forms or parts of the secular we mean.

S-zero

If we rewind our Western cultural history 500 years or so, we discover a time, Taylor believes, that was before the secular. I've called this Secular 0 (S-zero). Of course, even at that time there was some conception of the secular: even then, for instance, all people knew that a farmer's hoe was a profane and therefore secular tool, while the priest's cloak or the Eucharist chalice was sacred. Ultimately, however, there was no such thing as a secular imagination. To be French, for instance, was to be Catholic. The practices of faith and the larger cultural imaginary (i.e., presumed, nearly unthought, conception we had of how the world works) were inextricably fused with belief. To live in the ancien régime was to imagine belief and life as one whole cloth; to live in any of these S-zero societies *was* to believe: it was impossible to function within them and *not* believe.

Atheists, then, were nearly impossible to find in an S-zero world, for the whole society imposed belief. Paolo Sarpi, the Italian late sixteenth-century thinker, whose statue still stands in Venice, is notoriously called "the only unbeliever of his generation." Taylor's point is that if you were to turn back the clock 500 years or so, it would be hard to find anyone, other than good old Sarpi, who didn't believe. The secular was zero.

Yet, soon after Sarpi's day, the West began a great transformation, throwing off the orders of the ancien régime and dividing the whole cloth of belief and social life. The secular arrives when belief and participation in society are disconnected. Modernity brought the secular on the scene by doing this dividing.

S1

What brought the secular into the West was the imposition of a divide between public and private life. Belief was filed under the private; it was considered to have no direct impact on economic or political life, and as a consequence no relevance to, for instance, being a citizen. Taylor calls this stage Secular 1 (S1).

In S-zero belief determined the shape and safety of society itself. For instance, for someone to practice witchcraft or refuse to participate in mass put the whole village, maybe even the whole of the realm, at risk.[7] In an S1 world this is no longer the case. Those things that uphold political orders and shape the institutions of society are cut lose from belief itself. Now a few more Paolo Sarpis can be found—not a lot—but enough that no statues of notoriety are necessary. And these few can even be found running the state and shaping the societal institutions. Overall, belief is still important in an S1 world. It just lodged in the private sphere, and is even disconnected from the discoveries of the natural world. Enter believers like Kepler, Galileo (Sarpi's friend), and Newton, all three of whom confessed belief, but were no longer sure that belief had much to do with examining the natural world itself.

If we were to stop with S1, assuming it was the full definition of living in a secular age, then we'd have to assert that the United States is the most secular of Western societies. From its founding the United States imposed such a complete break with the old orders of the ancien régime that there could be *no* connection. There could only be complete separation between the church and the state—belief and societal operations were not, and never to be, linked. With the Revolution, the United States not only freed itself from King George's taxation, but from any memory, and therefore even tangential responsibility, to the imaginary of the ancien régime, to a time where the ordering of the institutions of society were linked with belief. While the other Western societies had their own transitions, slowly cutting the ties between belief and the ordering of society and shifting themselves into a S1 world, none would have as clear and complete a break as the United States.

But because this is the case, something odd occurs, which shows that we need Taylor's multivalent definitions to fully understand the secular. Oddly, because the United States was so committed to S1, it became a society where Secular 2 (S2) had less impact. Conversely, England and the Scandinavian countries, which could be thought of as S1 nations because they retained some of the ties between religious and political orders, the traces of ancien régime—these societies nevertheless became the most S2 nations.

S2

Taylor explains that S2 is an understanding of the secular in terms of the number of people participating in religious communities. In particular, in the late 1960s, when the countercultural movement arrived across the West, Canada and the other Western European societies had a "convenience" the United States lacked. When their young people realized that the state was corrupt, with one move they could turn their backs on both the church and the state. In these societies, the church and the state were connected enough (at least in memory), no matter how stretched the ligaments, that to refuse one was to refuse the other.

This wasn't the case in the United States. To turn your back on the state *was* to turn your back on mainline churches (turning them into what Hall calls "the once mainline"). And these churches, even in the United States, have never recovered in an S2 sense. Decline firmly wrapped itself around these institutions, squeezing slowly with force. Yet, being the most S1 society, American culture gave religious groups outside the mainline the space to "innovate," creating huge mega churches and other religious organizations (particularly in the western part of the country, far beyond the elite centers on the eastern seaboard). These new big churches and large organizations dammed the river of S2 in the United States, keeping from large-scale decline. This made the United States the least S2 society, because it was the most S1 society. Particularly, American Evangelicalism found unique ways, resting inside S1, to make the United States the least S2 society.[8] But to do this would necessitate a crisis.

Though the United States was the least S2 society—having the most people attending church on Sunday, for instance—the anxiety of loss needed to be ratcheted up. The crisis of decline became the mobilizing force for action (getting people to enact their religious lives).[9] In the 1980s, this began to stretch beyond concerns for church attendance and into conflict at the societal institutional level as well. Soon fundamentalists bit the hand that fed them (or at least the hand that let them be). They attacked the S1 composition of American society that gave them space to be, claiming that America had lost its sense of belief. Eventually, resentment of the fact that Paolo Sarpi-elite-types where running the societal institutions became a call to political arms. Loss was now an apocalyptic threat. Not only was there a call to worry about fewer people going to church, but there were new fears that secular forces where outlawing belief itself (enter Jerry Falwell and the Moral Majority). Inside these U.S. anxieties of the losses in S2, new Christendom dreams came to the fore. Hall was a prophetic theologian in pointing to the idolatry of ramping-up the anxiety of loss to win power. Even mainline pastors, who were sickened by the Christendom dreams of the moral majority and its attacks on S1, were anxious to find ways of beating back the decline of S2. Hall called them to look for something deeper, warning against something more central that needed to be wrestled with in our secular age.[10]

Even if the felt loses in S2 didn't lead to dreams of a new Christendom, they nevertheless became the defining mark of many denominations, pastors, and congregations. Decline as the loss of members, resources, and relevance was the apparent peril that had to be faced. The magnitude of this threat overwhelmed many pastors, who thought the way to respond to the secular was to find an ingenious program or strategy to upend decline (How can we grow membership? Keep young adults in the church? Be relevant in a new media culture?). Stuck in this S2 imagination, theology had little relevance. The issue, it was assumed, wasn't (isn't) our thinking, but our practical confrontation with decline. Yet, Hall saw something different, leading him to call us back to "thinking the faith." And what he saw, Taylor vividly articulates.

S3

To move the S2 conversation beyond its direct impact on church life and the existential experience of the pastor, we can see how S2 is intellectually bound within classic secularization theory—that is, the idea that as societies become more modern they become less religious. In classic secularization theory, the secular is S2. Yet, Taylor is skeptical of assuming this theory as the full story. He believes secularization theory doesn't really make sense of much of what's happened globally at the end of twentieth and beginning of the twenty-first century. It's not that belief is evaporating, but that it's shifting and contested. Therefore, Taylor doesn't believe that our ultimate issue—or what it really means or feels like to live in a secular age—can be fully understood by loss and decline. Though Protestant pastors and denominations keep looking for answers to S2 problems, Taylor believes what it really means to be living in a secular age is to find ourselves in Secular 3 (S3).

If S1 is the dividing out of belief from societal structures, placing belief in the private sphere, and if S2 is the decline of participation in the private institutions of belief, then S3 is the "fragilizing" of belief itself. Taylor explains that in S3 belief is not so much declining, as always and continually contested, making belief always fragile. We live in a secular age because we all know that we could be living a different way. So to say it again, our primary issue isn't that belief is in decline, but that belief is fragilized. This fragilizing is a reality that is much more important for the theologian and pastor to address than decline. I believe this is what Hall saw and sought to address.

FRAGILIZATION

The addressing of the fragilization of belief is what makes Douglas John Hall's theological project so dynamic and important. Hall senses and responds to what Taylor is articulating.[11] Our issue isn't necessarily that religious institutions are in decline, but that doubt is endemic. In an S3 world, there can be no belief without doubt, no faithfulness to the gospel without embracing fragilization. Pastoral ministry, Hall is informing us, will always be misguided when it seeks to puff its chest and stand against decline (this puffing chest always brings back dreams of Christendom's power and importance). Rather, our only way forward in an S3 world, Hall shows (and Taylor I think agrees), is to embrace fragilization itself.[12] Hall is a theologian of fragilization by calling us to peer into the eyes of doubts, and see what stares back—making doubt our companion.

Hall articulates this beautifully in the early parts of *Professing the Faith*. He says, "Faith is a continuous and unfinished dialogue with doubt."[13] Hall seeks to remind us that our journey of faith is always a journey with doubt, for the object of faith comes in its opposite. To quote Paul, "It is Christ, and [as Hall never fails to mention] him crucified" (1 Cor. 2:2). We believe not in a Christian state or in the relevance and multiplying of the resources of the congregation but in the personhood of Jesus Christ crucified. The cross itself fragilizes belief, making the object of belief seem initially unbelievable (it's strength is in its weakness [2 Cor. 12]). This is the thin tradition, the *theologia crucis*, in which Hall's theology is centered. It is a theology that Hall, quoting Jürgen Moltmann, says often "cannot be much loved."[14] It's a theology not much loved in the dispensation of S-zero, S1, and S2. But the whole of Hall's theology is to show that indeed its time has come.[15] The fragilization of belief in S3 makes the *theologia crucis* a contextual theology for our time, and in turn, makes Hall a theologian for S3.

As a theologian for S3, Hall shows that belief is constituted not in societal institutional power (a response to S1) or the building of big, busy congregations (a response to S2), but only by faith, hope, and love. Hall shows that faith, hope, and love are freed from being benign slogans for insignias, t-shirts, and thank-you cards by examining them through the *via negativa* (through their opposite, following the lead of the *theologia crucis*).[16] Christian belief is faith, hope, and love, which means it's not sight, consummation, and power.

Belief is fragile because its object, as pure subject, choses to be crucified, leading belief always to rest in the fragile forms of faith, hope, and love. So because belief is bound in faith, hope, and love over sight, consummation, and power, its companion is always doubt. Like the father in Mark 9 ("I believe, help my unbelief"), we always believe with doubt nearby, now more acutely in the secular age of S3. Taylor's articulation of what it feels like to live in a secular age reminds us it cannot be otherwise. Faith and doubt will always live together in an S3 world, making Hall's theology deeply important for its very starting point in fragilization itself. Taylor reminds us that to live in a secular age is to live with all our beliefs fragilized. And Hall shows how this fragilization can be the very context to encounter Christ, for he is the one crucified.

Yet now uneasy questions are bound to surface. Some might consider Hall's invitation to stare into the eyes of our doubts and see what stares back as a concession to the victory of unbelief over belief. Isn't this ultimately defeatist, giving up too much to the secular, playing the game by unbelief's rules? Neither Hall nor Taylor thinks so. Taylor contends that this is *not* defeatist, and ironically, he thinks it avoids defeatism because of how deeply doubt stretches in S3. To think only belief is fragilized in an S3 world is to misunderstand the nature of S3 itself. Taylor goes to great lengths to show that an S3 world not only fragilizes belief *but also unbelief*! Whether you're a believer or an unbeliever, Taylor holds, you're all mutually fragilized—this is the secular age we all share. So staring into the eyes of your doubts, seeing what stares back, isn't necessarily a concession to the void of meaninglessness, but can also be an openness (Taylor calls this an open take)[17] on what meaning might be staring back. This is to find the very thing, belief, in its opposite, as Hall would assert. To place this further within Hall's theological construction, we could say that because of the mutual fragilizing of both belief and unbelief, calling people into their doubts has both a kerygmatic and apologetic disposition. Yet, to make sense of this assertion, let's step back and look more closely at Taylor's contention that S3 mutually fragilizes both belief and unbelief.

CREATURES OF THE IMMANENT FRAME

Taylor explains that in an S3 world all who believe "can't help looking over our shoulders from time to time" wondering if our belief is just an evolutionary trick or maybe the result of socialization.[18] Taylor's point is that in our time there is no one who believes without doubt. It's impossible. We're all Paolo Sarpis to one degree or another.

In an S-zero world there were indeed creatures of belief who never doubted (maybe even a few of them remained in S1). Most people were beyond doubt because the environment they inherited blocked out doubt like the walls around Medieval Paris. The environment itself was a force field that keeps doubt out. These creatures inherited and continued a social order that was framed by the supernatural. Within that spiritual framework, most causes and fears had spiritual beginnings and ends, making belief obvious.

But we're creatures whose lives are framed not by a supernatural order but by a natural one. The causes and fears in our world have their source not in transcendence but in immanence. Indeed, we are creatures whose lives are framed by immanence. We live in what Taylor calls an "immanent frame." Because this is our environment, we are creatures who can't but doubt. All of us, whether church-goers or not, inherit an immanent frame. And doubt is an accessory you can't leave behind when your life is de facto framed by immanence. A society bound in an immanent frame has no need for statues to unbelief. There is no uniqueness in being an unbeliever. There are more Paolo Sarpis on the streets of Toronto than not, making the notoriety of a statue unnecessary, even ridiculous. Rather, it would be more noteworthy (though it would never happen), for a statue to appear in Toronto of Mary Morrison from Guelph, "The Only Believer of her Generation, who never doubted."

Living in an immanent frame obviously fragilizes belief. There is no escaping the immanent frame, so there is no escaping doubt. But Taylor's point is that fragilization not only strikes at belief but also at unbelief, making doubt a near universal reality. For instance, just when you are sure you don't believe, you doubt your doubts. This doubting of your doubts is what makes Taylor's articulation of the feel of a secular age so interesting. He explains that fragilization is just as true for those who confess unbelief.

For instance, a young woman states her unbelief; she contends that life is ultimately meaningless and in the end we're all just worm food. All there is is nothing! Yet her strongly held beliefs of unbelief are cracked and made fragile, like stepping on the early winter ice on a lake, when she holds her niece for the first time, or hears a certain piece of music, or journeys with that friend through her trauma. Staring into the eyes of her doubts of unbelief reveals a possibility of belief staring back at her. Such encounters are fragilization of her unbelief. Something more, something even ultimate, comes rushing to the surface, confronting her unbelief with something else. Taylor explains that in an S3 world *all* believers doubt. But in turn, Taylor explains, in this same S3 world all doubters sometimes believe. We're *all* fragilized in the secular age Taylor describes.

So taking us back to Hall, to stare into our doubts to see what stares back is both kerygmatic and apologetic. Hall's theology always lives between these two poles, never giving one up for the other. He says, "We must conclude, then, that the apologetic and the kerygmatic approaches are not an either/or but a both/and."[19] As the fragilized unbeliever looks into the doubts of her unbelief, the possibility of an apologetic moment appears. She needs to be invited to follow these doubts of her unbelief, journeying with a community of "open takes." Open to what such experiences could mean the community is humble enough to call them "takes." They are takes confessed enough to build our lives around, but nevertheless just takes—reasoned commitment to our experience of the more that meets our stare as we looked into our doubts.

In turn, though seemingly counterintuitive, as the believer struck by doubt looks into the eyes of these doubts, there is a possibility of a kerygmatic moment of proclamation. Looking into the fragilization of belief, one sees, or maybe better hears, the proclamation of the crucified Christ. This is the thin tradition of a God who is found on the cross, proclaimed by looking into the eyes of our own doubts, by embracing and seeking Christ in the fragilization of our belief. "I believe, help my unbelief" (Mark 9) is the kerygmatic pole of staring into doubt. "I did not know that the Lord was in this place" (Gen. 28:16) is the apologetic pole of following the doubts of our unbelief in a secular age.

CONCLUDING WITH CROSS PRESSURE AND REAPPROPRIATION

When these mutual events of fragilization occur—when we hear the ice fracturing beneath us—we find ourselves in the midst of what Taylor calls "cross pressure." Our belief or unbelief gets crossed up, and while we believe we doubt, or while we doubt we find ourselves believing (or wishing we could). Douglas John Hall's theology, I contend, is particularly directed toward those who are experiencing cross pressure. It's a theology that embraces cross pressure, believing that cross pressure is the fertile ground to find faith itself. Hall even asserts that this context of cross pressure may be the only ground in which to do so.

For Hall the saint of fragilized doubt is Martin Luther. Luther would build a whole new theological edifice out of the thin tradition. The cross of the crucified Christ is the only way for Luther to make sense out of his fragilization. The cross turns fragilization from a curse to the very locale of revelation.

Luther's story of fragilization as belief is the tale of a believer who looks directly into his doubts and finds new life coming out of death. Luther finds himself in soul-crushing cross pressure. Just when he believes, he finds he doesn't. Even in his devotion, working ever harder to please this God he worships, he is struck with doubt.

Trying to run from doubt, racing faster to up his effort, he finds only more cross pressure, his belief more and more fragilized. It isn't until he stops his racing to do more, and instead turns to stare down his doubts that he sees the crucified Christ, who gives faith not outside or beyond fragilization but right through it. Fragile belief—"calling a thing what it is," that belief itself is fragile—is where Luther discovers the only way to believe.[20] The gift of belief not around but through doubt.

Hall is a theologian for an S3 world, because no one has so creatively reappropriated Luther for late-modernity, naming and constructing a theological vision of a cross-pressured time of fragilization as Hall has done.

Douglas John Hall calls us to find faith *not* by reclaiming power or standing against decline, but by "calling a thing what it is." We find faith by calling our belief fragile and seeking the living Christ in this fragility. Douglas John Hall professes that if we do so, we'll find the living Christ right where Luther did, on the cross, giving us life through our deaths, even in a secular age.

NOTES

1. Taylor embodies the bilingual nature of Canada in his person—speaking equal French and English growing up.

2. I suppose it could also be argued that Hegel is this dialogue partner for Taylor. I think this would be accurate. However, from the early Philosophical Papers (see *Human Agency and Language: Philosophical Papers 1* [London: Cambridge University Press, 1999] and *Philosophy and The Human Sciences: Philosophical Papers 2* [London: Cambridge, 1999]) to the recent *The Language Animal: The Full Shape of the Human Linguistic Capacity* (Cambridge, MA: Harvard University Press, 2016), Herder is central. The very ethic of authenticity, which Taylors develop in his Massey Lectures, and which would take his career to another level, are indebted to dialogues with Herder.

3. See Berlin's spectacular *The Roots of Romanticism* (Princeton, NJ: Princeton University Press, 1999).

4. It's very interesting, and I believe opens up more space for the dialogue between Hall and Taylor, that when Taylor articulates the impact of the Reformation on bringing forth our secular age in *A Secular Age*, he mentions very little of Luther. For Taylor it's mainly the Calvinist stream that creates conditions for mutual regard and politeness, which in turn eventually produce a modern moral order that allows the existence of exclusively human flourishing. Of course, Taylor has much more to say about Luther in *Sources of the Self: The Making of Modern Identity* (Cambridge, MA: Harvard University Press, 1989).

5. Grand Rapids, MI: Eerdmans, 2009.

6. Of course these Catholic theologians were part of a movement called *ressourcement*, returning to the resources of ancient Christianity, particularly patristic thought, to find ways forward in late modernity. See the Dutch/Canadian theologian Hans Boersma, *A Return to Mystery: Nouvelle Theologie & Sacramental Ontology* (Oxford: Oxford University Press, 2009) for much more on this theological movement.

7. See *A Secular Age*, 89ff.

8. Of course this is a much longer story and more complicated one. The U.S. was least S2 nation even before the counterculture, but this had much to do with narratives of American victory coming out of the wars and ways religious communities responded to the Depression. World War I and World War II didn't bring the existential crisis to young people in the states that it did to those in England and Canada (and of course on the continent).

9. Taylor calls this "the age of mobilization," and it's a part of this story I simply don't have space to explore. See my other works for more on this (particularly *The Pastor in a Secular Age* [Grand Rapids, MI: Baker Academic, 2019]).

10. This statement by Hall shows he's more of a theologian of S3 than S2. He says, "Instead of providing easy answers to everything, it would be better for the church to concentrate on being a place to which questions could be brought." *The Reality of the Gospel and the Unreality of the Churches* (Philadelphia, PA: Westminster, 1975), 163.

11. There are so many other interesting connections between Taylor and Hall I can't explore here. For instance, Taylor has discussed the eclipse of grace (*A Secular Age*, 222ff). And Hall says this: "Surely the reason why Christianity has operated in our society primarily as a 'culture religion' (Peter Berger), a blend of religious denominationalism and nationalism, is that few have needed it for what it really is—a religion of radical grace. . . . The dominant culture of our society has felt no overwhelming need for the drastic reading of the human situation that is presupposed by a theology of radical grace." *Thinking the Faith* (Minneapolis, MN: Augsburg, 1989; paperback reprint: Minneapolis, MN: Fortress Press, 1991), 169. Another example of a similarity: Taylor in chapter 8 of *A Secular Age* discusses what he calls "the malaise of modernity." Hall sees something very similar, saying those in the suburbs are living with "covert nihilism." Hall says directly, "In short, the corrective to a social malaise whose neglect is threatening to transform it into virulent and perhaps violent forms of nihilism is—for the churches, too—that we must learn how to speak the truth about it in this more rudimentary sense" *Professing the Faith* (Minneapolis, MN: Fortress Press, 1993), 298.

Another similarity is their discussion of authenticity. These words of Hall echo Taylor's articulation of the positive elements of the ethic of authenticity. Both hold to some very important gains through our focus on authenticity, but also see some of authenticity's excesses. Hall sees Luther as an example of a person shifting us toward this ethic of authenticity. Hall says, "The question that emerges out of this existential refusal is whether it is possible to move beyond the refusal into some affirmative form of faith and theology. That was Luther's question, especially prior to 1517. He expressed his anguish in the language of a 'quest for a gracious God,' but it could as well be termed the quest for a faith that allowed him to be himself, completely, without abandoning him to self alone—for that would be no resolution of his dilemma." *The Cross in Our Context: Jesus and the Suffering World* (Minneapolis, MN: Fortress Press, 2003), 29.

A final example is Taylor's concern for what he calls "excarnation"—Christian faith that loses an embodied sense of living in the world and finding God in it. Hall's interpretation of the *theologia crucis* gives him a profound anti-excarnational theology (or better, a truly incarnational theology). For instance he says, "Luther's was the attempt to make Christian faith something different from that. He wanted a gospel that drove people into the world, not away from it; that opened their eyes to what was there, rather than assisting them to look past what was there. 'The theology of the cross calls the thing what it really is.'" *Lighten Our Darkness: Toward an Indigenous Theology of the Cross* (Lima, OH: Academic Renewal Press, 2001), 116.

12. Here is an example of Hall embracing the fragilization of S3. He says, "The only antidote to religious triumphalism is the readiness of communities of faith to permit doubt and self-criticism to play a vital role in the life of faith. *The Cross in Our Context*, 18.

13. *Professing the Faith*, 94.

14. See *The Cross in Our Context*, 6. Moltmann quote from *The Crucified God*.

15. This quotes points to how Hall sees the theology of the cross as a theological perspective for doubt: "A theology of the cross is not a theology of answers; it is a theology of the question. Besides, the whole thing is offered not as light but as a way into the darkness: the darkness that is, the darkness that must become the known context in every search for light." *Lighten Our Darkness*, 227.

16. "The most succinct and portable way that I have found to characterize the theology of the cross is to recall the three so-called theological virtues named by Paul in 1 Corinthians 13: faith, hope, and love. But, remembering the importance of the *via negative* for both Paul and Luther, the three positive virtues should be stated together with what they negate: faith (not sight), hope (not consummation), love (not power). Without the three negations, the three positives too easily devolve into platitudes." *The Cross in Our Context*, 33.

17. Hall's words here are so similar to Taylor's "open take." Hall says, "Any theology that bases itself on the theology of the cross is bound to be modest about its own claims; for it is faith, not sight—it points toward an ultimate reality that it can by no means contain." *The Cross in Our Context*, 117.

18. Taylor actually says it like this: "We cannot help looking over our shoulder from time to time, looking sideways, living our faith also in a condition of doubt and uncertainty." *A Secular Age*, 11.

19. *The Cross in Our Context*, 72.

20. Hall says this: "Luther found peace, relatively speaking, only when he was able to discern like Job an answering God—a God, paradoxically, whose answers were in fact questions, questions larger and more searing than his own, but a God whose questioning Presence was a real response to the Augustinian restless heart (*cor inquietum*) of this monk, the only response he would get, the only response he needed." *The Cross in Our Context*, 20.

WORKS CITED

Berlin, Isaiah. *The Roots of Romanticism*. Princeton, NJ: Princeton University Press, 1999.

Boersma, Hans. *A Return to Mystery: Nouvelle Theologie & Sacramental Ontology*. Oxford: Oxford University Press, 2009.

Hall, Douglas John. *The Cross in Our Context: Jesus and the Suffering World.* Minneapolis, MN: Fortress Press, 2003.

———. *Lighten Our Darkness: Toward an Indigenous Theology of the Cross.* Lima, OH: Academic Renewal Press, 2001.

———. *Professing the Faith.* Minneapolis, MN: Fortress Press, 1993.

———. *The Reality of the Gospel and the Unreality of the Churches.* Philadelphia, PA: Westminster, 1975.

———. *Thinking the Faith.* Minneapolis, MN: Augsburg, 1989; paperback reprint: Minneapolis, MN: Fortress Press, 1991.

Lundin, Roger. *Believing Again: Doubt and Faith in a Secular Age.* Grand Rapids, MI: Eerdmans, 2009.

Moltmann, Jürgen. *The Crucified God.* New York, NY: Harper & Row, 1974.

Root, Andrew. *The Pastor in a Secular Age.* Grand Rapids, MI: Baker Academic, 2019.

Taylor, Charles. *Human Agency and Language: Philosophical Papers 1.* London: Cambridge University Press, 1999.

———. *The Language Animal: The Full Shape of the Human Linguistic Capacity.* Cambridge, MA: Harvard University Press, 2016.

———. *Philosophy and the Human Sciences: Philosophical Papers 2.* London: Cambridge, 1999.

———. *A Secular Age.* Cambridge, MA: The Belknap Press of Harvard University Press, 2007.

———. *Sources of the Self: The Making of Modern Identity.* Cambridge, MA: Harvard University Press, 1989.

Chapter 4

Contextual Theology in Canada
Between Covenant and Treaty
Allen G. Jorgenson

CONTEXTUAL AND COVENANT

Douglas John Hall, North America's consummate contextual theologian, spent the bulk of his academic career at McGill University, whose website includes the following statement:

> McGill University is located on land which has long served as a site of meeting and exchange amongst Indigenous peoples, including the Haudenosaunee and Anishinabeg nations. McGill honours, recognizes and respects these nations as the traditional stewards of the lands and waters on which we meet today.[1]

I am also mindful that this institution, McGill University, was first funded using moneys from the illicit sale by Indian agents of land granted to the Haudenosaunee people (Six Nations of the Grand River) by virtue of the Haldimand Tract.[2] Sadly, this tale and variations on it are told across Turtle Island (North America). Settlers live on ill-gotten land, which includes that of my own home, workplace, and church. This is our context, the truth of which we too often resist acknowledging. Hall writes:

> That we resist the knowledge of our oppression of other peoples is of course a dimension of the same repressive mind-set which enables us to resist the knowledge of our own subtle oppression. We too are a broken people, covertly broken.[3]

Our context, then, demands an accounting of our situation, of our brokenness, and of our breaking others and the cosmos. The Truth and Reconciliation Commission (hereafter TRC) report's Call for Action and the Call for Justice emerging out of the Report of the National Inquiry into Missing and Murdered Indigenous Women and Girls (hereafter the MMIWG Inquiry) make clear the collusion of the churches in the praxis of colonization.[4] Alas, such collusion has been a world-wide phenomenon, but contextual theology demands that we attend to its contours in our locale. The TRC Calls to Action, in particular, have provided churches with some strong points of reference for finding their way into this conversation.[5] In addition to calling the churches to ensure that congregations understand the churches' role in the residential school system (Call to Action # 59) and to ensure that theological curricula be developed guided by the "need to respect Indigenous spirituality in its own right" (Call to Action # 60), all churches will also need to attend to TRC Call to Action # 48, which requests churches to adopt the UN Declaration on the Rights of Indigenous Peoples (UNDRIP) "as a framework for reconciliation," and to TRC Call to Action # 49, which repudiates the Doctrine of Discovery. This latter is especially germane to this paper.

The Doctrine of Discovery is informed by the papal bull *Inter Coetera* of 1493, and specifically references the supposedly divine right given explorers by the pope to claim for the king lands deemed "terra nullius."[6] While the doctrine had its birth in the decrees of the western Catholic church, its reach has been ecumenical—indeed interreligious. All settlers, no matter their creed, benefit from this teaching. It is clear, however, that Protestants too have contributed doctrinal motifs that have fueled both religious and secular quests for more: more souls, land, money, power, and so on. I think especially of the theme of covenant in this regard. Consider the following from *Thinking the Faith*:

> The most influential expressions of the Christian faith in North America were those which could provide a spiritual buttress to the secular mythology of progress and mastery.... [T]hat means, above all, Calvinism. For the peculiar brand of covenant theology in the Calvinist tradition could lend itself to the sense of divine election and destiny which capture the heart of the New World's citizenry almost from the outset.[7]

The particular, self-aggrandizing kind of covenantal theology to which Hall points is not that of Calvin but rather of the Puritans, whose thought drew on the Rhineland Calvinists.[8] The Rhineland Calvinists used the theory of social contract and natural law as hermeneutical keys for understanding God's relationship with humans—which was construed as conditional.[9] Calvin's single covenant is split into two for the Puritans, a covenant of works and a covenant of grace.[10] The covenant of works has a universal reach, so that all of humanity is deemed to be partners in this conditional relationship with God. The covenant of grace, however, is restricted to those chosen and enters into the theological discourse of its proponents as an organizing system. William Klempa identifies it as "the generative and organizing principle of a system of divinity."[11] This theological theme, however, has a reach beyond being "a system of divinity," for it is expanded and brought to bear on social and political realities.[12]

A piece of this covenantal, or federal, theology is seen in the tendency of Puritans—and others subscribing to this worldview—to pattern themselves after the people of Israel, and so to see themselves as a pilgrim people.[13] Robert Warrior, an indigenous scholar, points to the disastrous consequence of this teaching as it crossed the Atlantic:

> Many Puritan preachers were fond of referring to Native Americans as Amelkites and Canaanites—in other words, people who, if they should not be converted, were worthy of annihilation. By examining such instances in theological and political writing, in sermons, and elsewhere, we can understand how America's self-image as a "chosen people" has provided rhetoric to mystify domination.[14]

Warrior highlights this misused and dangerous understanding of covenant in an article exploring the danger of liberation theology's motif of "exodus" for First Nations, pointing out that the First Peoples of Turtle Island identify with the Canaanites, not the children of Israel. In so doing, he alerts us to the hazards of a theology of covenant that is engaged without a self-critical edge. In sum, he invites Christians to revisit this theme, which is foundational to the Hebrew scriptures and presumed in the Testament of Jesus, seeking out new resources that might open up for them some new perspectives.[15]

In what follows, I will attempt to construe a new view of covenant by first making a comparative theological detour whereby we consider a dynamic equivalent of covenant from another spiritual worldview: the theme of treaty from the First Nations of Turtle Island. After learning something about treaty from the First Nations of this Land, we will revisit the theme of covenant with an eye open for possible ways in which we might reconstrue this important theological category.

LESSONS FROM TREATY

Treaties did not begin with the arrival of Europeans on Turtle Island; they existed precontact and presumed a nation to nation basis.[16] Because they exemplify Indigenous political, social, and spiritual engagement across and between nations, they suggest some contours of "treaty" as a concept or practice that are pan-indigenous, even though particular treaties will be shaped by the nature of the agreements that they address. In what follows,

I outline a few characteristic understandings of treaties, taking leave from the words of Harold Cardinal and Walter Hildebrant: "The Elders begin by locating the history of their nations in a time continuum stretching thousands of years, starting with the beginning of time itself. The Elders view the treaties as part of that First Nation historical continuum."[17] In *Treaty Elders of Saskatchewan*, Cardinal and Hildebrant interview elders in order to discern the nature of treaties. They learn that the starting point of treaties is the relationship of the parties with the Creator, who alone can break a treaty.[18] Treaties are made for the purpose of living peacefully on the land and have the Creator as their foundation.[19]

Regarding the treaties with the Crown, the Elders affirm the following characteristics: the two parties shared in a joint fidelity to the Creator in the treaty; the treaty came with an irrevocable vow of peace; and the treaty mandated an irrevocable undertaking of "commitment to initiate and to create a perpetual familial relationship based on familial concepts based on FN principles."[20] Further, the agreement presumed an irreversible commitment to the survival and well-being of each party, as well as a promise of a continuing form of livelihood for the First Nations.[21] Treaties with the Crown, like all First Nations treaties, are also about relationships of peace and well-being before the Creator.

Hill and Coleman note that treaty-making was understood to be a sacred moment.[22] Cardinal and Hildebrandt note that the making of the treaties in Saskatchewan recognized this sacred characteristic, with both parties according a role to someone representing the spirituality of each.[23] Further,

> [e]lders refer to the spiritual ceremonies conducted and the spiritual symbols used by First Nations and the active participation of various Christian missionaries along with Christian symbols utilized by the Crown in those negotiations to assert that both parties anchored their goals and objectives on the values and principles contained in the teaching of each of their spiritual traditions.[24]

Treaties are, above all, spiritual. As time passed, however, treaties with the Crown were increasingly viewed as legal documents encoded in written form.[25] In contrast to the primacy of treaties-as-texts, in general First Nations understandings of treaties consider the following sources as important: diverse witnesses to the treaties, oral telling, treaty commission reports, eyewitnesses from both sides, and so on.[26] While Settlers tended to fixate on the written text of a treaty they signed, Indigenous signatories understood the treaty within a larger hermeneutic, indeed within the motif of process.[27] Anthony Hall comments that treaties should be understood more like verbs than nouns: treaties are replete with "invention, reinvention, and transformative interpretation" rather than "a fixed or static outcome; . . . it's more about the spirit than the letter of those sacred treaties," and so in need of constant reference and return.[28]

In setting the motifs of treaty and covenant alongside each other, then, it is clear that Settlers do violence to treaties when they reduced them to legal documents, and woodenly read them without undertaking the hermeneutical task of contextualizing them and considering their impact for the contemporary setting. Settlers abuse them when they forget that "treaties are living agreements."[29] In sum, First Nations view *treaty* as a sacred, living, and constantly renewed nation to nation agreement that has God as its witness.

Last January, Edna Manitowabi visited Martin Luther University College for the annual Circle of Dialogue. Toward the end of her talk, she mused a bit on the theme of treaty and shared with us a teaching from Peter O'Chiese: "The first treaty is made when the mother puts the newborn babe to her breast."[30] In the mother's act of sharing herself, as Edna later explained, the values of kindness and truthfulness are imparted to the child, and these are at the heart of making treaty.[31] This image has the power of forever changing our thinking about treaty, and possibly covenant too.

COVENANT, TESTAMENT, AND TREATY

The question before us, then, is how do we reclaim *covenant* after this biblical motif has been stained by human greed, by our propensity for demonstrating our value by devaluing the other, by our perverse capacity to commodify everything, even a child at the breast? Professor Hall notes that the "mythic interpretation of the genesis of America has informed the whole history of the United States. . . . What is not always noticed about this mythos, however, is that in subtle ways it makes 'God' dependent upon the success of the American experiment."[32]

Clearly what is needed, then, is a strong tonic, and it is a tonic that needs to start at home—since, as Dr. Hall has reminded us, there is no universal theology.[33] We have to ask how we can transform a concept of covenant that has enabled North Americans in general and North American Christian in particular to become a profoundly entitled people. Perhaps what is needed is some deconstruction of covenant in our context; what is demanded is the demolition of the self-certainty that accompanies a society drunk with manifest destiny—and so demonstrating what Gerald Vizenor calls "manifest manners."[34]

Manifest manners reflexively dismiss indigenous sensibilities as "savage." Manifest manners imagine the piety of sweetgrass to be "primitive," if not demonic. Manifest manners trade in the conceit of claiming the land as a commodity—to be bought and sold. Manifest manners indulge the Doctrine of Discovery in concert with a conceited sense of covenant. Such an indulgence is to be protested. And so now I turn to my old friend Luther for some help in reforming covenant.

Kenneth Hagen notes that Luther distinguished a *covenant* from a *testament*. A covenant is bilateral, with promises accruing to both parties to the covenant; by contrast, a testament is unilateral.[35] In "A Treatise on the New Testament, that is, the Holy Mass" (1520), Luther identifies Holy Communion as *the* testament toward which the gospel points.[36] The gospel points to Jesus at the table on the eve of his death promising forgiveness and life to those who are about to inherit him. The Eucharist is the testament par excellence, since a testament is contingent on the testator dying, as Jesus promises to do. A testament is dependent on the will to give to the inheritor, as Jesus does as he gives bread and cup, body and blood. A testament intends heirs, which includes all who hear the words "given for you."[37]

Luther saw the Eucharist as a strong tonic for the view of covenant operative in his day, whose bilateral character, as Luther saw it, hampered God's scope for divine action by making God dependent on human works.[38] God had become subject to the human.

For Luther, the idea that God was dependent upon humanity was operative in two developments. The first was the understanding of the mass as a sacrifice of Christ, rather than as a sacrament. When Christ is a sacrifice rather than a sacrament, he ceases to be the subject of the divine saving activity. The second was the nominalist framing of justification, whereby the faithful were encouraged to *facere quod in se est* ("do what is in you"). In this conception of justification, God meets sinners half-way, with the result that God has become dependent on us doing our part. This arrangement accords with Luther's concept of a bilateral covenant, in which God can meet us only after we have made our best effort.

By contrast, Luther's theology of the promise turns on the observation that God alone is able to promise unconditionally, and only an unconditional promise can evoke faith. According to Luther's theology of the testament, we go to the meal and receive Christ, who gives the divine self to us unconditionally. This gift we accept in faith, and this gift transforms us in love. Such a love evolves in acts of care for the neighbor and cosmos. Luther believed that only a unilateral testament of unconditional love from God empowers the faithful to act with justice and compassion. The bilateral covenant theology operative in late medieval Christianity paradoxically undermined care for the neighbor by causing Christians to fixate on what they needed to do to be justified before God. Care for the neighbor was thereby sabotaged.

In his "Treatise on the New Testament, that is, the Holy Mass," Luther notes how the collect, the thanksgiving over the bread, and the offertory are all traces of the ancient practice of bringing food to the meal to share with the needy.[39] But Luther notes that "all this is reversed" in the mass as it was actually practiced.[40] Instead of offering food for the poor, the priest sacrificially offers Christ again and again, but all in vain since faith was not preached, and works cannot receive Christ; and instead of the poor receiving food from the breadbasket of the church, the poor bring their offerings to a church already flush with riches.[41] Luther sees this reversal of what ought to be as the consequence of a theology of works, a conditional theology that he identifies as a *theologia gloria* in the Heidelberg Disputation.

A theology of testament—a theology of the cross—reverses this. The faithful, who receive grace from God unconditionally, now bring their gifts for the poor to the meal, and at the meal they receive again God's gift of acceptance. This is gospel. This is grace. But the TRC reminds us that we have replayed the reversal Luther lamented in the popular piety of his day. Just as church of the Holy Roman Empire emptied the bread baskets of the pious poor, the churches in the "New World" were willing partners with colonial powers in stripping the First Peoples of their territory, their rights, their language, their hope. And just as the church that Luther lamented made God's unconditional offer of acceptance into a conditional offer tied to the penitential promise of works, so the churches accepted the First Peoples of this land into their midst on the condition of their assimilation into the dominant culture, an assimilation convincingly called genocide by many.

And lest Canadians pride ourselves in moving beyond this state of affairs with our varied efforts at responding to the TRC Calls to Action and the MMIWG Inquiry Calls for Justice, consider the following from a news article about Chief Justice Murray Sinclair: "The monster that was created in the residential schools moved into a new house," Sinclair said. "And that monster now lives in the child-welfare system."[42]

How might a theology of testament respond to this reality? What is the church to do in this situation?

TESTAMENT AND A THEOLOGY OF THE CROSS

A church that is shaped by a theology of testament—that is, by a theology that begins with grace taking the shape of the cross—will be pushed to the limits of its experience. Such a church, then, lives a liminal existence, and so lives at the edges of society. In the Canadian context, the church at the edge encounters people who model what it means to live in treaty, which is "sacred, living, and constantly renewed." It learns from First Nations that treaties of every sort are grounded in the Creator's will for the well-being of all, and so comes to know that a healthy theology of testament is baptismally grounded.[43] Such a theology is appropriately bilateral in living in peace with other humans and all of creation in reciprocity because of the unilateral motion of grace from the Creator. Further, from those who can teach us the way of treaty, the church learns how this theology of the testament is to be shaped by the particular contours of the land where it lives. And it knows that it can only live faithfully on this land by living in harmony with the people of this land, who alone can school us in loving this land.

Testament in conversation with treaty is theology in situ; a theology of the testament is a *grounded* theology. This is theology that has begun to do what Douglas John Hall lamented our inability to do when he wrote *The Canada Crisis*, in which he rued our inability "to think our theology indigenously."[44] But what will this indigenous theology look like? Again we turn to Professor Hall. What we will discover in this theology thought Indigenously is a *"theologia crucis,"* which is "in its most rudimentary expression a theology of 'divine pathos' (Heschel) and covenantal faithfulness vis-à-vis the world."[45] Moreover, Hall notes that such a theology in a time such as ours is marked by that perdurable phenomenon of *Anfechtung* (trial, temptation, tribulation).[46] To understand better a theology of the cross marked by *Anfechtung*, we consider again Luther, this time in his "Preface to German Writings (1539)."[47]

In this document, Luther locates *Anfechtung* within the threefold strategy of studying Christian theology as *"oratio, meditatio* and *tentatio*, or *Anfechtung."*[48] With *oratio* Luther bids us begin theology on our knees, despairing of our reason as the faculty to guide us through life. He then considers *meditatio*, wherein the faithful pore over texts, reading them aloud "so that you may see what the Holy Spirit means by them."[49] And then Luther comes finally to the third step in studying theology:

> Thirdly, there is *tentatio, Anfechtung*. This is the touchstone which teaches you not only to know and understand, but also to experience how right, how true, how sweet, how lovely, how mighty, how comforting God's Word is, wisdom beyond all wisdom.[50]

We might be first surprised at such a description of *Anfechtung*, most often referenced as if it is hell on earth, a kind of Christian correlate of existential dread. But something else seems to be at work in Luther's understanding of *Anfechtung*, a correlate of his *theologia crucis*, so eloquently described in the Heidelberg Disputation. Here we read

> He, however, who has been emptied through suffering no longer does works but knows that God works and does all things in him. He neither boasts if he does good works, nor is he disturbed if God does not do good works through him. . . . [T]o be born anew one must consequently first die and then be raised up with the Son of Man. To die, I say, means to feel death at hand.[51]

Suffering the despair of being self-sufficient in this experience of *Anfechtung*, then, becomes the pang of the new birth ever bearing upon those finding themselves strangely in a place of faith.

Perhaps, in some fashion, this concept speaks to the experience of the dying church. The church in the West is dying; but in dying faithfully it finds itself again in need of the grace of testament. Here, as the church dies, we despair of our capacity to think our way out of our collective sin against the First Peoples of Turtle Island, and against the land itself. Here we return to our scriptures with a chided hermeneutic. Here, according to Luther, we "stop this senseless talk and consult experience."[52] And what is it we experience as we find ourselves born anew in the place of testament—sacred, living, and constantly renewed on this land called "mother"? We experience our death as an entitled church and experience birth as a church on this land. As we lift the bread to our mouths and taste the wheat of the fields of Saskatchewan; as we raise the cup to our lips and taste the grapes off the Niagara Escarpment; as we slide our hand into the baptismal bowl and feel the St. Laurence slip between our fingers, we feel ourselves being carried to the breast of our mother. And as we suckle from this land, treaty begins, here, in this place.

NOTES

1. "Traditional Territories," McGill University, accessed November 16, 2019, https://www.mcgill.ca/edu4all/other-equity-resources/traditional-territories.

2. "Six Nations' funded colleges and universities and never repaid," *Two Row Times,* December 28, 2016, https://tworowtimes.com/historical/six-nations-funded-colleges-universities-never-repaid/.

3. Douglas John Hall, *Thinking the Faith: Christian Theology in a North American Context* (Minneapolis, MN: Augsburg, 1989; paperback reprint: Minneapolis, MN: Fortress Press, 1991), 35.

4. See "They Came for the Children," Truth and Reconciliation Commission of Canada, accessed November 15, 2019, http://publications.gc.ca/collections/collection_2012/cvrc-trcc/IR4-4-2012-eng.pdf, and "Calls for Justice," Reclaiming Power and Place: The Final Report of the National Inquiry into Missing and Murdered Indigenous Women and Girls, accessed November 15, 2019, https://www.mmiwg-ffada.ca/wp-content/uploads/2019/06/Calls_for_Justice.pdf.

5. See "Truth and Reconciliation Commission of Canada: Calls to Action," Truth and Reconciliation Commission of Canada, accessed November 15, 2019, http://publications.gc.ca/collections/collection_2012/cvrc-trcc/IR4-4-2012-eng.pdf.

6. Jennifer Reid, "The Doctrine of Discovery and Canadian Law," *The Canadian Journal of Native Studies* 30, no. 2 (2010): 338.

7. Hall, *Thinking the Faith*, 165.

8. Leonard J. Trinterud, "The Origins of Puritanism," *Church History* 20, no. 1 (1951): 37, 38.

9. Trinterud, "The Origins of Puritanism," 38.

10. Trinterud, "The Origins of Puritanism," 45

11. William Klempa, "The Concept of Covenant in 16th and 17th Century Continental and British Reformed Theology," in *Major Themes in Reformed Theology*, edited by Donald K. McKim (Grand Rapids, MI: Eerdmans, 1992), 94.

12. Klempa, "The Concept of Covenant," 98.

13. Trinterud, "The Origins of Puritanism," 50.

14. Robert Warrior, "Canaanites, Cowboys, and Indians," in *Voices from the Margin*, edited by Sugirtharajah R.S. (Maryknoll, NY: Orbis, 1991), 240.

15. G.E. Mendenhall, "Covenant," in *The Interpreter's Dictionary of the Bible, Volume 1*, edited by G.A. Buttrick (Nashville, TN: Abingdon, 1962), 723.

16. Kiera L. Ladner and Michael McCrossan, "The Road Not Taken: Aboriginal Rights after the Re-Imaging of the Canadian Constitutional Order," in *Contested Constitutionalism, Law and Society* (Vancouver, BC: UBC Press, 2009), 265–66.

17. Harold Cardinal and Walter Hildebrandt, *Treaty Elders of Saskatchewan* (Calgary, AB: University of Calgary Press, 2000), 2.

18. Cardinal and Hildebrandt, *Treaty Elders*, 7, 25.

19. Cardinal and Hildebrandt, *Treaty Elders*, 39.

20. Cardinal and Hildebrandt, *Treaty Elders*, 7–32.

21. Cardinal and Hildebrandt, *Treaty Elders*, 34–35.

22. Richard W. Hill Sr. and Daniel Coleman, "The Two Row Wampum-Covenant Chain Tradition as a Guide for Indigenous-University Research Partnerships," *Cultural Studies—Critical Methodologies* 19, no. 5 (2018): 9.

23. Cardinal and Hildebrandt, *Treaty Elders*, 7.

24. Cardinal and Hildebrandt, *Treaty Elders*, 7.

25. Cardinal and Hildebrandt, *Treaty Elders*, 49.

26. Cardinal and Hildebrandt, *Treaty Elders*, 50.

27. "As Long as the Sun Shines, the Grass Grows and the River Flows," Faculty Blog, Faculty of Law University of Alberta, January 9, 2018, https://ualbertalaw.typepad.com/faculty/2018/01/as-long-as-the-sun-shines-the-grass-grows-and-the-river-flows.html.

28. Anthony J. Hall, "Creation, Original People, and the Colonization of a Hemisphere," in *Buffalo Shout, Salmon Cry: Conversations on Creation, Land Justice, and Life Together*, edited by Steve Heinrichs (Waterloo, ON: Herald Press, 2013), 45.

29. Adam Gaudry and Danielle Lorenz, "Indigenization as Inclusion, Reconciliation, and Decolonization: Navigating the Different Visions for Indigenizing the Canadian Academy," *AlterNative: An International Journal of Indigenous Peoples* 14, no. 3 (September 1, 2018): 22, https://doi.org/10.1177/1177180118785382.

30. Edna Manitowabi, "Indigenous Way of Knowing," Circle of Dialogue Public Lecture, Martin Luther University College, Waterloo, ON, March 19, 2019.

31. Edna Manitowabi, telephone conversation with the author, November 18, 2019.

32. Douglas John Hall, *Professing the Faith: Christian Theology in a North American Context* (Minneapolis, MN: Fortress Press, 1993), 112.

33. Douglas John Hall, *The Canada Crisis: A Christian Perspective* (Toronto, ON: Anglican Book Centre, 1980), 9.

34. Gerald Robert Vizenor, *Manifest Manners: Narratives on Postindian Survivance* (Lincoln, NE: University of Nebraska Press, 1999), xi.
35. Kenneth Hagen, "The Testament of a Worm: Luther on Testament and Covenant," *Consensus* 8, no. 1 (January 1, 1982): 16.
36. Martin Luther, *Luther's Works—American Edition*, 55 vols. (St. Louis, MO and Philadelphia, PA: Concordia Publishing House and Fortress Press, 1955), hereafter cited as LW volume number, page number. For the present reference see LW 35, 106.
37. LW 35, 86
38. Hagen, "The Testament of a Worm," 16.
39. LW 35, 95.
40. LW 35, 96.
41. LW 56, 96, 97.
42. Lauren Krugel, "Child Welfare System Is the New Residential School 'Monster,' Senator Says," *The Globe and Mail*, October 26, 2018, https://www.theglobeandmail.com/canada/article-residential-school-monster-now-lives-in-child-welfare-system-2/.
43. Hagen, "From Testament to Covenant," 8.
44. Hall, *The Canada Crisis*, 40.
45. Douglas John Hall, *Confessing the Faith: Christian Theology in a North American Context* (Minneapolis, MN: Fortress Press, 1996), 29.
46. Hall, *Thinking the Faith*, 110.
47. LW 34, 279–88.
48. LW 34, 285.
49. LW 34, 285.
50. LW 34, 286, 287.
51. LW 31, 55.
52. LW 31, 68.

WORKS CITED

Cardinal, Harold, and Walter Hildebrandt. *Treaty Elders of Saskatchewan*. Calgary, AB: University of Calgary Press, 2000.

Gaudry, Adam, and Danielle Lorenz. "Indigenization as Inclusion, Reconciliation, and Decolonization: Navigating the Different Visions for Indigenizing the Canadian Academy." *AlterNative: An International Journal of Indigenous Peoples* 14, no. 3 (September 1, 2018): 218–27. https://doi.org/10.1177/1177180118785382.

G.E. Mendenhall. "Covenant." In *The Interpreter's Dictionary of the Bible, Volume 1*, edited by Buttrick George Arthur, 714–23. Nashville, TN: Abingdon, 1962.

Hagen, Kenneth. "The Testament of a Worm: Luther on Testament and Covenant." *Consensus* 8, no. 1 (January 1, 1982): 12–20.

Hagen, Kenneth George. "From Testament to Covenant in the Early Sixteenth Century." *The Sixteenth Century Journal* 3, no. 1 (April 1972): 1–24.

Hall, Anthony J. "Creation, Original People, and the Colonization of a Hemisphere." In *Buffalo Shout, Salmon Cry: Conversations on Creation, Land Justice, and Life Together*, edited by Steve Heinrichs, 33–46. Waterloo, ON: Herald Press, 2013.

Hall, Douglas John. *Confessing the Faith: Christian Theology in a North American Context*. Minneapolis, MN: Fortress Press, 1996.

———. *Professing the Faith: Christian Theology in a North American Context*. Minneapolis, MN: Fortress Press, 1993.

———. *The Canada Crisis: A Christian Perspective*. Toronto, ON: Anglican Book Centre, 1980.

———. *Thinking the Faith: Christian Theology in a North American Context*. Minneapolis, MN: Augsburg, 1989; paperback reprint: Minneapolis, MN: Fortress Press, 1991.

Hill Sr., Richard W., and Daniel Coleman. "The Two Row Wampum-Covenant Chain Tradition as a Guide for Indigenous-University Research Partnerships." *Cultural Studies—Critical Methodologies* 19, no. 5 (2018): 1–20.

Krugel, Lauren. "Child Welfare System Is the New Residential School 'Monster', Senator Says." *The Globe and Mail*. October 26, 2018. https://www.theglobe andmail.com/canada/article-residential-school-monster-now-lives-in-child-welfare -system-2/.

Ladner, Kiera L., and Michael McCrossan. "The Road Not Taken: Aboriginal Rights after the Re-Imaging of the Canadian Constitutional Order." In *Contested Constitutionalism*, edited by James B. Kelly and Christopher P. Manfredi, 263–86. Law and Society. Vancouver, BC: UBC Press, 2009.

Luther, Martin. *Luther's Works—American Edition*. 55 vols. St. Louis, MO and Philadelphia, PA: Concordia Publishing House and Fortress Press, 1955.

Reid, Jennifer. "The Doctrine of Discovery and Canadian Law." *The Canadian Journal of Native Studies* 30, no. 2 (2010): 335–59.

Trinterud, Leonard J. "The Origins of Puritanism." *Church History* 20, no. 1 (1951): 37–57. https://doi.org/10.2307/3162047.

Vizenor, Gerald Robert. *Manifest Manners: Narratives on Postindian Survivance*. Lincoln, NE: University of Nebraska Press, 1999.

Warror, Robert. "Canaanites, Cowboys, and Indians." In *Voices from the Margin*, edited by R. S. Sugirtharajah, 235–41. Maryknoll, NY: Orbis, 1991.

Chapter 5

Indian Residential Schools and the Churches

An Exercise in the Theology of the Cross

Brian Thorpe

RESIDENTIAL SCHOOLS—A CHRISTENDOM PROJECT

As waves crashed against the western coast of Vancouver Island, a small boat transported three church bureaucrats to an offshore island that had been the ancestral home of the Ahousat First Nation since time immemorial. The task of the church officials was to enter into conversation with elders regarding an irritant in the historical relationship between the nation and the United Church of Canada. Until the early 1940s the United Church (and, prior to church union in 1925, the Presbyterian Church) had operated an Indian Residential School on the island. When the school burned down during World War II it was not replaced, and in 1953 the church had sold the property on which the school had sat to a nonindigenous individual. While for the church in that era this was a simple matter of a fee simple sale, for the Ahousat the loss of the land represented a broken oral promise made by missionaries in the late nineteenth century, who had assured the Ahousat that if the land were no longer used for educational purposes it would be returned to the Ahousat nation.

When the church folk arrived on the island, they were met not only by elders but also by the entire grade of class 12 from the local high school, who were anxious to witness a contemporary encounter between a mission church and their colonized nation. At several points during the elders' recounting of the history between themselves and the church, reference was made to an early twentieth-century commission that had created reserve boundaries in British Columbia. At one point in the dialogue, one of the young students asked one of the elders why this government body kept being referenced, since that particular day's encounter was between the nation and the church only. The elder replied by stating that to the Ahousats, along with any of the other First Nations in North America, when it came to the church and the state, "they were all the same people." While this might have been literally true—the reserve boundary commission was named, after its leaders, the "McKenna-McBride Commission" and the school was run by the Presbyterians—in a much more profound way the elder was acknowledging the reality of a Christendom much more easily recognized by those on the margins of both church and society than by the dominant society that took for granted the notion that the Christian church was a simply handmaiden to political power.

The creation in the late nineteenth century, of the federal Indian Residential Schools system was enabled by a partnership between government and four Christian denominations—Anglican, Methodist, Presbyterian, and Roman Catholic—that would be unthinkable in our contemporary post-Christendom era. The government of the day assumed that the colonizing goal of separating children from their families and culture could be best achieved through indoctrination in the religious traditions of the colonizer. For the Protestant churches, on the other hand, the opportunity to be the educators of indigenous children fit well with the evangelical zeal so characteristic of late-nineteenth-century Protestantism. For Roman Catholic entities, meanwhile, taking a leadership role in the schools would contribute to the protection of institutional Roman Catholicism against what was seen in both the United States and Canada as Protestant hegemony.

The participation of two of the founding denominations of the United Church of Canada—the Methodists and the Presbyterians—in the residential schools system reflected not only an uncritical approach to the relationship between church and state, but also the dominance of those traditions in the shaping of the cultural ethos of both the United States and Canada. With regard to the Reformed tradition, Douglas John Hall states,

> Incongruous as they may appear when considered in their original forms, Calvinism and Renaissance/Enlightenment humanism become co-partners in the formation of the North American spirit. While the triumphalism of later Calvinism was based upon an interpretation of the sovereign deity of the scriptures and the triumphalism of humanism found its rationale in the "laws" of nature and history, both of these chief inspirational sources of the North American experiment shared a highly positive view of human meaning.[1]

The marks of election in a secularized Calvinist system are worked out in different ways in the United States and Canada—the American emphasis is on entrepreneurialism and material success ("life, liberty, and the pursuit of happiness"), while the loyalist Canadian mantra urges duty and sobriety ("peace, order, and good government"), the positivism about which Hall speaks binds the two nations in a civic consciousness shaped by the Reformed tradition of western Europe.

Methodism, Hall argues, made its own contribution to the dominant cultural ethos of English Canada through its focus on the doctrine of perfection. "The Methodist doctrine of perfection could certainly find a place in such a social scheme; besides, Methodism, like its parent body, Anglicanism, lacked a searching doctrine of human sinfulness, on whose basis it might have been more skeptical of anthropocentric pretension."[2] This insight is confirmed by the fact that Egerton Ryerson, one of the leading Methodist leaders in nineteenth-century Upper Canada, seems not to have seen any contradiction between his championing of a nonsectarian public system of education for settlers in the colony and his support for a sectarian system of education for indigenous children. The uncritical acceptance of a cohesion between Christianity and the western European culture of the settlers was such that public education would never be seen as a threat to the Christian identity of the settlers, while sectarian education was seen as an essential ingredient in the assimilation of indigenous children into that culture.

The time period in which the modern residential school system was birthed—the late nineteenth century—is also significant.[3] The so-called age of progress in Western culture had nurtured an optimistic vision of human agency and a corresponding disregard for human limitation. For the Protestant churches of the era, the theological liberalism that had migrated from Europe to the shores of North America seemed particularly suited to the aspirations of nation-building and colonial conquest, especially for the United Church's founding denominations. Weaned on the early social gospel and theological liberalism, the church often fell into the trap of confusing its call to shape its actions in anticipation of the coming realm of God with the assumption that its good works would bring about that realm within human history, with God as a benign bystander. It was this temptation to self-sufficiency and power that led the churches into an unholy alliance with the principalities and powers. More important still in relation to the churches' role in the residential schools system was the neglect, in a theology rooted in an age of progress and optimism, of the ambiguous nature of every human act. In its actions in support of the colonizing project, and in its commitment to education as a salvific tool in the evangelistic mission, it resisted the notion that even the most selfless acts carry with them the risk of that sin which Jesus so despised: self-righteousness. This neglect and resistance often led to an easy conscience on the part of the churches, which were able to keep the focus on their good intentions, while ignoring the social and political assumptions informing those intentions.

THE CHANGING CONTEXT: THE END OF CHRISTENDOM

While the end of Christendom in Europe can trace its roots to the "thin tradition" in the Reformation and the Age of Enlightenment, it can be argued that Christendom lingered much longer in North America. In a similar vein, the tragedy of World War I, which in Europe brought an abrupt end to the naïve optimism of the late nineteenth century, did not have the same impact on the other side of the Atlantic. As a result, the myth of Christendom continued to influence the thought and actions of the church in Canada long after it had ceased to have much hold in Europe. It can be argued that this situation in liberal churches such as the United Church of Canada, buoyed by the culturally significant but theologically vacuous growth of suburban churches in the post–World War II period, existed until the 1960s.

The reality of the end of Christendom was not broadly acknowledged until the 1960s—which helps to explain why a church such as the United Church took so long to divest itself of an archaic partnership with the Canadian government. In 1947, the United Church presented a brief to a joint committee of the House of Commons and the Senate, which was charged with making changes to the Indian Act. In its brief, the church acknowledged the problems of institutionalized education and recommended what, for the time, would have been considered a progressive alternative. However, in a telling comment, the church also stated that it was proud of the work it had done to combat paganism in indigenous culture. In other words, the United Church of Canada was still unable to separate its mission from the assimilationist policies of the government. It would take another four decades for it to articulate the central Christendom error in its relationship with indigenous peoples, when it finally confessed that "we confused Western ways and culture with the depth and breadth and length and height of the gospel of Christ. We imposed our civilization as a condition of accepting the gospel."[4]

RESIDENTIAL SCHOOLS AND THE THEOLOGY OF THE CROSS

If the creation of the residential schools system and the churches' involvement therein can be perceived through the lens of Christendom, then the impact of the schools on indigenous peoples and on the integrity of the churches involved in the system can be viewed through the theology of the cross. In contrast to the uncritical assumptions about human history that characterize a Christendom church, a theology of the cross drives us toward an understanding of history and the human condition that is informed by the tragedy of crucifixion. The suffering of Jesus on the cross finds its correlation in human experience in the suffering of the world. This theological perspective will prove to be much more open to the suffering experienced by survivors of the residential schools systems and communities devastated by colonialism than would be the case for a Christendom church, for which an understanding of the reality of the human story is restrained by institutional success and doctrinal certitude. Martin Luther labeled the theology emerging from such a church as *theologia gloriae*. In the twenty-first thesis of the Heidelberg Disputation, Luther contrasts this theology with *theologia crucis*: "A theologian of glory calls evil good and good evil. A theologian of the cross calls the thing what it actually is."[5] Participation of churches in the residential schools system reflected an uncritical identification of the Christian gospel with Western civilization, at the behest of the principalities and powers of the day. Ignored in this process were the voices of those marginalized and broken by the policies of church and government. A theology of the cross that focuses on the suffering caused by political and religious power opens us to the possibility that when we speak about the impact of residential schools, we might begin to "call the thing what it actually is."

Douglas John Hall articulates an anthropology that is informed by what he calls "a single thesis with three prongs: *The cross of Jesus Christ represents simultaneously a high estimate of the human creature, a grave realism concerning human alienation, and the compassionate determination of God to bring humankind to the realization of its potentiality for authenticity.*"[6] In the biblical narrative these three prongs correspond to creation, the reality of sin in the human condition and the promise of redemption. To view the impact of residential schools through the lens of the theology of the cross is to consider each of these prongs and the way in which they inform the experience of residential schools survivors and the contemporary response of the church to the legacy of its role in this colonizing project.

The Theology of the Cross and the Goodness of Creation

The biblical narrative begins in Genesis with a powerful affirmation of the goodness of creation. What follows, however, is a story of infidelity, dishonesty, and violence, which pervade the story of Israel and of the emergence of the Christian movement. In spite of such disappointments and setbacks, the goodness of creation does not disappear from the scene. Through covenant and grace, the essential blessing of creation is restored again and again. What this means in terms of our understanding of the human condition is that we live in a dialectic tension in which the horror and beauty of human existence coexist. Nowhere is this more evident than in the symbol of the cross. The cross exists both as a symbol of human cruelty and injustice and as an affirmation of divine presence with us in the midst of suffering.

Douglas Hall articulates this dialectical understanding of the cross in this way: "Faith . . . sees behind and beyond the brutality and ugliness of the crucifixion as such; it sees the glory (*doxa*) 'hidden beneath its opposite' (Luther). The resurrectional-pentecostal perspective that is faith's presupposition sees in this scene of ultimate human degradation the ultimate identification and solidarity of the Creator with the creature."[7]

During the first four years of the twenty-first century, a group of twenty-eight survivors of the Edmonton Indian Residential School gathered with representatives of the government of Canada and the United Church of Canada in the Gitxsan Nation in northern British Columbia. The purpose of these meetings was to seek justice and restitution for harms done in the school. An attempt was made to replace the adversarial nature of the courtroom with a more culturally sensitive approach to truth telling and resolving conflict. In the process, each of the survivors was given as much time as was needed to tell his or her story. The stories were filled with the pain of separation and abuse. There were also horrific stories of lives marred by the aftermath of the trauma created by the institutionalization of young children. In the testimony of the survivors, the suffering symbolized by the cross was made incarnate.

However, there was another dimension of narrative present among that group of survivors. During the 1950s and 1960s a sexual predator was present among the staff at the school. His modus operandi was to prey on younger boys in the school. Observing this, some of the older boys banded together to form a clandestine organization which they called "The Older Brothers." When they observed the predator getting close to one of the younger boys, they would find ways to insert themselves between the predator and his intended victim.

As the men recounted these acts of defiance and protection, one could sense the pride and love which emerged in the midst of stories of pain and violence. In an institutional setting in which government-appointed officials should have protected their charges and in which church employees should have exercised compassion, the government was more concerned about administrative issues—and the church's chaplain was, in fact, the predator! In this tragic drama, it was those with the least power within the institution who were the agents of protection and healing.

In the theology of the cross, the grace and the presence of God is imbedded in the tragedy and violence of crucifixion. Thus, the essential goodness of creation is revealed in that which would negate goodness—the cross.

In the human narrative, the creation of the residential schools system represents one more chapter in which the negation of the essential goodness of creation—in this case, the essential goodness of the relationship, culture, and spirituality of First Nations—results in the reliving of crucifixion. However, embedded in this particular tale of crucifixion is the story of the Older Brothers. Although they had so little agency within the institution in which they had been placed, through acts of solidarity and courage, the Older Brothers brought about the protections that neither the church nor the state had been able or willing to provide. In this way, the essential goodness of creation was revealed in a system which would negate that very goodness.

It is this dialectic, in which goodness and its negation coexist, and in which the value and beauty of existence itself cannot be overcome, that the hope of redemption for all creation is sustained. It is in this dialectic, in which the courage and compassion of boys coexists with an institution that is dehumanizing, and in which the value and beauty of a particular form of existence—that of indigenous peoples—cannot be overcome, that the hope of right relations and justice is sustained.

The Theology of the Cross and the Sin of Estrangement

The end of the churches' involvement in the residential schools system in 1969 was followed by two decades of cultural in both indigenous and non-indigenous communities. When the silence was broken by the public testimony of survivors of the schools, the most prominent of whom was Chief Phil Fontaine of the Assembly of First Nations, a forgotten chapter of the churches' role in the colonization of First Nations slowly came to the fore. For the United Church the most dramatic way in which the consciousness of the church was stirred took the form of a lawsuit in which survivors of the Alberni Indian Residential School who had been sexually and physically abused sued the federal government and the church. While the accounts of abuse witnessed in the courtroom were horrific, another dimension of survivors' testimony struck to the core of Christian sensibility regarding individual and corporate sin: the wrenching stories of young children being separated from family and community. Trips of hundreds of miles by rail or bus brought children from close-knit and remote communal environments into an institution in which the language and customs were alien.

From the perspective of Western law, the focus of the wrongs remained the instances of physical and sexual abuse and the impact of these on the future lives of the victims. The loss of family relationships, spirituality, and community solidarity are not considered as "torts" in Canadian law. From the point of view of Christian narrative, however, these losses should be considered as central to what could be labeled as sin in this story.

In his exposition of the theology of the cross in a North American context, Douglas Hall points to the centrality of estrangement in any understanding of sin. It is the estrangement of Christ from God (the "forsaken" cry) on the cross that elicits the human *sitz im leben* (setting in life) to which the cross and Christ. the representative of estranged humanity, is related. In the Christendom version of the gospel, this important message is often lost. Hall comments, "No word in the Christian vocabulary is so badly misunderstood both in the world and in the churches as the word *sin*. Christians have allowed this profoundly biblical conception, which refers to broken relationship, to be reduced to *sins*—moral misdemeanors and guilty 'thoughts, words and deeds,' especially of the sexual variety, that could be listed and confessed and absolved."[8]

In the courtroom in which the United Church and the government of Canada stood together as codefendants, the sins of sexual and physical abuse were named and compensation (insignificant in relation to the harm done) was ordered. However, the sin of broken relationship would require repentance on the part of the church, which would go far beyond what a Western court might demand.

The Theology of the Cross and the Gift of Authenticity

When Douglas John Hall speaks of the third prong of his articulation of the Theology of the Cross, he uses the term "authenticity" to define what in Christian nomenclature is often called "redemption." This choice of terminology represents a deliberate attempt to move away from an Anselmic-Calvinist notion of the atonement representing a payment by God through Christ of the debt incurred by human sinfulness. As Hall argues, while this transactional analysis might appeal to the emerging capitalist models that accompanied the growth of Protestantism, it fails to adequately encompass the reality of divine grace for those whose lives reflect the way of the cross more directly than the privileged inheritors of both capitalism and the individualism and easy conscience engendered by the Enlightenment. Rather, Hall suggests, the concept of authenticity reflects an understanding of atonement in which the suffering of Christ is not simply a divine transaction but is, rather, a divine-human relationship in the midst of suffering. Thus redemption becomes the divine "yes" to the essential goodness of humanity, and, indeed, of all creation. Hall encapsulates this notion in this profound statement: "The object of divine grace in the life, death and resurrection of Jesus Christ is the justifying of the human."[9]

Resolution of claims against the government and the church by the courts, or even through alternative dispute resolution processes could be seen as simply transactional processes. Crimes were committed. If those who were responsible for the institutions in which the crimes were committed were found to be responsible, compensation to victims was paid.

However, these processes were never sufficient. It was not just the case that the monetary compensation was too small (although this was often the case), but rather that the humanity of the survivors was always much greater than the acts of violence committed against them. The transactional response to civil suits found in Western legal systems might have satisfied those living in comfort and relative security. For those for whom the way of the cross continues to be a lived reality, the response was profoundly inadequate.

It was for this reason that the Truth and Reconciliation Commission was formed. The hope engendered by this public policy response was that in allowing survivors and others in the residential schools system to tell their story and to have that story acknowledged by church and state, their essential humanity and its particular expression in indigenous culture might be upheld.

In the terms of the Theology of the Cross, the settlement of claims in a court of law represented the payment of a debt. The testimony of a complete life, on the other hand, whose tragedy is held in tension with a culture, spirituality, and individual acts of courage that tragedy could not destroy, represents an affirmation of human authenticity.

THE THEOLOGY OF THE CROSS AND THE CONTEMPORARY CHURCH

As the impact of the churches' Christendom project, in which they acted as spiritual handmaidens the state and participated in the state's colonizing practices in relation to indigenous peoples, began to be understood in the post-Christendom era of the late twentieth century, the reactions of those faithful souls still left in the churches varied. Two of the most common responses to the emerging narrative of residential schools were denial and incapacitating guilt. Neither of these responses, however, offered either comfort or justice to the survivors of the schools.

These responses did also reflect the church's need for a new theological imagination in respect to its identity and mission. The expressions of denial more often than not reflected a nostalgia for the lost realm of Christendom, in which the mission of the church was indistinguishable from the dominant culture in which it lived—and in which those on the margins of that culture might, at best, receive charity, but their stories would never inform the mandate of either church or state. On the other hand, those who were incapacitated by guilt in response to the legacy of residential schools did indeed experience the tragedy of the cross in the testimony of survivors, but they missed the redemptive power of that same narrative of the cross.

In one of those circles of survivors and government and church representatives in which the stories of residential schools were told, one incident occurred that encapsulates the reality of that redemptive power. This particular circle listened as one survivor of the Edmonton Indian Residential School recounted years of abuse in the school. After the testimony concluded, a monetary settlement was offered and accepted. Once again, if this resolution were seen as simply a transactional matter, the drama of the day would have concluded. Yet there was another part to the story. The psychologist in the circle offered to drive the survivor home, and then returned to the circle. The survivor had told him, said the psychiatrist to the group, that he never thought the day would arrive when his story would be believed by those in authority. And then the survivor had paused, and then added, "I was just getting to know those guys and I'll probably never see them again."

At first glance, the survivor's reflection expresses a grim reality: historically, both the Indian Agent and the missionary would arrive in a community, have an impact for good or ill, and then leave. But there is another, deeper layer here. From person who would have the least reason in the world to offer it comes the offer of relationship. The story does not end, after all, with a transaction. Rather it begins again with the offer of relationship.

The story of the cross is shallow if it ends with a transaction between sinful humanity and a merciful God. It takes on power if it does not end, but rather begins again with the divine-human relationship in the suffering and beauty of creation. Douglas John Hall concludes his discussion of the three prongs of the Theology of the Cross by lovingly repeating the words of Martin Luther, which reflect both the ongoing promise of the cross and, in our context, the hope of a survivor who was "just getting to know these guys":

> Christian living does not mean to *be* good but to become good; not to *be* well but to get well; not being but becoming; not rest but training. We are not yet, but we shall be. It has not yet happened. But it is the way. Not everything shines and sparkles as yet, but everything is getting better.[10]

For the contemporary church, the story of residential schools can be seen as a historical narrative that has little to do with the current mission and identity of the Christian community. However, to relegate the story of our colonizing past to the confines of history would be akin to seeing the cross as nothing more than a prelude to resurrection. What is missed when we speak of either crucifixion or the story of residential schools as past events is the fact that these cruelties of the human story keep recurring in different forms.

More important, what is missed when we treat crucifixion and the injustices perpetrated by the church as past events is the hope of relationship embedded in the human tragedy. In the cross, the intimate relationship between sacred and secular is enacted in the death of God at the hands of religious and political authority. In the residential schools system, the colonial relationship between oppressors and oppressed lies at the center of the enterprise. Embedded in both of these relationships is the hope of repentance and redemption. The divine-human relationship in the cross engenders the promise of the accompaniment of God in the suffering of humanity. The relationship between the church and First Nations children in the residential schools offers the promise that, through acts of repentance on the part of the church, right relationships between settlers and First Nations peoples might mark the identity and mission of a postcolonial Christian movement.

NOTES

1. Douglas John Hall, *Thinking the Faith: Christian Theology in a North American Context* (Minneapolis, MN: Augsburg, 1989; paperback reprint: Minneapolis, MN: Fortress Press, 1991), 166.
2. Hall, *Thinking the Faith*, 166.
3. Residential schools largely operated by churches had existed in Canada since the eighteenth century, but the national system only came into being with the implementation of the 1879 Davin report. See J. R. Miller, *Shingwauk's Vision: A History of Native Residential Schools* (Toronto, ON: University of Toronto Press, 1996), 101–3.
4. The United Church of Canada, "Apology to First Nations Peoples" (General Council, 1986).
5. Douglas John Hall, *The Cross in Our Context: Jesus and the Suffering World* (Minneapolis, MN: Fortress Press, 2003), 20.
6. Hall, *The Cross in Our Context*, 91.
7. Hall, *The Cross in Our Context*, 93.
8. Hall, *The Cross in Our Context*, 104.
9. Hall, *The Cross in Our Context*, 106–7.
10. Hall, *The Cross in Our Context*, 109.

WORKS CITED

Hall, Douglas John. *The Cross in Our Context: Jesus and the Suffering World*. Minneapolis, MN: Fortress Press, 2003.

———. *Thinking the Faith: Christian Theology in a North American Context*. Minneapolis, MN: Augsburg, 1989; paperback reprint: Minneapolis, MN: Fortress Press, 1991.

Miller, J. R. *Shingwauk's Vision: A History of Native Residential Schools*. Toronto, ON: University of Toronto Press, 1996.

The United Church of Canada. "Apology to First Nations Peoples." General Council, 1986.

Chapter 6

Hall's Eco-Theology of the Cross in a Climate-Changed World

Harold Wells

This chapter is an appreciative exposition and analysis of Douglas John Hall's thought and its relevance to the climate crisis. Perhaps the best place to begin is with a story Hall tells about waiting for a bus to go to work on a hot, smoggy summer morning in Montreal. Car after car went past, usually inhabited only by the driver. As he stood there inhaling noxious fumes, he wanted to paint a big sign and hold it up: "Take the bus, dammit!" But as he stood there he had bleak apocalyptic thoughts:

> Are we at the beginning of a really dangerous period in the history of our planet? Is the global warming about which so many have warned us quite literally real . . . ? Is this maybe the onset of planetary catastrophe?—How do you know when you are at the beginning of a really dangerous period in the history of our planet? When is the point of no return? Is it already too late to alter the tragic course of a planet in the throes of repression, self-deception and delusions of ideological progress-theory?[1]

Hall's passionate concern for the future of humanity and the planetary biosphere is evident throughout his writings. But how is this ecological concern integrated into his whole, many-faceted theology? Even the slightest acquaintance with his work makes it obvious that Hall's theology is, from beginning to end, a theology of the cross. We could also describe it as an innovative "neo-orthodoxy," or even as "neo-Niebuhrian." In a recent brief writing, Hall lamented that "too much that passes for theology in North America, perhaps especially in Canada, is fragmentary, obscure or driven by one-issue preoccupation." Certainly he has not been preoccupied with one issue. In that little essay, he indicates his aspiration: "To see life whole." He also regrets theology's withdrawal from the public sphere. "Where," he cries, "is Reinhold Niebuhr when we need him?"[2]

In this paper I shall consider Hall's published work as ecological theology. Then I shall explore his *theologia crucis*, to see how the ecological theme and theology of the cross are mutually illuminating. Hall's theology demonstrates that in our time, a theology of the cross needs to be an ecological theology, and a Christian ecological theology needs to be a theology of the cross. However, I begin with some brief comments on our present context, that is, specifically, our present global context of climate crisis, to which, I believe, Hall's theology is highly relevant.

THE CONTEXT: A NEW DARK AGE?

One of Hall's greatest contributions to theology is the effective way that he has pressed upon us the need for an intentional contextuality; that is, his insistence that engagement of the milieu in which theology is done is an essential dimension of the theological task. He recognizes that dialogue with other disciplines must include the physical sciences.[3] In our time of climate crisis it is especially the geo-physicists, biochemists, marine biologists, and glaciologists to whom theologians and preachers must listen. In the *Toronto Journal of Theology* (1985), Hall writes that contextuality becomes most acute in theology "when the theological community has been hit over the head by very tangible and unsettling facts of contemporary existence." He mentions at that time nuclear war, world hunger, environmental and technological crises, and economic inequality.[4] Now, as we approach the third decade of this twenty-first century, we are "hit over the head" with the real possibility that we are moving toward "a new dark age."[5] This is the judgment of James Lovelock, the distinguished British multidisciplinary scientist and inventor, eminent for his contribution to dealing with ozone depletion. Hall himself refers appreciatively to Lovelock, especially his concept of the planet Earth as Gaia, "whose being throughout is relational."[6] Lovelock speaks of Earth as a "live, self-regulating planet."[7] He was among the first to warn of the drastic global warming that is occurring because of our human use of fossil fuels—coal, oil, and natural gas—to the tune of 40 billion tons of carbon dioxide every year.[8] Lovelock is optimistic that humanity will survive the oncoming disasters. But what does optimism mean to Lovelock? He believes that the number of human beings surviving will not be in the billions, but unlikely "less than millions; this is more than enough," he says, "for the survival of our species."[9] Such is the optimism of a distinguished scientist in our time.

Lovelock is not alone in these dire warnings. A leading American climatologist, James Hansen, imagines a "Venus Syndrome"—a world so overheated with carbon dioxide, methane, and other greenhouse gases as to render the Earth finally "uninhabitable."[10] Again, Elizabeth Kolbert, telling the story of the great five extinctions that have afflicted our planet, whether through frequent ice ages, global warming, or through volcanic eruption or asteroid strike, warns of a coming "sixth extinction" perpetrated by the planet's most intelligent creatures.[11] Most importantly, the UN Intergovernmental Panel on Climate Change (IPCC) brings together the research of hundreds of scientists of many disciplines from all over the world. According to the IPCC report of 2018, if humanity continues on its present trajectory, we are on track to exceed a global average of 1.5°C, and to approach 2°C above preindustrial levels by 2030.[12] This is generally regarded as a tipping point into global, chaotic circumstances never before recorded in human history. It will mean much more of what we have already begun to see: excessive heat, melting of the polar regions, rising seas, inundation of islands and coastal lands, rampant fires and floods, and violent weather. We should imagine before the end of this century a planet convulsed with so much suffering, from physical disasters, mass migrations, food and water shortages, and economic and institutional collapse, that the whole notion of human progress will seem laughable. "The dark age would arrive within one generation," writes one author.[13]

The practitioners of political and economic sciences also make their indispensable contribution. In her recent books, Naomi Klein, a multi-disciplinary public intellectual, argues that any serious attempt to deal with climate change would involve major regulation of national economies—regulations completely contrary to deregulated capitalism, which has a stranglehold on the economic, political, and economic processes. "Market capitalism," she says, "has systematically sabotaged our collective response to climate change."[14] Climate action looks like socialism to an elite who detest any kind of government restriction of their ability to make profits, so that "profit for private companies always trumps climate action."[15] In her most recent book, Klein comments that the required solutions to the climate crisis "make some kind of left-wing revolution virtually inevitable, which is precisely why they [the elites] are so determined to deny its reality."[16]

Not only humans are threatened. In 2019, a report of the UN Intergovernmental Science Policy-Platform on Biodiversity informs us that human activity is mainly responsible for an unprecedented decline in biodiversity. Some 680 vertebrate species have gone extinct since the sixteenth century. One million biological species are now threatened by extinction, including 40 percent of all amphibians, a third of both reef-building corals and marine mammals, and 10 percent of all insects.[17]

But humanity has not yet reached the peak of its technocratic hubris. Already scientists and technicians are contemplating various forms of "geo-engineering" to combat foreseeable climate holocaust through, for example, solar radiation management technologies, which would inject sulfate particles into the upper atmosphere to reflect the heat back into space and so manipulate planetary temperatures and rainfall. In the view of critics of geo-engineering, such schemes will have unforeseen consequences, and would seem to "trespass in a domain properly beyond the human."[18] Another author suggests that eventually, geo-engineering will give us "designer climates, localized to very particular needs."[19] This would take to a new level the power and control of planetary life by human beings, in a new epoch which scientists have now labeled "the Anthropocene." This word names the era wherein human beings have initiated a new geological epoch by altering the composition of the atmosphere.[20]

ECOLOGICAL THEOLOGY IN AN "OFFICIALLY OPTIMISTIC SOCIETY"

Authors like Lovelock, Hansen, and even the UN agencies, are often dismissed as prophets of gloom and doom. It is difficult for the general public to take seriously the dark warnings of these soothsayers, especially in what Hall calls "the officially optimistic society." As early as 1976, in Hall's first major volume, *Lighten Our Darkness*, he laments the "drummed up determination to think positively" so basic to North American cultural rhetoric. Although our most characteristic experience is now "one of impending catastrophe, disintegration, chaos, negation," we North Americans are the "least capable of encountering this abyss."[21] After all, North Americans did not suffer the worst of the great wars that so disillusioned the European world about inevitable human progress. Moreover, the two northern nations of this continent began to take shape just as the age of science and modern technology began, with its sense of unlimited opportunity and growing assurance that humans were, in the words of Descartes, "the lords and possessors of nature."[22] Citing Canadian philosopher George Grant, Hall points out that the idea of progress derives from the linear view of history implicit in the biblical doctrine of divine providence.[23] Already in the eighteenth century, European Enlightenment thinkers asserted the perfectibility of humanity and of the human social order. But it was in the New World that faith in progress truly took hold. It was faith in history itself, history as redemptive, that shaped and formed our distinctively North American modern culture.[24] And, of course, it is humanity's mastery through advanced technology that reinforces the technocratic "religion of progress," increasingly replacing divine providence with an anthropocentric optimism, which becomes, as Hall says, a compulsory and "official" optimism in North American culture.

All of this makes it nearly impossible, he argues, for North Americans to face the darkness that threatens. As early as the mid-1970s he speaks of the possible "end of the human race," and even more, "the prospect of a planet unable to support life of any kind."[25] At that time he had in mind not the threat of climate change, but the specter of nuclear holocaust, which remains today a very real possibility. We have developed, Hall says, a kind of "programmed indifference to much of the data of despair."[26]

Hall is well aware of the accusations leveled at historic Christianity regarding environmental destruction. Famously, the historian Lynn White wrote that Christianity, "the most anthropocentric religion" the world has ever seen, bears a huge burden of guilt, for it taught "man's transcendence of, and rightful mastery over, nature." By destroying pagan animism, White argued, "Christianity made it possible to exploit nature in a mood of indifference."[27] Hall believes we cannot easily dismiss this charge. Not that biblical faith itself endorses such a view of humanity's relation to creation, but that Christian rhetoric has so often legitimized the right of human beings to dominate nature and thus to foster the technocratic image of humanity.[28] It is doubtful, he thinks, that such a view of humanity could have arisen except on Christian soil; nevertheless it is a distortion of the biblical view. In scripture, the divine dominion is always prior to any human dominion, for "the earth is the Lord's and the fullness thereof" (Ps. 24:1). Especially in the Hebrew scriptures, humans are to live in God's creation in an attitude of thanksgiving. The modern technocratic view of human mastery, which has produced the nuclear bomb and now global warming, cannot be defended biblically without distortion.[29]

We note, then, that Hall's ecological theology is clearly grounded in scripture, and that it remains Christ-centered. He does not adopt a so-called creation spirituality such as that which we might associate with, for example, Matthew Fox.[30] He avoids an "eco-spirituality," or "nature-romanticism," insisting that nature is not divine, nor always benign.[31] He does not concur with the cosmo-centrism of Thomas Berry, who proposes that we should set aside the Bible for twenty years, for "the universe, the solar system and the planet Earth should constitute . . . the primary revelation of that ultimate mystery whence all things emerge into being."[32] Differing from these views, Hall resists any "soft-peddling of our christocentrism," opting rather for "deepening it."[33]

Hall therefore articulates a biblical and christological foundation for his ecological theology, for example in his exegesis of one of the most abused biblical texts, namely Genesis 1:28, wherein human beings, created in God's image, are given "dominion" over other creatures. This text, notorious among environmentalists, must be read in light of other scriptures, and in light of the lordship of Christ. First, the text does indeed bear witness to what Halls calls a dialectical tension in humanity's relation to the natural realm. Humans do indeed stand above nature; they are not merely part of it. In "remembering, hoping and speaking," they are "united, yet not united with nature." Nevertheless, humans are also within nature, shaped from the dust of the earth, and utterly dependent on other creatures for their existence.[34] Hall insists, in his book *Imaging God* (1986), that the dominion or rule of God the Creator is one of love, not domination. Most clearly, for Christians, the dominion of God is disclosed in the Servanthood of Jesus.[35] His dominion as Lord is that of "the healer of the sick, the seeker of the lost, the one who forgives and seeks the restoration of the sinner."[36] Our human dominion, then, must be understood from our christological center.

Already in *Lighten our Darkness*, Hall expounds the biblical concept of the human as "steward," which he believes best expresses the meaning of humanity's dominion.[37] Again, in *The Steward: A Biblical Symbol Come of Age* (1982) he points out that the steward in the Hebrew scriptures is a servant, but a superior servant, a person of authority and power. Yet the steward remains a servant, accountable to another. In the parable of stewardship in Luke 12, the stewards of the Son of Man are characterized as managers and caretakers of their master's Kingdom. Terrible judgment follows for stewards who forget their servant role. Hall argues that Christ himself can be seen as the faithful steward of God, the exemplar and foundation of our stewardship.[38]

In *The Stewardship of Life in the Kingdom of Death* (1985), written in the midst of the Reagan presidency in the United States, and at the height of the Cold War arms race, Hall speaks darkly of humanity's flirtation with death, which he calls a kind of "social necrophilia." He has in mind "multifold disasters," including the disappearance of whole species of animals and plants. "The bomb," he writes, is only "the most potent symbolic and real of these concretizations of death." Hall confronts the phenomenon of a Christian Religious Right, which looks with gleeful excitement toward an apocalyptic holocaust which will bring about "the Rapture."[39] Over against this, Hall insists that the "this-worldliness" of biblical faith means that this world really matters. He cites Dietrich Bonhoeffer's *Letters and Papers from Prison*: "This world must not be prematurely abandoned. In this, the Old and New Testaments are at one."[40]

When we come to Hall's later work, for example *Waiting for Gospel* (2012), we find that he is deeply alarmed by the overwhelming ecological crisis that is global warming. While he is aware of many crises facing human civilization, he says, this "radical deterioration of the environment is both the most ubiquitously threatening . . . and the most difficult for the possessing peoples of the planet to grasp and admit."[41] How does Hall address this crisis theologically? It is evident from his earliest work that the chosen method and perspective of his theology as a whole is a "theology of the cross." We now turn to see how Hall's ecological theology of stewardship informs, and is informed by, his *theologia crucis*.

THEOLOGY OF THE CROSS: A THEOLOGICAL AND FAITH POSTURE

This minority genre is, as he explains in *Thinking the Faith*, the basic "point of view" of his theology as a whole. From the beginning in *Lighten our Darkness*, in *Thinking the Faith* (1989), and every subsequent volume, it is evident that theology of the cross is Hall's basic "theological and faith posture."[42]

Theologia crucis, of course, is a concept and perspective named by Martin Luther, which, however, has deep roots in both testaments of the Bible. With reference to the Jewish theologian Abraham Heschel, Hall points out that the God of the theology of the cross is the God of the Hebrew prophets, the passionate God of pathos, who weeps, laments, and suffers with the people.[43] This is the God of Paul the apostle, who speaks in 1 Corinthians of the weakness and foolishness of God, which is nevertheless stronger and wiser than human strength or human wisdom (1 Cor. 1:25). Luther's theology of the cross is fundamentally about the doctrine of God, and about God's love and free grace for sinners. It was Luther who first spoke of "the crucified God."[44] It was he who broke decisively with the dominant theological tradition regarding the "impassibility" of God. In this Luther departed from a major element of classical theism, affirming explicitly that God suffers:

> God wished again to be recognized in suffering . . . so that those who did not honour God as manifested in his works should honour him as he is hidden in his suffering. . . . Now it is not sufficient for anyone, and it does him no good to recognize God in his glory and majesty, unless he recognizes him in the glory and shame of his cross.[45]

Luther contrasted theology of cross with a theology of glory. *Theologia gloriae* was the term by which he named the ruling theology of the Catholic church of his day—a theology that emphasizes God's absolute power and control, and thereby legitimizes domineering political powers, along with a powerful and glorious ecclesiastical institution. Hall stands with Luther on the crucial question of the suffering of God. The true God is the hidden One, the kenotic, self-limiting One who suffers with and for us in Christ. In a lengthy chapter of *Professing the Faith*, Hall articulates his faith in Jesus Christ as Emmanuel, God with us, which is the essential premise of this theology.[46] However, he does not merely repeat Luther's theology of the cross, but contextualizes and enriches it for our twentieth and twenty-first centuries. Specifically, Hall develops the potential of *theologia crucis* as a political theology in the post-Christendom era. He explains in *Thinking the Faith*:

> This of course has been facilitated greatly by the disestablishment of the Christian religion. Under the conditions of the Constantinian arrangement, . . . to offer a political gospel so thoroughly at odds with empire was virtually unthinkable. Even a mind as prolific and critical as Luther's could not undertake, in such a context, the full exploration of this tradition for its larger, public meaning.[47]

The development of theology of the cross by numerous authors in the post–World War II era has been described as "theology after Auschwitz."[48] In view of the unspeakable horrors of the Nazi holocaust of the Jews, theology could never be the same again. As Hall indicates, theology post-Auschwitz sees the dominant theological traditions of Christendom as forms of theology of glory. Over against this, today theology of the cross must be a political theology "at odds with empire." Hall, like others, is inspired by Dietrich Bonhoeffer, who wrote compellingly from a Nazi prison about the weakness and suffering of God:

> The God who is with us is the God who forsakes us . . . God lets himself be pushed out of the world and on to the cross. He is weak and powerless in the world, and that is precisely the way, the only way, in which he is with us and helps us.[49]

While Luther's theology of the cross was overwhelmingly concerned with the forgiveness of sin, Hall's contemporary *theologia crucis* is concerned with the social, ethical, and political implications of Christology and the doctrine of the self-emptying God. The theodicy question is key for us here: How, in light of theology of the cross, should we understand the providence of a loving God who fails to intervene in the most horrific of circumstances? Specifically, how are we to understand the providence of God in the face of unprecedented natural disasters, the potential end of civilization through nuclear war or climate change, and even, possibly, an uninhabitable Earth?

CLIMATE CRISIS AND THE PROVIDENCE OF GOD

In the Christian tradition, providence is about God's dominion, preservation, and governance of the world. As we have seen, in his earlier work Hall had commented that the Christian doctrine of providence has been replaced in modernity by an optimistic doctrine of progress through technology. He draws upon George Grant, who has written profoundly about the dehumanization that results from the subservience of humans to "technique."[50] In *Confessing the Faith* (1996) Hall strongly rejects, with Grant, what he calls "the optimistic anthropology of liberalism," or "the religion of progress." He insists: "Christians do not believe in progress, they believe in providence."[51] But how should providence be understood in a theology of the cross? And how does it relate to the climate crisis? Can we trust in God's providence to deliver us from climate catastrophe?

We note first that, for Hall, God's providence is a matter of faith—faith and not sight. "That the world is being preserved from beyond its own internal processes is a matter of faith." Faith in providence follows upon the doctrines of God and of creation. The eternal God creates ex nihilo, for "the being of creation is a matter of pure gift. It is God's possibility. There was no preexistent potentiality for it apart from God's creating love."[52] God, then, is unquestionably sovereign, and this sovereignty must be seen in terms of "constant, overseeing care."[53] It is basic to Christian faith that the God who has loved the world in Christ not only creates but also sustains and preserves the world. The God of cross and resurrection is not, after all, an absent, uncaring deity (as the Deists would have it) but the One who passionately loves the world and is at work in the world to preserve and to redeem it.[54] But how does God's sovereignty relate to the loving care of God in a world of so much suffering and evil?

What can be said about the "being of God" that throws light upon God's providential presence in creation? First, theology of the cross is always, necessarily, Trinitarian. In a rich and substantial discussion of the Trinity, Hall writes, "Trinitarian monotheism insists that there is dialogue (dynamism, relatedness . . .) within the one God." This God is always the "Being-with." Both testaments of the Bible, he contends, exhibit an ontology of communion, or relationality, rather than of substance. This ontology of relationality is opposed to an undialectical, or monarchial, monotheism, which "is by contrast static and unbending." Failing to see this clearly, the dominant theism of Christendom speaks of a deity "from whom all traces of suffering, or even of movement, have been expelled." But, because God *is* love, God engages deeply, and suffers with the creation, in Christ and through the Spirit. The alternative monarchial monotheism serves all too well as an ideological tool in the suppression of diversity. Hall rejects, therefore, a "one sided single-minded theism in the service of a dominant culture and an imperial state."[55] It is this triune God, then, who is from the beginning a "Being-with," whose providence preserves and sustains creation, and who suffers and is at work with and within creatures in the suffering and struggles of the world.

That is why Hall devotes a whole lengthy chapter to "Questioning the Father Almighty." He is critical of the historically dominant Christian doctrine of God "which has tended to accentuate the aspects of transcendence and power, as befits a patriarchally conceived deity in the service of empire." He offers, then, a "general critique of power as the primary concept informing the Theological tradition."[56] This emphasis on transcendent power, characteristic of Constantinian theology, derives, in part, from the encounter of the church with the tradition of Athens, but was developed also by the "theological servants" of Constantine to render the church useful to the empire. Hall writes:

> A deity who "stoops to our weakness" and actually becomes weak for our sake, such is not the blueprint for a god designed for empire, any empire. If the aims of those who, like Arius, were deeply influenced by Greek philosophic Theology, were to preserve the Christian God from a compromising participation in mundane materiality, the struggle of Constantine and his theological servants was to exploit the power potential of the Christian God and minimize everything reminiscent of divine vulnerability and self-emptying.[57]

Hall contends that, in our predominantly secular, post-Christendom society, most people, especially the young, find it impossible to relate to a God whose main characteristic is might, success, or winning. A growing underclass finds untenable a "Father Almighty," who "functions mainly to insulate people from the reality of their situation."[58] Over against this, it is necessary today to return to the God of both biblical testaments, for "the whole biblical testimony to this deity involves something like a *kenosis*—an emptying of that which prevents or could prevent God's full communion with the covenant partner." As a practitioner of theology of the cross, he believes that *kenosis* is "the foundational dimension of deity as deity is conceived in this tradition."[59]

How is *kenosis* relevant to our climate crisis? *Kenosis* pertains not only to the incarnation of God in Christ, but also to creation and providence. Surely Hall is right about this: In view of what we know of evolutionary science, and of the history of the planet, with its mass extinctions and developmental dead ends, the all-controlling deity of a classical Christian monotheism lacks credibility in our time.

Does this mean, then, that God is powerless and does not act to sustain or preserve the world? Is this self-emptying God irrelevant to the struggle against planetary catastrophe? Or, to put the question differently: How may we expect God to act, or not to act, to preserve the planet Earth in our time of climate crisis?

As we have seen, Hall considers that an end of human civilization, and even an uninhabitable earth is possible. We have no guarantees. In Bonhoeffer's terms, he holds out no hope that a deus ex machina will descend from above to rescue us in some supranatural manner from such a disaster. Again, Hall quotes Bonhoeffer: "The Bible directs man to God's powerlessness and suffering. Only a suffering God can help."[60] Hall wrote, in *The Stewardship of Life in the Kingdom of Death*:

> God makes no promise to protect and preserve life over against the human decision that it is not worth protecting and preserving. It is a facile and unbiblical interpretation of the meaning of divine providence that assumes any such thing.[61]

Hall does not expect the Creator to set aside the laws of nature to accommodate human foolishness. For biblical faith, he believes, the laws of nature, including, presumably, those that govern the processes of climate change, are means by which God sustains and preserves the creation.[62] While in scripture God is sometimes depicted as working outside the natural processes of the physical world, he argues that

> God's mode of relating to the creature in the literature of the older Testament is not normally through ostentatious display of power; rather, the biblical God works within the historical processes, honoring the laws of nature as well as human freedom, and altering the course of events through subtle and quiet intervention, usually involving the calling and activity of some human being.[63]

God is not absent or indifferent to what happens to the Earth. Hall speaks hopefully about the mode of God's providence in *God and Human Suffering*, when he writes that

> faith perceives patterns of meaning and direction. To speak more accurately, it perceives the miraculous! Not crass and gaudy shows of supranatural power in which the laws of nature are ignored, but true miracles of the everyday sort: the miracle of life going on, the miracle of something and not nothing, the miracle of purpose.[64]

He writes in a similar vein in *Professing the Faith*, emphasizing the human task of dominion as stewardship:

> Nothing is more needful in our present context than a new appreciation for the human "dominion" that God our Creator exemplifies in the authentic human being, Jesus, the shepherd who lays down his life for the sheep. Over against a domineering, manipulative, smug technological humanity that tries to control the whole world . . . it is precisely human "dominion" that is called for. Neither

domination of the world, nor withdrawal from the world meets the requirements of this tradition under the impact of the contemporary situation. More than ever the human being is called by God today to assume "dominion"—only this refers not to the dominion exemplified by Caesar but to that exemplified by Jesus Christ.[65]

In *Confessing the Faith*, Hall laments the failures of the churches to "take up causes" in a concrete way regarding matters of social justice and environment, a reluctance to concretize its concerns, perhaps because of its commitment to "an upbeat message," and a reluctance to confront the powerful with serious critical reflection.[66]

I conclude, then, that a Christian ecological theology today is deepened and illuminated by a theology of the cross, and that a theology of the cross becomes relevant and effective in our present global context of climate crisis when linked to an ecological theology. Douglas John Hall has admirably shown us how this can be done.

We should give the last word to Hall, who offers no optimism about the future, but does offer hope. He writes, in *The Stewardship of Life in the Kingdom of Death*:

> There is a grace abroad in the world that introduces new possibilities . . . even at the edge of the Red Sea. And against the people who want to believe that *everything* is possible, faith says: Keep your eyes open and don't give in to the urge to cheer prematurely.[67]

NOTES

1. Douglas John Hall, *Waiting for Gospel: An Appeal to the Dispirited Remnants of Protestant "Establishment"* (Eugene, OR: Wipf and Stock, 2012), 106.
2. Douglas John Hall, "Christian Theology in a Post-Christendom World," in *Christian Thought in the Twenty-first Century: Agenda for the Future* (Eugene, OR: Cascade Books, 2012), 86.
3. Douglas John Hall, *Thinking the Faith: Christian Theology in a North American Context* (Minneapolis, MN: Augsburg, 1989; paperback reprint: Minneapolis, MN: Fortress Press, 1991), 75, 310–17.
4. Douglas John Hall, "Contextuality in Christian Theology," *Toronto Journal of Theology* 1, no. 1 (Spring 1985): 3–16.
5. James Lovelock, *The Revenge of Gaia* (London: Allen Lane, 2006), 11; note also Hall's discussion of "The Rebellion of Nature," in *Thinking the Faith*, 219–23.

6. Douglas John Hall, *Professing the Faith: Christian Theology in a North American Context* (Minneapolis, MN: Fortress Press, 1993), 310, 322.

7. James Lovelock, *A Rough Ride to the Future* (London: Penguin, 2015), 75.

8. Bill McKibben, *Falter: Has the Human Game Begun to Play Itself Out?* (New York: Henry Holt, 2019), 22.

9. McKibben, *Falter*, 122–23, 155. See his earlier work *The Vanishing Face of Gaia* (London: Allen Lane, 2009), 92–104.

10. James Hansen, *Storms of My Grandchildren* (New York: Bloomsbury, 2009), 223–36; see also Hansen, "Young People's Burden: Requirement of Negative CO2 emissions," *Earth System Dynamics* (September 2016): www. Insideclimatenews/ hansen.org

11. Elizabeth Kolbert, *The Sixth Extinction: An Unnatural History* (New York: Henry Holt, 2014).

12. United Nations Intergovernmental Panel on Climate Change, "Special Report on Global Warming of 1.5 Degrees C," *Technical Summary* (October, 2018): 32, 37.

13. David Wallace-Wells, *The Uninhabitable Earth: Life after Warming* (New York: Tim Duggan, 2019), 202.

14. Naomi Klein, *This Changes Everything: Capitalism vs. the Climate* (New York, and Toronto, ON: Simon and Schuster, 2014), 19, 154–55.

15. Klein, *This Changes Everything*, 72.

16. Klein, *On Fire: The Burning Case for a Green New Deal*, 77.

17. UN Intergovernmental Science Policy-Platform on Biodiversity, "Global Assessment Report on Biodiversity and Ecosystems Services;" www.unitednations .global-biodiversity-assessment-reports/2019.

18. Clive Hamilton, *Earthmasters: The Dawn of the Age of Climate Engineering* (New Haven, CT: Yale University Press, 2014), 180.

19. Wallace-Wells, *The Uninhabitable Earth,* 153.

20. Kolbert, *The Sixth Extinction,* 107–10.

21. Douglas John Hall, *Lighten Our Darkness: Toward an Indigenous Theology of the Cross* (Philadelphia, PA: Westminster, 1976), 39.

22. Hall, *Lighten Our Darkness*, 49.

23. George P. Grant, *Philosophy in the Mass Age* (Toronto, ON: Copp Clark, 1966).

24. Reinhold Niebuhr, *Faith and History* (New York: Charles Scribner's Sons, 1959), 3.

25. Hall, *Lighten Our Darkness,* 61, 228.

26. Ibid., 5.

27. Lynn White, Jr., "The Historical Roots of Our Ecological Crisis," *Science* 155 (March 10, 1967): 1203–07.

28. Hall, *Lighten Our Darkness*, 215.

29. Ibid., 84–86.

30. Matthew Fox, *Creation Spirituality* (San Francisco, CA: HarperSanFrancisco, 1991).

31. Douglas John Hall, *Professing the Faith: Christian Theology in a North American Context* (Minneapolis, MN: Fortress Press, 1993), 174. Also, *Confessing*

the Faith: Christian Theology in a North American Context (Minneapolis, MN: Fortress Press, 1996), 441.

32. Thomas Berry, "Twelve Principles for Understanding the Universe and the Role of the Human in the Universe," in *Thomas Berry and the New Cosmology*, eds. A. Lonergan and C. Richards (Mystic, CT: Twenty-Third Publications, 1987), 107.

33. Douglas John Hall, "Confessing Faith on the Edge of Empire," *Touchstone* 23, no. 3 (September 2005): 12.

34. Ibid., 80.

35. Douglas John Hall: *Imaging God: Dominion as Stewardship* (Grand Rapids, MI: Eerdmans; New York: Friendship Press, 1986).

36. Ibid., 83.

37. Hall, *Lighten Our Darkness*, 85–86.

38. Douglas John Hall, *The Steward: A Biblical Symbol Come of Age* (New York: National Council of Churches Commission on Stewardship, 1982), 17–22.

39. Douglas John Hall, *The Stewardship of Life in the Kingdom of Death* (New York: Friendship Press, for the Commission on Stewardship, National Council of Churches, 1985), iii–vi, 32–38.

40. Hall cites Bonhoeffer in *Thinking the Faith*, 28.

41. Hall, *Waiting for Gospel*, 106.

42. Hall, *Thinking the Faith*, 24.

43. Abraham J. Heschel, *The Prophets*, Vol. 2 (New York: Harper and Row, 1962); Hall, *Thinking the Faith*, 26–27.

44. Martin Luther wrote: *"theologia crucis est de deo crucifixo et abscondito." Resolutiones disputationum de indulgentiarum virtute*, in *D. Martin Luthers Werke*, Vol. 1 (Weimar: Hermann Bohlau, 1883), 613.

45. Martin Luther, *The Heidelberg Disputation*, in *Luther's Works*, Vol. 31, ed. H. J. Grimm (Philadelphia, PA: Muhlenberg, 1957), Thesis 20, 52–53.

46. See Hall's major treatment of Christology in *Professing the Faith*, Part III.

47. Hall, *Thinking the Faith*, 31.

48. Jürgen Moltmann, "The Pit—Where Was God? Jewish and Christian Theology after Auschwitz," in *God for a Secular Society: The Public Relevance of Theology*, trans. M. Kohl (Minneapolis, MN: Fortress Press, 1999), 169–90.

49. Dietrich Bonhoeffer, *Letters and Papers from Prison*, ed. Eberhard Bethge (London: SCM Press, 1967), 360–61.

50. See George Grant, "We Are Technique," *Technology and Empire* (Toronto, ON: Anansi, 1969), 137. Hall, *Professing the Faith*, 17, 84; Hall, *Lighten Our Darkness*, 59, 178, 182.

51. Hall, *Confessing the Faith*, 494.

52. Hall, *Professing the Faith*, 76.

53. Ibid., 86.

54. Ibid., 85–90.

55. Ibid., 68–71.

56. Ibid., 92.

57. Ibid., 106.

58. Ibid., 130–33.

59. Ibid., 149–50.
60. Bonhoeffer, *Letters and Papers from Prison,* 361; quoted by Hall, *Professing the Faith,* 182.
61. Hall, *The Stewardship of Life in the Kingdom of Death,* 72.
62. Hall, *Professing the Faith,* 83.
63. Ibid., 449.
64. Douglas John Hall, *God and Human Suffering: An Exercise in the Theology of the Cross* (Minneapolis, MN: Augsburg, 1986), 110–11.
65. Hall, *Professing the Faith,* 351.
66. Hall, *Confessing the Faith,* 182.
67. Hall, *The Stewardship of Life in the Kingdom of Death,* 84.

WORKS CITED

Berry, Thomas. "Twelve Principles for Understanding the Universe and the Role of the Human in the Universe." In *Thomas Berry and the New Cosmology.* Edited by A. Lonergan and C. Richards. Mystic, CT: Twenty-Third Publications, 1987.

Bonhoeffer, Dietrich. *Letters and Papers from Prison.* Edited by Eberhard Bethge. London: SCM Press, 1967.

Fox, Matthew. *Creation Spirituality.* San Francisco, CA: HarperSanFrancisco, 1991.

Grant, George P. *Philosophy in the Mass Age.* Toronto, ON: Copp Clark, 1966.

———. *Technology and Empire.* Toronto, ON: Anansi, 1969.

Hall, Douglas John. "Confessing Faith on the Edge of Empire." *Touchstone* 23, no.3 (September 2005), 7–21.

———. *Confessing the Faith: Christian Theology in a North American Context.* Minneapolis, MN: Fortress Press, 1996).

———. "Contextuality in Christian Theology." *Toronto Journal of Theology* 1, no. 1 (Spring 1985), 3–16.

———. *God and Human Suffering: An Exercise in the Theology of the Cross.* Minneapolis, MN: Augsburg, 1986.

———. *Imaging God: Dominion as Stewardship.* Grand Rapids, MI: Eerdmans; New York: Friendship Press, 1986.

———. *Lighten Our Darkness: Toward an Indigenous Theology of the Cross.* Philadelphia, PA: Westminster, 1976.

———. *Professing the Faith: Christian Theology in a North American Context.* Minneapolis, MN: Fortress Press, 1993.

———. *The Steward: A Biblical Symbol Come of Age.* New York: National Council of Churches Commission on Stewardship, 1982.

———. *The Stewardship of Life in the Kingdom of Death.* New York: Friendship Press, for the National Council of Churches Commission on Stewardship, 1985.

———. *Thinking the Faith: Christian Theology in a North American Context.* Minneapolis, MN: Augsburg, 1989; paperback reprint: Minneapolis, MN: Fortress Press, 1991.

———. *Waiting for Gospel: An Appeal to the Dispirited Remnants of the Protestant "Establishment."* Eugene, OR: Wipf and Stock. 2012.

Hamilton, Clive. *Earthmasters: The Dawn of the Age of Climate Engineering.* New Haven, CT: Yale University Press, 2014.

Hansen, James. *Storms of My Grandchildren.* New York: Bloomsbury, 2009.

———. "Young People's Burden: Requirement of Negative CO2 Emissions." *Earth System Dynamics* (September 2016): www.Insideclimatenews/hansen.org.

Heschel, Abraham J. *The Prophets,* Vol. 2. New York: Harper and Row, 1962.

Klein, Naomi. *On Fire: The Burning Case for a Green New Deal.* Toronto, ON: Alfred A. Knopf Canada, 2019.

———. *This Changes Everything: Capitalism vs. the Climate.* New York and Toronto, ON: Simon and Schuster, 2014.

Kolbert, Elizabeth. *The Sixth Extinction: An Unnatural History.* New York: Henry Holt, 2014.

Lovelock, James. *A Rough Ride to the Future.* London: Penguin, 2015.

———. *The Revenge of Gaia.* London: Allen Lane, 2006.

———. *The Vanishing Face of Gaia.* London: Allen Lane, 2009.

Luther, Martin. "The Heidelberg Disputation." *Luther's Works.* Edited by H. J. Grimm, Vol. 31. Philadelphia, PA: Muhlenberg, 1957.

———. *Resolutiones disputationum de indulgentiarum virtute. Luthers Werke,* Vol. I. Weimar: Hermann Bohlau, 1883.

McKibben, Bill. *Falter: Has the Human Game Begun to Play Itself Out?* New York: Henry Holt, 2019.

Moltmann, Jürgen. "The Pit—Where Was God? Jewish and Christian Theology after Auschwitz." *God for a Secular Society: The Public Relevance of Theology.* Translated by Margaret Kohl. Minneapolis, MN: Fortress Press, 1999.

Niebuhr, Reinhold. *Faith and History.* New York: Charles Scribner's Sons, 1959.

United Nations Intergovernmental Panel on Climate Change. "Special Report on Global Warming of 1.5 Degrees C." *Technical Summary,* October 2018. www.IPCC.2018.

United Nations Intergovernmental Science Policy-Platform on Biodiversity. "Global Assessment Report on Biodiversity and Ecosystems." www.unitednations.global-diversity-assessment.reports/2019.

Wallace-Wells, David. *The Uninhabitable Earth: Life after Warming.* New York: Tim Duggan, 2019.

White, Lynn, Jr. "The Historical Roots of Our Ecological Crisis." *Science* 155 (March 10, 1967).

Chapter 7

What Are People For?

Reimaging Theo-anthropology in the Anthropocene

Pamela R. McCarroll

What time is it? Where are we? These two questions are central to the contextualizing work of theologian Douglas John Hall. How we respond to these questions as theologians, as church, as people of faith and global citizens locates our perspectives, our beliefs and practices in real life. I join with many others in identifying the *Anthropocene* as the most pressing reality of our time and place. We are living during the epoch of the Anthropocene, the period during which human activity has irrevocably altered the geology, the biosphere, and the climate of the planet.[1] There is no going back. Nearby and far away, the effects of the climate crisis have become part of a yearly cycle of environmental disasters—floods, fires, drought, heat waves, hurricanes, and so on. We are having "100 year floods" and fires almost yearly. The worsening environmental destruction calls theologians and people of faith to engage the crisis and to discern a way forward that we may live faithfully in these harrowing times.

Douglas John Hall is one of the earliest voices in theology in the area of the environmental crisis, and he has inspired many others. Along with a growing chorus of thinkers, he argues that the environmental crisis is an external manifestation of an internal crisis regarding the meaning and purpose of human life—a crisis about what it means to be human, a spiritual crisis.[2] Distorted notions of the meaning and telos of human life have successfully tempted humans to presume mastery and domination over the earth and its creatures—to colonize the earth and other life to serve human ends. For Hall, reorienting our thought—the metaphors, images, and narratives by which we live—is an important part of altering the destructive path we are on.

In an effort to explore and reimagine a theo-anthropology for today's context, this paper engages the work of Douglas Hall in dialogue with that of eco-theologians Panu Pihkala and Sallie McFague. Hall's work articulates a three-fold pattern for a contextual theology of the cross that addresses those with power and privilege, "the possessing peoples of this planet."[3] The first move, *calling the thing what it is*, is a critical move that seeks to unmask the lies (the theologies of glory) by which those of us with power and privilege live. The second move, *the journey to the cross*, is a decolonizing journey toward the vulnerability, finitude, and the limits of creaturely life. The third move, *becoming human*, is constructive and imagines concrete ways to live the fullness of our humanity, both its vulnerability and beauty, in relationship with others, as part of creation. The thought of Panu Pihkala and Sallie McFague are presented through this three-fold pattern as they intersect with and build upon Hall's work. The paper concludes with a descriptive reimaging of a theo-anthropology that reflects a reordering for human life and practice today.

DOUGLAS JOHN HALL

Calling the Thing What It Is

Inspired by the work of Martin Luther, especially as presented in the *Heidelberg Disputation*, Hall unmasks the deceptions of the theology of glory that serve those with power and privilege. The theology of the cross is suspicious of intimations of human power, mastery, and self-sufficiency that deny the suffering and pain of creation, for both human and nonhuman being. This first critical move, for Hall, includes several elements, each of which reflects the intrinsic alienation of the human creature from our own creatureliness and leads to the distortion of relationships with other creatures, with the larger creation, and with the Creator. Hall asks, "Is it Christianity that has taught us to love consumption and overabundance and waste? Is there come link between our trust in God and our astonishing prosperity, our being 'First,' our superpower-dom?"[4]

Hall outlines how this false *imago hominis*, drawn from a theology of glory, has authorized humans to function as lords and masters over the creation. The supremacy of the human will and reason over otherness is embedded within assumptions of Western modernity's "religion of progress"[5]—the quintessential theology of glory in the North America context. Among other things, the religion of progress presupposes that human will and reason lean toward goodness and participate in the coming-to-be of God's reign on earth. This, of course, is a lie the evidence of which is all around us, from the extinction of species to the rising levels of carbon dioxide to the contamination of fresh water by industry, and so on.

Hall draws on the myth of Prometheus, the one who steals fire from the gods, to illustrate how theologies of glory have functioned in our context. Prometheus represents the image of the human common in the modern West, especially in North America, wherein heroic narratives frame the settler story on this land. Humans, particularly of the European white male "possessing" variety, are imaged almost as demigods, capable of wielding mastery over creation.[6] As the creatures who are "a little less than the angels"[7] (Psalm 8), and as the creature made in G-d's likeness, with G-d imaged as "almighty," the human exertion of power over earth is seen to image divine power on earth, a Promethean *imago hominis*. This "power-over," hierarchical image of the human in relation to creation is the distorted gospel of Christendom, the theology of glory writ large. In part, the total environmental devastation that is upon us, then, is the result of hubris, human pride, idolatry, the "yearning to be as gods" based on a theology of glory that places (some) humans as masters at the center of conceptions of reality.

This is not the end of Hall's analysis, however. Indeed, the North America social imaginary is far more complex, particularly through recent decades. The image of the human as master, as heroic, as the height of creation has become suspect. We live amidst the experience of "future shock"[8] in which the terrors of war, of inequality, of environmental destruction and nuclear capability have undermined our capacity to envision a future or to preserve any sense of the goodness or "heroic" destiny of the human creature. Rather than the heroic savior of this realm, the human creature is the villain—the primary cause of the multiple crises of the earth.

Hall draws on the existentialist's use of myth of Sisyphus to represent the alienation, the crisis in meaning and purpose, undergirding much of human life today.[9] Sisyphus is an image of fatalism, despair, and meaninglessness. At some level, he argues, those of us with power and privilege know we are Sisyphus endlessly rolling the boulder up the hill only to have it fall back down again. However, on another level, because the Promethean narrative (religion of progress) has so dominated our imaginations, we keep mouthing its promises of growth and progress even when everything around us tells a different story. We seem incapable of imagining anything beyond its illusion of triumphant progressive futurity.

This complicated combination of "Sisyphus imitating Prometheus"[10] is lethal, as it involves humans wreaking havoc on the earth through prideful compulsions of the Promethean will combined with the slothful despair of Sisyphus, who is unable to take responsibility in the midst of a palpable sense of impending doom. We are confused, anxious, and disoriented, and we do not know where to turn. So, we deny, repress, and avoid the reality of the bad news because it is too overwhelming, too much to bear. Hall is not afraid to say how bad the bad news is.

The Journey to the Cross

The second move within the three-fold pattern is the journey to the cross. For those with power and privilege, the journey to the cross includes surrendering and letting go of all pretensions to self-delusion, to power, control, and mastery. It is a decolonizing journey[11] that moves from colonizing mastery over otherness to vulnerability, mutuality, and interrelationality with others. It is a recognition of all the many ways we humans, especially the powerful and privileged among us, seek to run from our own creatureliness, our essential nakedness and neediness. It is a journey to discover ourselves as human creatures in relationship and as part of a much larger whole. In the face of the Anthropocene, this is a journey that will include lament and grief as we discern how much has already been lost. For Hall, this movement is empowered by the promise of G-d-with-us—the divine solidarity of the Creator with the creature as revealed through the cross. We make the journey to the cross, knowing that G-d meets us there.

The journey to the cross entails being called out of the illusionary heroic narratives of the theology of glory and called toward the cross where the fullness of humanity hangs—vulnerable, finite, suffering; the image of love, forgiveness, and solidarity. Hall looks to the places of suffering to seek out the hidden face of G-d, whose love—divine pathos, *Mitsein*, *agape*[12]—meets us in the darkest darkness and calls us to ourselves.

The image on the cover of Hall's book, *The Cross in Our Context*, powerfully illustrates the critical and decolonizing movements of Hall's *theologia crucis*.[13] In the foreground Jesus hangs on a cross, silhouetted in darkness and shadows, surrounded by dark smokestacks pumping out toxins. Cross and smokestacks extend upward from a blackened earth—a powerful image for the cross in our context today. Creation and savior are killed at the hands of the unwieldy human creature in their quest for power, immortality, and god-likeness. The suffering savior amidst the suffering creation functions as a symbol of the reign of death, of how far we have fallen, of the sheer destructive potentiality of the human will. It is a symbol also of human vulnerability, limit, finitude, and death. The very world has become Golgotha! But a closer gaze reveals something behind the disturbing shadows, light refracted from a hidden sun contrasting the darkness of the scene, illuminating the background with pastel green, orange, blue. Is it a sunrise or a sunset that lightens our scene? How might the promise revealed in the background invite us to imagine new ways of becoming human given the truth revealed in the foreground?

Becoming Human

The final movement in the three-fold pattern of the cross is the call to becoming human.[14] While the second movement is a deconstructive, decolonizing movement by which we are stripped of the *accoutrements* of glory, power, and privilege, and in which we recognize our own nakedness, the third movement is more constructive. The emphasis is on how to live as creatures, in the fullness of our humanity in mutuality and right relationship, part of the "ontology of communion."[15] Hall challenges us to recognize our responsibility and role as distinctive creatures within the larger creation—called "to be human, nothing more and nothing less."[16]

To the question of whether creation would be better off without humans, Hall responds a resounding "no."[17] Rather, he reclaims the biblical image of the steward as a way to explore the purpose and meaning of human life in the North American context today.[18] The steward, he argues, provides a way for the human creature to image G-d, both by embodying the "with-being" love of G-d for creation and by acknowledging the distinctions between Creator and creature. The steward is a servant who has both responsibilities to creation and accountability to G-d.[19] The steward serves G-d by serving creation.[20] It is an image that neither elevates the human creature (like the Promethean power-over image) nor degrades the human creature (like Sisyphus' fatalism). The steward is a creature who is capable of compassion, empathy, solidarity, and suffering with and for others, and is, thus, able to live into these possible heights of becoming human[21]—called to "steward life in the kingdom of death."[22] Increasingly through his work, Hall is drawn to the work of James Lovelock and William Golding, whose Gaia theory images the earth as a living reality within which all that exists participates.[23] Within this system, he argues, drawing on Genesis 2–3, God calls representative humanity to a vocation of care—to sacrifice for, to tend, and to know creation.[24] Even after the expulsion from the garden into the wilderness, he says, this vocation does not change. Drawing on the post-expulsion myth paired with creation's demise today, Hall suggests that today we are called to be "stewards in the wilderness."[25]

With the wilderness—or the Anthropocene—as our context, how might we participate in, steward, and care for the earth and its creatures? How might this image provide contours for a contextual theo-anthropology for today? How might it inspire a renewed sense of meaning and purpose, a re-oriented spirituality, to invite people of faith to live meaningfully even in the face of powers of death that threaten to overwhelm? To engage these questions dialogically, I turn now to an emerging eco-theologian of the cross, Panu Pihkala.

PANU PIHKALA

Calling the Thing What It Is

Panu Pihkala is doing important work on theo-anthropology in the context of the environmental crisis, interweaving theology of the cross and systematic theology with existential psychology and other psychodynamic theories.[26] Like Hall, he argues that the cross of Christ stands amidst the suffering of creation and calls on people of faith to have the courage to face the suffering for what it is. He too affirms that G-d's hidden presence is revealed within suffering—within the suffering creation, communities struggling under environmental crises, of those individuals caught in lives they know are environmentally damaging, and of activists who despair because of these challenges.[27] The call to people of faith is to resist defeatism and to find meaning and even hope in the face of the tragedy that is upon us.[28] Pihkala unpacks the complexity of human culpability, of our sense of being overwhelmed, of our fatalism, guilt, and outrage in relation to the environmental crisis.

Pihkala agrees that humans have lost a sense of their purpose and meaning in life, and as a consequence their heedless actions are driving the reign of death upon the earth. Drawing on similar notions of "future shock" as adopted by Hall, he identifies a primary *problematique* for many today: the existential angst or eco-anxiety that subliminally dominates the social imaginary in the face the climate crisis and the very real losses and changes in the earth's ecosystems. "Climate change feels like death," he writes.[29] Eco-anxiety is a form of death, or of existential anxiety, that overwhelms people's abilities to cope healthfully. It is a sense of doom looming as a shadow over everything as the threat of environmental collapse injects itself into daily life. The extent to which people experience eco-anxiety depends to a degree on the extent to which they are vulnerable to the extreme changes in climate. Eco-anxiety may be contributing to the increased clinical diagnoses of anxiety disorders, he asserts, precisely because it reflects the extent to which larger horizons of meaning are collapsing, undermining people's resilience and ability manage day-to-day anxiety.

To make things worse, Pihkala says, there is mounting recognition that an underlying sense of eco-anxiety is triggering unhealthy coping mechanisms, such as denial, repression, and avoidance; these in turn further exacerbate the crisis. A "socially constructed silence"[30] resists acknowledging that the crisis even is a crisis, resists "calling the thing what it is."[31] As a result, we find ourselves "calling evil, good and good evil."[32] From individuals to governments, from religious communities to businesses, the tendency is to avoid, repress, and deny the climate crisis. Defense mechanisms, intended to help protect people in situations of threat, have been triggered to such a degree that avoidance, denial, and repression have become commonplace, even at upper levels of governments. A false hope that everything is fine, that we can just carry on as usual, settles people into compliance, even when at some level they know they are living a costly lie. The same coping mechanisms that help enable survival in the face of an immediate crisis become destructive as they become habitual, as we know through trauma theory, causing disconnection, avoidance of responsibility, and alienation from reality. These dynamics are characteristic of the Sisyphus/Prometheus phenomena described by Hall. Humans are disoriented, caught in a web of lies, and fearful of our own vulnerability, culpability, and helplessness in the face of an overwhelming crisis—a crisis for which many of us feel responsible and from which we want to flee.

The Journey to the Cross

The decolonizing journey to the cross, for Pihkala, is found in having courage to recognize the powers of death for what they are. At the same time, Pihkala and others in the larger field of Ecotherapy[33] argue that motivation for change cannot come out of fear or threat, because (as we have seen) more often than not, such motivators trigger defense mechanisms. Rather, motivation for change must grow out of love, out of a sense of awe and reverence for life, and from courage to love even in the face of death. The theo-anthropology embedded here suggests that as humans are enabled to stop running away from our own vulnerability, finitude, and sense of absolute dependence—all of what death represents—and begin to accept these aspects of our human condition, the capacity for love compassion, gratitude, and new life can open up.

For Pihkala, like Hall, the journey to the cross in the Anthropocene means opening ourselves to enter into the fullness of the suffering of creation—to feel, to lament, and to express the grief, sadness, and pain associated with the loss of so much of our natural world. Grief that is repressed and has no way to be released becomes destructive. Tending to the deep sadness over loss is an expression of love. Such action opens up space for new life and bears witness to the meaningfulness of all of life in its particularity and wholeness. How might we as communities of faith discover courage to stand at the foot of the cross, to grieve, and to stand in solidarity with the suffering creation, knowing that G-d meets us there? Creating ritualized opportunities for the public sharing and acknowledgement of grief may well be an important role for the church and other religious communities in the years ahead.[34]

Becoming Human

Pihkala and others insist that even in the face of environmental destruction—a tragedy beyond which we cannot see—the call to nurture life, to engage in acts of faith, hope, and love persists. In the field of Ecotherapy, a primary "treatment" for eco-alienation/eco-paralysis is to join in actions with others that manifest concrete ways of nurturing and being nurtured by the environment—planting trees, cleaning up garbage in parks and walkways, making our worship spaces eco-friendly, learning about the eco-systems of our area, contributing to policies that make a difference.[35] Even if such actions do not result in changing the future of the earth, the actions themselves bear witness to life, to the larger horizon of existence, to hope against hope. Quoting Martin Luther,[36] in a statement important for the Confessing church in the face of Nazi powers of death, Pihkala writes, "Even if I knew that the world would go to pieces tomorrow, I would still plant my apple tree today." Let us plant trees.

SALLIE MCFAGUE

Calling the Thing What It Is

As a close friend and contemporary of Hall, the late Sallie McFague has also been an important voice in the eco-theology movement. She agrees that the environmental crisis is a spiritual problem[37] tied up with distorted notions of what it means to be human in relation to the larger world. In her earlier work on the body of God[38] she also argues that the metaphors we use to understand human life and our ways of thinking theologically are distorted and need a complete reimagining. She offers a panentheistic conception of the world as God's body in a way that re-sacralizes matter, calling on people of faith to honor the sacred in all things.[39]

In her final monograph, McFague was inspired by the *State of the World 2010* report that calls on world religions to draw people back to a message central to all the world's religions—that consumerist materialism does not provide happiness or comfort. Rather, she says, religion's "special gift [is] the millennia-old paradoxical insight that happiness is found in self emptying, that satisfaction is found more in relationships than in things, and that simplicity can lead to a fuller life."[40] In her later writings she acknowledges that changing the way we image ourselves, creation, and G-d may not be enough to stem our eco-destructive behavior. She argues that we must also follow concrete, theologically based practices of simplicity and discipline in order to change our behavior. Neoliberal capitalism's implicit image of the human as "consumer," she asserts, is a big problem, wreaking havoc on the earth. She challenges the churches and other religious institutions to "return home" to the core of their teachings and to a radical critique of materialism and "the reigning anthropology of insatiable greed."⁴¹ Instead, religious institutions can take the lead in the spiritual disciplines of compassion, simplicity, and "restraint, not for the sake of ascetic denial of the world, but in order that 'abundant life' might be possible for all."⁴²

McFague urges people of faith to focus on what G-d requires of us, individually and collectively, in this time and place.⁴³ We are not here to fulfill our own insatiable desires; we are here to respond to a something "beyond ourselves that is both our hearts' deepest desire and our most profound duty."⁴⁴ She implores religious traditions to fulfill their vocation to resist the principalities and powers in offering a radical alternative to the incessant greed and consumption of neo-liberal capitalism, which, of course, is killing us.

The Journey to the Cross

While McFague does not specifically reference the theology of the cross, her focus on kenosis and her affirmation, following Moltmann, that the "cross is the centre of all Christian theology," places her own theology very much within this tradition. Turning to the lives of some of the saints—John Woolman, Simone Weil, Dorothy Day—for inspiration and direction, she invites us to follow the path of kenosis, or self-emptying, as a way to live in the face of environmental destruction, consumptive greed, and the societal fixation on feeding individualistic ego needs. Drawing on forms of nature and on religious and other teachings, McFague submits that kenosis is "the recognition that restraint, openness, humility, respect for otherness, and even sacrifice (diminishment and death) are part of life *if* one assumes individual well-being takes place within political and cosmic well-being."⁴⁵ Importantly, she argues that the path of kenosis—of sacrifice and death opening to new life—is commonly evident in nature among animals and within the rhythms of the seasons. While not the same, the kenotic movements of nature, she says, are in some ways analogous to the central message of all major religions. She focusses on the theology of kenosis in Christianity as a deeply incarnational theology that points to the character of the divine and the essence of the human.⁴⁶

"It is a theology that starts with need," she writes, "both God's need and ours, a need that runs all the way from the most elemental biological processes of energy transformation to understanding the Trinity (the being of God) as one of continuous and total exchange of love."⁴⁷ Like Hall's distinctions regarding Prometheus and Sisyphus and his call to a different way of being, McFague also insists "that 'another way is possible' from either passive acceptance or violent aggression. . . . [Instead with] self emptying (limiting the ego's selfish desires), space is given for others to flourish, flourishing that not only is good for them, but, in a strange way, is good for oneself as well."[48] She distinguishes kenotic theology (theology of the cross) based on divine self-giving incarnational love, from other "traditional" theologies (theologies of glory) that emphasize God's power and control over creation, wherein human submission to God's ultimate sovereignty is required. Drawing on the metaphor of the world as God's body and building on the story of Jesus, the message is about "the God who empties the divine self into human being both in his life of radical service to others and in his death on a cross, thus revealing that all God's relations are kenotic in character."[49]

Becoming Human

What is most interesting for our purposes, however, is McFague's focus on what this kenotic theology "looks like," how it is lived, how it is incarnated in the practice (if you will) of life and death.[50] She identifies some key practices for kenotic living based on an anthropology that begins with a profound sense of interconnectivity and grace. Life is a gift from G-d and from all others on earth.[51] The fact of our life, of our few conscious years on this planet, is not something of our making. It is given. We are entirely dependent upon others. Life is an unexpected and unearned gift that did not have to be. Our basic stance, therefore, ought to be gratitude. Such a stance helps us to feel *at one with the world* in such a way that we do not fear death, and do not get so caught up in the anxieties related to death (not having control, for instance). At one with the world, our capacity for empathy with all creatures is opened up as we are enabled to perceive other parts of creation not as resources to serve our needs, but as subjects with intrinsic value, calling for reverence. We begin to experience ourselves as "on loan," here for a while and for the sake of the whole.[52] We are the only creature who knows we live only through interdependent relationships. For those who identify as middle class North Americans, this kind of living will include practices of restraint, of voluntary poverty and simplicity as a means to both resist rampant individual consumerism and to bear witness to a different order for life.[53]

Like Hall, McFague sees a deep link between thought and action. How we image ourselves and how we live in the world are intrinsically related. As followers of the crucified one we are called to manifest a way of being in the world that is of a different order from, and thereby resists, the consumerism of neoliberal capitalism that feeds on fear, competition, and greed. We are called to a kenotic way of being, premised on gratitude, of giving back, of reciprocity, of love and paying attention to the other, of sharing, sacrifice, and openness, and of acceptance the rhythms of life and death.[54]

CONCLUSION: BECOMING HUMAN IN THE ANTHROPOCENE

Dialogically engaging the work of these three theologians in the context of the Anthropocene makes it clear that the human creature needs to undergo a transformation, a change of heart, mind, and practices of being. This transformation, this "reimaging," must be decolonizing in its nature, relocating the human creature in relation to the larger world, part of and dependent upon creation. This transformation must be a movement from power over to being with, from consuming to reverencing, from control to vulnerability, from denying our intrinsic creatureliness to embracing it as a gift, from fearing death to trusting and having courage in the face of death.

Following the way of the cross today means being committed to engage in practices that nourish, honor, and reverence life, even and especially when the larger movements of our world are moving toward death. Our hope must not be based on our need to reach the goal of changing the world (though this, of course, would be nice). Such outcome-oriented hope only disappoints, and ultimately feeds anxiety, nihilism, and despair. Rather, our hope must be a "hope against hope" (as Hall so often says): a hope that acknowledges the tragic cycles of death dominating the world, and recognizes the insidious ways humans are caught in these cycles, and yet acts with courage in the face of such tragic realities to confront death's ubiquitous presence and there to bear witness to life. Such a hope also means reverencing life where it is—paying attention—to the beauty of creation and allowing it to feed and nourish the soul.

As we have seen, the human creature both is and is not like the rest of creation. We have a unique capacity for destruction, domination, and control of creation—using it to serve our own purposes. And we have as well a unique capacity for love and reverence, for understanding, knowledge, remembrance, and anticipation.

In reflecting on Hall's image of the steward in the wilderness in connection with Pihkala's and McFague's reflections, we have been wrestling with important questions: What does it mean to be stewards in the wilderness, in the face of death? What does it look like? Drawing on the inspiration of these thinkers, I have been pondering creation-centered images to help ground and extend Hall's image of the steward in the wilderness. Let us consider pollinating bees as creatures from whom we may learn something of what it means to be a human in a time and place such as ours.[55] It requires a kind of humility, akin to that of the journey to the cross, to learn from other creatures about how to be human.

Bees are the greatest of pollinators. By their pollination they draw forth the fruit of plants, enabling reproduction and the growth of food—grains, fruits, vegetables. In their service to life, how might we learn from the bees?

Bees go about their business connected with all that is. They live, most often, communally and interconnected. They work cooperatively with each other and with other species. Their work ensures long-term sustainability for themselves and other species. In their mutual interconnectivity, how might we learn from the bees?

Bees are attracted to the beauty of flowers and are strengthened and fed by the diversity of plants and other creatures. Growth and regeneration for other species are enabled and mediated by their pollination. In their way of tending to beauty, diversity, and otherness, how might we learn from the bees?

Bees make their homes together, building on that which is already there, not tearing down and re-building. They eat and release into the earth only that which is wholesome and pure. When they land on something, they do not break or ruin it.[56] In their gentle practices of being, of treading lightly, of giving back what they take, how might we learn from the bees?

Like humans, bees are also under stress right now. Their populations are diminishing drastically. Yet, they go on being bees—caring for, feeding, and mediating life for so many other species. Even our human survival is wrapped up in the work of the bees. In their practices of stewarding life in the kingdom of death, how might we learn from our neighbors, the bees?

NOTES

1. "Planetary Health in the Anthropocene," Editorial, *The Lancet* 393 (June 8, 2019): 2272. See also, "Anthropocene," Google Dictionary, accessed March 15, 2019, https://www.google.ca/search?q=anthropocene&rlz=1C1CHBF_enCA771CA 771&oq=anthropocene&aqs=chrome..69i57j0l5.3116j0j7&sourceid=chrome&ie= UTF-8. See also Jennifer Baichwal, Nicholas de Pencier, and Edward Burtynsky, *Anthropocene: The Human Epoch* (Mongrel Media, 2018), accessed March 15, 2019, https://theanthropocene.org/film/.

2. Douglas John Hall, *Professing the Faith* (Minneapolis, MN: Fortress Press, 1993), 253–300.

3. Douglas John Hall, *The Cross in Our Context* (Minneapolis, MN: Fortress Press, 2003), 51.

4. Hall, *Cross in Our Context*, 50.

5. Douglas John Hall, *Thinking the Faith* (Minneapolis, MN: Augsburg Books, 1989; paperback reprint: Minneapolis, MN: Fortress Press, 1991), 164.

6. Douglas John Hall, *Waiting for Gospel* (Eugene, OR: Cascade, 2012), 110–11.

7. Douglas John Hall, *Professing the Faith*, 212; Hall, *Cross in Our Context*, 50.

8. Douglas Hall often references Alvin Toeffler's notion of "future shock" to reflect the generalized anxiety regarding the future in the age of climate change and nuclear weaponry. See *Cross in Our Context*, 97.

9. Albert Camus, *The Myth of Sisyphus* (New York: Alfred A. Knopf, 1955).

10. Douglas John Hall, *Professing the Faith*, 261.

11. Pamela McCarroll, "Keeping it Real: De-colonizing Christian Inter-Religious Practice as an Exercise in a Practical Theology of the Cross," *Religions* 10, no. 203 (2019): 1–13.

12. Hall, *Professing the Faith*, 130–83.

13. Sam Kittner, *Crucifix and Refinery Stacks* (photo), National Geographic Society, 2003.

14. Douglas John Hall, *Imaging God* (Grand Rapids, MI: Eerdmans, 1986), 180.

15. Hall, *Professing the Faith*, 218.

16. Hall, *Professing the Faith*, 212.

17. Douglas John Hall, *Waiting for Gospel*, 114.

18. Pamela R. McCarroll *Waiting at the Foot of the Cross* (Eugene, OR: Pickwick, 2014), 172–73.

19. Hall, *Waiting for Gospel*, 105–16.

20. Hall, *Waiting for Gospel*, 111–15.

21. Hall, *Waiting for Gospel*, 115–16.

22. Douglas John Hall, *The Stewardship of Life in the Kingdom of Death* (New York: Friendship Press, 1985).

23. Douglas John Hall, *What Christianity is Not* (Eugene, OR: Cascade, 2013), 14.

24. Hall, *Imaging God*, 161–205.

25. Hall, *Waiting for Gospel*, 116.

26. Panu Pihkala is a Finnish theologian. His work is influenced by other eco-theologians of the cross (Cynthia Moe-Lobeda and Vitor Westhelle) and the work of Paul Tillich, Douglas Hall, Joseph Sittler, and Larry Rasmussen. His monograph, *Eco-Anxiety and Hope*, is in the process of being translated into English.

27. Panu Pihkala, "The Pastoral Challenge of the Environmental Crisis," *Dialog* 55, no. 2 (2016): 137.

28. Panu Pihkala, "Eco-Anxiety, Tragedy and Hope: Psychological and Spiritual Dimensions of Climate Change," *Zygon* 53, no. 2 (2018): 545–69.

29. Panu Pihkala, "Death, the Environment, and Theology," *Dialog* 57 (2018): 287.

30. Panu Pihkala, "Eco-Anxiety, Tragedy and Hope," 549. Pihkala is quoting Norgaard, 2011, and Zerubavel, 2006.

31. Martin Luther, *Heidelberg Disputation*, Thesis 21, translated by Harold James Grimm, in *Luther's Works*, edited by Harold J. Grimm, 31:54.

32. Martin Luther, *Heidelberg Disputation*, Thesis 21, 54.

33. See, for example, Howard Clinebell, *Ecotherapy* (Minneapolis, MN: Fortress Press, 1996; republished London: Routledge 2013).

34. See Panu Pihkala, "Eco-Anxiety, Tragedy and Hope," 545–69.

35. See Clinebell, *Ecotherapy*.

36. This quotation is considered "apocryphal" in that it does not appear in any of Luther's published writings. However, it does resonate with his notion of the hope of the cross.

37. Sallie McFague, *Blessed Are the Consumers: Climate Change and the Practice of Restraint* (Minneapolis, MN: Fortress Press, 2013), xi.

38. Sallie McFague, *The Body of God: An Ecological Theology* (Minneapolis, MN: Fortress Press, 1993).

39. McFague, *Body of God*.
40. McFague, *Blessed Are the Consumers*, x–xi.
41. McFague, *Blessed Are the Consumers*, xi.
42. McFague, *Blessed Are the Consumers*, xi.
43. McFague, *Blessed Are the Consumers*, 12.
44. McFague, *Blessed Are the Consumers*, 13–14.
45. McFague, *Blessed Are the Consumers*, 144.
46. McFague, *Blessed Are the Consumers*, 171–205.
47. McFague, *Blessed Are the Consumers*, 172.
48. McFague, *Blessed Are the Consumers*, 145. Douglas Hall similarly emphasizes the kenotic teaching, "losing one's life to find it," and the role of sacrifice for humans within the larger creation. See *Imaging God*, 193–204.
49. McFague, *Blessed Are the Consumers*, 173.
50. McFague, *Blessed Are the Consumers*, 174.
51. While Hall also emphasizes that we are not our own as the starting point for a spirit of gratitude, he focusses most on us belonging to G-d. See *Imaging God*, 160–205.
52. McFague, *Blessed Are the Consumers*, 208. Hall acknowledges a similar movement. See *Imaging God*, 160–205.
53. McFague, *Blessed Are the Consumers*, 209.
54. McFague, *Blessed Are the Consumers*, 214.
55. I am grateful to Caleb McCarroll-Butler, an environmental scientist, for sharing with me his insights and knowledge about pollinating bees.
56. "The believer is like the bee which eats that which is pure and wholesome and lays that which is pure and wholesome. When it lands on something it does not break or ruin it." The Prophet Mohammed, accessed February 2, 2020, https://parliamentofreligions.org/project-home/climate-commitments-project.

WORKS CITED

Baichwal, Jennifer, Nicholas de Pencier, and Edward Burtynsky. *Anthropocene: The Human Epoch*. Mongrel Media, 2018. Accessed March 15, 2019. https://theanthropocene.org/film/.
Camus, Albert. *The Myth of Sisyphus*. New York: Alfred A. Knopf, 1955.
Clinebell, Howard. *Ecotherapy*. Minneapolis, MN: Fortress Press, 1996. Reprinted London: Routledge, 2013.
Hall, Douglas John. *Imaging God*. Grand Rapids, MI: Eerdmans, 1986.
———. *Professing the Faith*. Minneapolis, MN: Fortress Press, 1993.
———. *The Cross in Our Context*. Minneapolis, MN: Fortress Press, 2003.
———. *The Stewardship of Life in the Kingdom of Death*. New York: Friendship Press, 1985.
———. *Thinking the Faith*. Minneapolis, MN: Augsburg, 1989; paperback reprint: Minneapolis, MN: Fortress Press, 1991.
———. *Waiting for Gospel*. Eugene, OR: Cascade, 2012.

———. *What Christianity is Not*. Eugene, OR: Cascade, 2013.

Luther, Martin. *Heidelberg Disputation*, Thesis 21, translated by Harold James Grimm, in *Luther's Works*, edited by Harold J. Grimm, 31:54.

McCarroll, Pamela R. "Keeping it Real: De-colonizing Christian Inter-Religious Practice as an Exercise in a Practical Theology of the Cross." *Religions* 10, no. 203 (2019): 1–13.

———. *Waiting at the Foot of the Cross*. Eugene OR: Pickwick, 2014.

McFague, Sallie. *Blessed Are the Consumers: Climate Change and the Practice of Restraint*. Minneapolis, MN: Fortress Press, 2013.

———. *The Body of God: An Ecological Theology*. Minneapolis, MN: Fortress Press, 1993.

Pihkala, Panu. "The *Pastoral* Challenge of the Environmental Crisis," *Dialog* 55, no. 2 (2016): 131–40.

Pihkala, Panu. "Eco-anxiety, Tragedy and Hope: Psychological and Spiritual Dimensions of Climate Change." *Zygon* 53, no. 2 (2018): 545–69.

Pihkala, Panu. "Death, the Environment, and Theology." *Dialog* 57 (2018): 287–94.

"Planetary Health in the Anthropocene." Editorial. *The Lancet* 393 (June 8, 2019): 2272. See also "Anthropocene," Google Dictionary. Accessed March 15, 2019. https://www.google.ca/search?q=anthropocene&rlz=1C1CHBF_enCA771CA771&oq=anthropocene&aqs=chrome.69i57j0l5.3116j0j7&sourceid=chrome&ie=UTF-8.

Chapter 8

God and the Church after Christendom

Rethinking "Power" through Douglas Hall's Theologia Crucis

Harris Athanasiadis

What is Christianity's relationship to power? By "power" I mean the capacity to dominate, impose, control, and shape history, and to mold the world around me. The history of the Western world is the history of this kind of power. The history of Christianity in the Western world is the history of how this religion was shaped by its relationship with such power.

Christianity was one of many religious options in the first centuries of the Common Era. Beginning with the Roman emperor Constantine in the fourth century, however, Christianity became the most powerful religion in Western society and the one official religion of the empire, rendering all other religious options illegal. Becoming all-powerful also meant centralizing doctrine and unifying it, rather than allowing for diversity. All theology not officially approved, and all churches not officially sanctioned, were outlawed and branded "heretical." The penalty was severe punishment, even death. Christendom was all-powerful, and its sanctioned leaders and theologians were also all-powerful.[1]

How did such power shape Christianity's doctrine from its earliest church councils onwards? How much was such doctrine faithful to the theology of original Christianity when it was a persecuted minority movement? Douglas John Hall is one voice among others who have argued that Christianity's transformation into Christendom was a mistake, even a betrayal of Jesus Christ. But beyond that, Hall has identified the major theological fault-lines in Christendom and has developed an alternative Christian theology. In particular, Hall rethinks Christianity outside "power" as defined above and develops it on a very different foundation, a foundation rooted in a theological tradition named *theologia crucis* (theology of the cross). Through his own creative appropriation of the *theologia crucis*, Hall offers a profound theological vision for the North American Church of today.

This chapter will not only present Hall's argument, but also lay out the radical implications of Hall's *theologia crucis* for the doctrine of God and the church.

WHAT TIME IS IT?

For Hall, a theologian's location in time and place, as well as personal history and situation, is critical in shaping his or her theology. Hall identifies his own context, then, as that of a white, middle-class, English-speaking, Canadian, and North American male, recognizing in that identity and location a history of privilege and power. Such privilege and power have also been associated historically with the Protestant churches of this continent and especially the once main-line churches. Finally, such privilege and power have made this social location highly influential in shaping popular North American culture in terms of its hopes, dreams, ambitions, values, and vision for life and society.

"What time is it?" Hall asks this question repeatedly as he offers a narrative that lays out where we as North Americans are and how we got here. This narrative has seven parts.[2]

1. The history of Western civilization is a history of the desire for and worship of power in order to dominate, control, and conquer the world. "Mastery of human and non-human nature" is a phrase Hall often uses, borrowed from the Canadian philosopher George Grant.[3] While civilizations differ in their quest for truth, beauty, and goodness, among the leading classes of Western civilization the desire for power has dominated all other desires. The modern era's rapid advances in science and technology, moreover, have increased exponentially the capacity for such power to dominate, control, and shape the world. Coupled with the rise of a Western "Enlightenment" in all areas of the human mind and spirit, such advances have led to a growing confidence in the human species over against a dependence on God, to a faith in history as human progress rather than divine providence, and to a hope that Western civilization's conquest of the world would lead to greater freedom and peace for all. In essence, then, social and technological power, combined with growing human intellectual and spiritual confidence, has accelerated a movement in which humanity—specifically, humanity as centered in the powerful classes—becomes God in God's place.
2. Such faith and hope, however, have come crashing down in the twentieth century, as war, genocide, and destruction have revealed another side of

such power. Even while the West is capable of dominating, controlling, and shaping the world, the human spirit is also revealed to be full of twisted motivations that are destructive of the world and destructive of humanity, leading to mass suffering and global peril of unprecedented proportions. Whether it's the threat of nuclear or environmental annihilation, cold war, or global economic crises, modern science and technology coupled with a hunger for power and the blinding illusions of the inevitability of moral progress have led human civilization to the point of an unprecedented crisis.
3. While many in the West continue to hope and dream that power (primarily science and technology) will save the world and fix all that has broken in the twentieth century, a growing number of more sensitive Westerners have become disillusioned, and such disillusionment has led many to despair about any larger good purpose and meaning for human civilization. While there is an overt kind of despair that is experienced by those who are the victims of power—the millions who are impoverished and suffering from marginalization of one form or another—there is also a covert kind of despair, a despair often hidden beneath the surface of popular culture, yet increasingly emerging in artistic, literary, and musical expressions, and in philosophical movements like existentialism. This covert despair is rooted in a loss of human purpose. Once the promise of power coupled with faith in human moral progress in history is confronted as the colossal failure it is, and once the voices of the victims of such power are truly heard, it is difficult not to despair of finding genuine purpose and meaning in the world.
4. The church in the West has always served as the official religion of power, and therefore as a cheerleader for power, even while the effects of the Enlightenment displaced it from its central location in society. At the same time that Europe as a whole faced the twentieth century, the churches faced a further crisis: growing disillusionment and despair produced a loss of faith, both in God and in the institutions that had aligned themselves with power. Even as post-war ecclesiastical participation surged in the mid-century, the steady erosion of the church's social influence continued apace.
5. Unlike in Europe, where twentieth-century destructiveness has been lived up close, and where movements like existentialism became more mainstream in popular culture, North American culture has continued to live in denial about the failure of Western civilization. Many continue to carry an optimism about the future through science, technology, and a moral positivity about the human spirit. The alternative for others is escape into a private oblivion of consumption and pleasure. Nonetheless, even in North America there have been signs of covert despair, loss of

meaning and purpose, and a growing nihilism that, when coupled with power rooted in science and technology, portends even greater danger to the planet.
6. The North American churches (primarily those English-speaking, Protestant, and once-main-line churches most aligned with power in North America) have continued to offer a triumphalist, stained-glass version of the broader optimism, or an escapist, individualist, and personalist spirituality in denial of the covert despair and nihilism hidden beneath the surface of North American society. As Hall has framed this narrative in his work over the decades, he has become more and more conscious of how expressions of covert despair have been increasing in popular culture manifestations, while at the same time traditional forms of optimism and triumphalism are becoming ever hollower and more pathetic.[4]
7. To add to this failure to address and engage with the hidden despair in the wider culture, the main-line churches of North America have been suffering a growing humiliation as numbers, money, social influence, and respect all dwindle. They are now increasingly sidelined, as evangelical/charismatic churches strengthen, as religious pluralism grows, and as more and more people claim to have no religion. The old church has lost its power and influence, and because its gospel, vision, and purpose proceeded from that power and influence, it is suffering its own despair even as it is called to respond to people who themselves are suffering their own despair, to whom it has all too little to offer.[5]

Therefore, whether it is the popular mainstream culture overseen historically by the "waspish" dominant class, or the churches that were made up of and supported this class, Prometheus confident and optimistic in his power has been transformed into Sisyphus who has lost his purpose and meaning in the face of a colossal failure to save the world and himself.[6] Where, then, is hope to be found?

THEOLOGIA CRUCIS

In his first major book, Hall poses these questions:

> Is there a gospel that, without offering unbelievable earthly answers or unacceptable heavenly ones, will nevertheless help me to live in this world without ultimate despair? Is it possible to discover a faith that does not require me to repress the unbelief that rises up in me, as I contemplate the present and future

of this world? Is it possible to hope, without embracing the official optimism of this society and its religion?[7]

What is needed, according to Hall, is not a theology that continues to buttress church and society with confident certitudes of triumphalist faith, hope, power, and glory, which become ever more pathetic as the churches decline in social influence, numbers of adherents, and finances. Neither is it a theology that encourages a denial or escape from the darkness of despair overt and covert through individualistic spirituality, or through worship turned into entertainment, or through the reduction of a thinking faith to social justice imperatives. Rather, what is needed is the kind of theology that can engage the darkness and enter into it, trusting that a fresh word of faith and hope will be given from within to light the way.

Such a theology, according to Hall, is what the theological tradition known as *theologia crucis* can provide. In his words, "While the theology of glory vanquishes (that is, claims to vanquish) all that negates by presenting a triumphant positive, the theology of the cross provides a basis of trust and courage enabling faith to enter more deeply into the sphere of the negative and to engage it."[8] Engaging it doesn't mean conquering it, but redeeming it and overcoming it from "within."[9] The *theologia crucis* does this by eschewing completely power as domination, control, and conquest (what we might call "domination power") in favor of a different kind of power, a power that is often mistaken as weakness. This different power is a way characterized by "waiting," "being-with," and "suffering-with," all of which point to a very different way of saving. It identifies the cross of Christ as the heart of the redemptive "power" of God—and not some triumphant resurrection that regards the cross as something to be conquered rather than redeemed.

While the phrase *theologia crucis* originates with the Protestant reformer Martin Luther, it also points to a theological tradition that can be traced back to the Apostle Paul, the School of Antioch, certain medieval mystics, the early Karl Barth, Reinhold Niebuhr, and Jürgen Moltmann, among others. Hall also locates this tradition in the Older Testament, naming it the "Tradition of Jerusalem." He notes that it is what might be called a "thin tradition," because in Christendom's love affair with domination power, any theology that privileges the cross rather than the resurrection as the heart of the revelation of God and God's saving work cannot be taken seriously.[10]

The cross is both a symbol and a concrete reality that embodies all that is evil, unjust, and destructive in the world.[11] In addition, the cross captures all the covert and overt despair created by the oppressive failure of domination power to bring about paradise on earth. Furthermore, domination power cannot be conquered effectively by a greater force of the same kind. It can be undone only by a very different kind of power, which the world sees as weakness. Cruciform power is the only power that can truly shine new light into the darkness of despair, that can transform despair into genuinely new resurrection possibilities.[12] What is this "cruciform power" like? How specifically is it able to redeem?

REDEMPTION FROM WITHIN

Hall develops and uses a whole terminology derived from the Bible and other sources to describe what redemption must look like to heal, save, and transform in the North American context. A *theologia crucis* recognizes that in a context where domination power has created overt and covert despair, redemption is possible only when healing, salvation, and transformation emerge from within the situation. It cannot impose itself forcefully, paternalistically, or condescendingly from above or outside. Power exerted from above or outside cannot conquer, fix, wipe away, or overcome pain of failure, loss of purpose, brokenness of spirit, or any of the other manifestations of the experience of despair that are endured in our world today. A different kind of power, a power from within, is what's needed.

In Hall's own words:

> There are . . . situations in which power simply does not work. Such situations are not foreign to any of us. Even the most macho of males (and females) experience such situations, and it may well be asked whether their resort to power and brute force is not frequently a consequence of their frustration over knowing in the depths of their souls that power does not change anything but usually only complicates existing problems. . . . Who, through power tactics, can eliminate the self-destroying habits of a son or daughter who has fallen prey to hard drugs? What nation, through power alone, can ensure world peace?

Not only are there "situations where power is of no avail. They are most of the situations in which as human beings we find ourselves!"[13]

What is needed, according to Hall, is a "*metanoia*"[14] of spirit that can only come from within the human spirit individually and collectively. Such a *metanoia* must be

> aimed at the anxiety that seeks security in the building of "greater barns," at the collective fear which is always busy fashioning images of the enemy, . . . at the false pride which sets race against race and sex against sex and generation against generation, and at the economic concupiscence which tries to find permanence and meaning in amassing possessions. How can power . . . meet and transform this anxiety, this fear, this false pride, this concupiscence? Such

spiritual qualities, which belong not only to individual persons but describe the spirit of our First World, can be altered only through an encounter with a judgement (*krisis*) which convicts from within and an alternative which commends itself through forgiveness and love.[15]

And once love is introduced as the key to redemption or conquest from within, Hall adds this:

The anatomy of human suffering is infinitely more complex than triumphalism of every variety conceives it to be, and it defies the "answers" of the powerful. The only power that can address suffering humanity is the power of love, and that is a power "made perfect in weakness" (2 Cor. 12:9). . . . What Reinhold Niebuhr called "the logic of the cross" . . . must interpret power in terms the world calls weakness, and victory in terms of what the world calls failure, because the thing that this power would overcome and this victory win is delicate indeed: it is the human spirit. The root causes of our suffering . . . being inseparable from our very selves, the conquest of them must be an intensely subtle one—a conquest from within.[16]

Love does not redeem by taking over but by standing beside the other, becoming an agent that empowers the other in and through her or his suffering, instead of rendering the other passive—and dependent for rescue on a dominating power.

"BEING-WITH": THE ONTOLOGY OF COMMUNION

In order to serve as a redemptive agent with the other, then, the other's distinctiveness and difference must be respected and treasured—not extinguished by being taken over in the redemption journey. True love respects another's distinctiveness and difference, and true love approaches the other in mutual creational vulnerability. In Hall's words:

Love means difference: I am not you, and you are not me. . . . We evoke and support each other's individuality even as we discover our fundamental solidarity. We do not disappear into each other's being. . . . Rather we become all the more present, real, and solid as persons . . . in the process of being united with one another. What is forfeited in our relatedness is not our individual "thouness". . . but the hostility, the suspicion, the bid for self-sufficiency that belong to the distortion of our personalities in their separation from the other.[17]

Hall refers to such love as "being-with." Whether it is God coming to be with us through the incarnation and "suffering-with" us through the cross, or whether it is us being "saved"[18] through God's being with us, and then being inspired and empowered so that we seek in our turn to be with others, this kind of relationality is the only way despair can be redeemed. DJH also describes such being-with as the "ontology of communion"—a term he borrows from the Lutheran theologian Joseph Sittler.[19] According to Hall the ontology of communion, of "being-with" (*mitsein* in German), is essential in defining both God and us humans. We are created as essentially relational beings by a God who is essentially relational in the divine being. Hall argues that this ontic relationality is deeply rooted in the tradition of Jerusalem (already mentioned earlier) over against the tradition of Athens (and the Western tradition since the Enlightenment). Being-with is contrasted with being-alone, being-against, being-over, or being-under, all of which reflect relational distortions that derive from the corrosive effects of power, which corrupts and destroys what we, through love, are created to be.

Being-with also leads necessarily to suffering-with (*mitlied* in German)[20] when the creature with whom God wants to commune is suffering. God's love for the human creature and for creation as a whole "groaning in travail" (Romans 8) is a suffering love. Such suffering love may appear weak in comparison with domination power, which overtly controls the world and promises to be the only means of overcoming suffering. But in the face of the overt and covert despair so rampant in our world, "only a suffering God can help" (Bonhoeffer)—a God who redeems from within by being-with and suffering-with and alongside those in despair. This is how the power called love redeems, and it is the *only* power than can redeem.

Moreover, as already intimated, the power that pertains to being-with and suffering-with love lies paradoxically in empowering the other to participate in his or her redemption journey; it refuses to render the other a passive victim who must depend totally on domination power to conquer and overcome despair, a power which always fails in the end. In his soteriology, anthropology, and ecclesiology, Hall introduces the term "representation."[21] According to Hall, representation is a contemporary term, accessible to North Americans, that helps describe how God (revealed and embodied in Jesus the Christ) encounters us in our despair and works through us in the face of our despair. Our own encounter with a being-with God inspires and empowers us to mediate God's love to others in their despair and to carry that despair before God in a way that does not extinguish these others but instead draws them forth on the redemption journey.

When we are inspired, empowered, and enabled to find hope and meaning in such a way that what we have suffered shapes us positively—in who we become, how we mature, and how we see; and when such maturity and insight become the kind of compassion we can carry with us in the way we *are* with others, then God is redeeming the world from within—beginning with us and then, through us, redeeming others. God is represented to others through us and we are representing others before God in our prayerful, worshipful, and compassionate being-with.

Finally, though, we may ask: what are the larger implications of the *theologia crucis'* negation of domination power in favor of a cruciform power of love as the means to divine redemption for the doctrine of God and the church in North America?

RETHINKING GOD AND THE CHURCH AFTER CHRISTENDOM

For all the reformations that have taken place in the history of Christian thought, the primary attribute of God as power to dominate, control, direct, or at the very least permit whatever happens, has until very recently never been questioned fundamentally to the point of a major rethinking. After the twentieth century, though, such rethinking has begun. What Hall has done toward the end of the century, along with other theologians and theological movements (such as process theology), is no less than a complete reformation of the doctrine of God. The radical nature of this rethinking, according to Hall, has meant replacing domination power with cruciform, being-with love as the primary attribute of God, even to the point of extinguishing domination power as an attribute of God.

According to Hall, in the traditional doctrine of Western Christendom,

> God is depicted as one, who, unlike us, does not exist under threat of nonbeing in any of its manifestations. Thus the divine power (omnipotence) is not challenged by any lack or weakness; the divine knowledge (omniscience) is not circumscribed by ignorance, uncertainty, or inherent limitation; the divine presence (omnipresence) is not subject to the constraints of time and space; and God is not vulnerable to change or prey to passions that may be aroused by any external eventuality (immutability).[22]

Indeed, argues Hall, such attributes of power in God have been so consistently applied doctrinally that it has been virtually impossible to appreciate attributes more faithful to the bible that "entail a subordination of power as it is normally conceived to its apparent opposite, weakness." In fact, argues Hall,

> As soon as God loves—loves, namely, a world and creatures whose condition is that of being-threatened-by-nonbeing—then God too must be seen to participate vicariously in nonbeing. For love, if it is genuine, assumes as its own the condition of the beloved. The loving God of the Bible is evidently not interested in a personal triumph of being over nonbeing, but only in a triumph that incorporates the salvation of the beloved; and that is no facile matter.[23]

Hall then reflects on this salvific/redemption journey in the now familiar language of the biblical ontology of communion, of being-with us and suffering-with us, and also being present to us, alongside us, face-to-face with us, even within us.[24] The distinctive difference of cruciform power from domination power is that redemption always remains a communion in which neither we nor the other is ever extinguished. Rather, we participate with God as we are represented before God (through Christ our representative), and then are called in grace to be representatives ourselves on behalf of God to others and on behalf of others before God. Suffering does not destroy us when our despair can find new meaning in how we are able to be redemptively present with and for others as God is with and for us. We develop new maturity, strength, insight, and hope in ways we would never have known or experienced before through the very suffering we have faced and lived. This is why Hall can state, "God does not will the fall of the creature; yet God graciously anticipates it as one who is able to make of this tragic turn of events a new beginning that is even, perhaps, more glorious than the first."[25] God does this both from within and beside, as redemptive source and participant: "The God of the whole Bible is a suffering God. God suffers because God loves. And until that which God loves—the creation—is healed, the glory of God can only be glimpsed by those who in some measure are given to participate in God's suffering love."[26]

The theological door Hall has opened in his rethinking of the doctrine of God is, I would argue, a complete elimination of the attribute of power as domination power from the being and working of God. To interpret any event in the world or in our personal lives as an act of God—as if God is somehow effecting healing or redemptive change outside any human agency/participation—has become incredible to those sensitive to the overt and covert despair in our world. Hall does argue for some mystery in how divine providence may be working in the world; he even expresses a version of the kenotic-theory of divine self-limitation, in which God is described as making a deliberate choice to hold back power "for our sake, becoming accessible to us within the parameters of our creatureliness."[27] He also follows theologians like Jürgen Moltmann and Gregory Baum, among others, and mystics like Simone Weil via George Grant, who express the divine kenotic self-limitation as an act of divine love in withdrawing or restraining God's sovereign power, creating space for freedom in creation and human history.[28]

The problem with this way of describing divine sovereignty, however, is that it conceptualizes power as domination power within God whether as assertive action, domination, and control on the one hand, or self-limitation, restraint, and withdrawal on the other. Cruciform love, however, is a totally different kind of power that exercises itself from within rather from without creation. Cruciform love is powerless in the world when hearts are hardened and closed. But once activated from within through the persuasion of the divine Spirit, it becomes an active agent of transformation and justice in the world. Can God be anything other than cruciform love—and can God be any other kind of being and power than such love? If the answer is no, then does it make sense to separate God from such love conceptually, as a being who loves rather than that very Love itself—especially in a post-Christendom, secularized context, in which any talk of God as some independent being is met with incredulity or considered idolatrous?[29]

If talk of God as a distinct being is no longer credible in a secularized world, and we move further toward identifying God as a mystery that is cruciform love redeeming from within, then God is both like and unlike us human beings in several ways. God cannot choose not to love and still be God. Moreover, if God is to heal and transform creation, then God/love can work only from within. We humans, on the other hand, are given the freedom to *choose* communion with such love and to *choose* to receive and be transformed by it. Freedom to choose, however, also means freedom to resist, indeed even to choose domination power as our way—perhaps because we fear our own vulnerability and lack of control. What is more, there are situations in history and in the world when we must negotiate the use of domination power without becoming corrupted by it, knowing that its benefits are limited and its possibilities dangerous. Domination power may be necessary for us humans at times (for instance to protect the weak and vulnerable and to rescue the abused), but is it really needed as an attribute of God, even as negation, weakness, or self-limitation? We humans must choose love freely if our love is to be genuine, but does God have to have choice, if indeed God actually *is* that movement, force, or energy of love that transforms from within?

And what, then, of the church in the world? A radical rethinking of the doctrine of God, one that completely repudiates domination power as a divine attribute and completely embraces the power of cruciform love as *the* defining attribute of God, is possible only from the new vantage point of a post-Christendom church painfully aware of its own social humiliation and vulnerability. When the church not only accepts that it has now become emptied of social privilege, power, and influence, when it embraces such "humiliation" as the providential hand of God (working from within), it is then opened, able to rethink God and God's working in, through, and as the body of Christ in the world.

From his earliest books on the church, Hall has consistently made several key arguments: (1) disestablishment is not a curse but a divine gift; (2)

disestablishment is faithful to the biblical images Jesus uses of his fellowship (i.e., salt, yeast, light, little flocks), which recognize in smallness a capacity for authenticity, attentiveness to truth, and being-with love not possible when the church is big, powerful, and wealthy; (3) the disestablished church, appreciative of its vulnerability yet also of its fidelity to its crucified/risen Lord, recognizes that God is working in the world outside the church as much as in and through it; and (4) the disestablished church struggling to survive and find new meaning and purpose in its mission is more faithful not only in representing its crucified/risen Lord in its vulnerability, but also in being-with and representing the world's overt and covert despair in its own life.

Thus, the disestablished church carries a new freedom and commitment to be with and for others, and to align itself with critical and constructive liberation and protest movements within society.[30] It can finally incarnate the priesthood of Christ, both in its own priestly representation of Christ in the world and in its intercession before God of the world's suffering and need.[31] It no longer needs to stake an exclusive claim to furthering God's work in the world, but finds a renewed call to participate in what cruciform love is already doing in the world, which it could neither appreciate nor recognize earlier, when it was so attached to domination power.[32]

While humanity must negotiate power in a world of sin and injustice, the church's mission is to convict the world of the limits of domination power, inspiring instead the choice for being-with others who are the victims of power. To do this, the church must also find its purpose and meaning by communing with cruciform love in the face of its own despair arising from failure, humiliation, and uncertainty about its future. Finally, the church must find new life by prayerfully, worshipfully, and contemplatively offering up such despair before the eternal love who can heal and transform from within. Can the North American church, finally, become the "wounded healer"?[33] In fidelity to its cruciform Lord, can it itself embody cruciform love?

CONCLUSION

At its heart, Hall's theological vision is a response to a narrative of what has happened to Western civilization since modernity, and what has happened to the churches of the West as well. Naming the central malaise of our context as "despair," and discerning that it manifests itself in both overt and covert forms, Hall argues that only a *theologia crucis* can engage such despair honestly, meaningfully, and redemptively. Hall appropriates this "thin tradition" as he develops conceptual language for it in the concept of the "Ontology of Communion," Which has profound implications for the doctrines of God and the Church, raising key questions about the nature of God and the future of the church. In a context where talk of "God," let alone of any faith in God, is increasingly questioned and widely dismissed, where churches are increasingly marginalized and ignored, "power" in Christian thinking about God and the representational life of the church in the world must be rethought completely. Unless we engage that "still small point where battle is raging"[34] in our North American context today, the church has no meaningful future in its communal life and witness in the world. Only in communion with Cruciform Love, whom we Christians name "God," and only through participation in the "being-with" representational life of Cruciform Love in the world, can the church finally fulfill its purpose and find its salvation.

NOTES

1. Douglas Hall makes this argument throughout his work. For a more recent example, see *Waiting for Gospel: An Appeal to the Dispirited Remnants of Protestant Establishment* (Eugene, OR: Cascade, 2012), 51–53.

2. These seven points are found throughout Hall's corpus, beginning with *Hope against Hope: Towards an Indigenous Theology of the Cross* (Tokyo: World Student Christian Federation, 1971).

3. The importance of Grant's influence on Hall's analysis of the North American Context cannot be underestimated, beginning with *Lighten Our Darkness: Toward an Indigenous Theology of the Cross* (Philadelphia, PA: Westminster, 1976). For more on the connection between Grant and Hall, see Pamela McCarroll, *Waiting at the Foot of the Cross: Toward a Theology of Hope for Today* (Eugene, OR: Pickwick, 2014). See also Harris Athanasiadis, *George Grant and the Theology of the Cross: The Christian Foundations of His Thought* (Toronto, ON: University of Toronto Press, 2001).

4. What about more liberal mainline churches focused on "justice"? Moral imperatives and larger criticism of systemic and personal injustice may be a much better alternative to optimistic denials of the gravity of social injustices or escapist individualistic spirituality and worship as entertainment, because they address the overt despair in the world. Yet moral imperatives of justice do not in themselves engage the deeper malaise of covert despair growing among the middle classes of North America. Nor have the liberal churches meaningfully faced their growing humiliation and loss of power to influence change in government policy or society at large.

5. This is because mainline liberal churches have abandoned theology by reducing it to ethics. See *What Christianity Is Not: An Exercise in "Negative" Theology* (Eugene, OR: Cascade Books, 2013), 57–58, 69–71, 78ff.

6. *Professing the Faith: Christian Theology in a North American Context* (Minneapolis, MN: Fortress Press, 1993), 255; *Waiting for Gospel*, 98.

7. *Lighten Our Darkness*, 97.

8. *The Cross in Our Context: Jesus and the Suffering World* (Minneapolis, MN: Fortress Press, 2003), 30.

9. *Cross in Our Context*, 32. Also, *Waiting for Gospel*, 84–85.

10. *Lighten Our Darkness*, 107. Also, *Waiting for Gospel*, 77–79; *What Christianity Is Not*, 91, 94, 134, 160.

11. *Waiting for Gospel*, 84–85.

12. *Lighten Our Darkness* (Revised edition, 2001), xviii.

13. *God and Human Suffering: An Exercise in the Theology of the Cross* (Minneapolis, MN: Augsburg, 1986), 98–99.

14. *Metanoia* is a Greek word meaning repentance, conversion, or transformative kind of inner change. See *What Christianity Is Not*, 89, 144, 156.

15. *God and Human Suffering*, 102.

16. *God and Human Suffering*, 106–7.

17. *The Steward: A Biblical Symbol Come of Age* (New York: Friendship Press, 1982), 208.

18. Salvation is not a state of being but a journey of becoming.

19. *The Steward*, 207. See also *What Christianity Is Not*, 136ff.

20. Hall has a preference for German over English renditions of being-with and suffering-with, because they draw forth the unique relationality of meaning in a way English cannot. See *What Christianity Is Not*, 136, 140, 142.

21. *Professing the Faith*, 347ff, 506ff. Also, *Confessing the Faith: Christian Theology in a North American Context* (Minneapolis, MN: Fortress Press, 1996), 44ff.

22. *Professing the Faith*, 96.

23. *Professing*, 97.

24. *Professing*, 158–62.

25. *Professing*, 89.

26. *Professing*, 183.

27. *Thinking the Faith: Christian Theology in a North American Context* (Minneapolis, MN: Augsburg, 1989; paperback reprint: Minneapolis, MN: Fortress Press, 1991), 100.

28. *God and the Nations* (Minneapolis, MN: Fortress Press, 1995, with Rosemary Radford Ruether), 18–25; *Confessing the Faith*, 330; Jürgen Moltmann, *The Trinity and the Kingdom: The Doctrine of God* (San Francisco, CA: Harper and Row, Publishers, 1981), 59–60; Gregory Baum, *The Oil Has Not Run Dry: The Story of My Theological Pathway* (Montreal, QC: McGill-Queen's University Press, 2017), 59–60; Simone Weil, *Waiting for God* (London: Collins, 1951), 34, 114; Athanasiadis, *George Grant and the Theology of the Cross*, 88–100.

29. *What Christianity Is Not*, 135.

30. *The Reality of the Gospel and the Unreality of the Churches* (Philadelphia, PA: Westminster, 1975. Reprint: Minneapolis, MN: Fortress Press, 2007), 161–63.

31. *Has the Church a Future?* (Philadelphia, PA: Westminster, 1980. Reprint: Minneapolis, MN: Fortress Press, 2009), 124–26. See also *What Christianity Is Not*, 96129, 138.

32. *What Christianity Is Not*, 162. Also, *The End of Christendom and the Future of Christianity*, (Valley Forge, PA: Trinity Press International, 1997. Reprint: Eugene, OR: Wipf and Stock, 2002), 65.

33. Henry Nouwen, *The Wounded Healer* (New York, Doubleday, 1979).
34. This saying is attributed to Luther and referred to throughout DJH's corpus.

WORKS CITED

Athanasiadis, Harris. *George Grant and the Theology of the Cross: The Christian Foundations of His Thought.* Toronto, ON: University of Toronto Press, 2001.

Baum, Gregory. *The Oil Has Not Run Dry: The Story of My Theological Pathway.* Montreal, QC: McGill-Queen's University Press, 2017.

Hall, Douglas John. *The Cross in Our Context: Jesus and the Suffering World.* Minneapolis, MN: Fortress Press, 2003.

———. *The End of Christendom and the Future of Christianity.* Valley Forge, PA: Trinity Press International, 1997. Reprint: Eugene, OR: Wipf and Stock, 2002.

———. *God and Human Suffering: An Exercise in the Theology of the Cross.* Minneapolis, MN: Augsburg, 1986.

———. *Has the Church a Future?* Philadelphia, PA: Westminster, 1980. Reprint: Minneapolis, MN: Fortress Press, 2009.

———. *Hope against Hope: Towards an Indigenous Theology of the Cross.* Tokyo: World Student Federation, 1971.

———. *Lighten Our Darkness: Towards an Indigenous Theology of the Cross.* Philadelphia, PA: Westminster, 1976.

———. *Professing the Faith: Christian Theology in a North American Context.* Minneapolis, MN: Fortress Press, 1993.

———. *The Reality of the Gospel and the Unreality of the Churches.* Philadelphia, PA: Westminster, 1975. Reprint: Minneapolis, MN: Fortress Press, 2007.

———. *The Steward: A Biblical Symbol Come of Age.* New York: Friendship Press, 1982.

———. *Thinking the Faith: Christian Theology in a North American Context.* Minneapolis, MN: Augsburg, 1989; paperback reprint: Minneapolis, MN: Fortress Press, 1991.

———. *Waiting for Gospel: An Appeal to the Dispirited Remnants of Protestant Establishment.* Eugene, OR: Cascade Books, 2012.

———. *What Christianity is Not: An Exercise in "Negative" Theology.* Eugene, OR: Cascade Books, 2013.

Hall, Douglas John, and Rosemary Radford Ruether. *God and the Nations.* Minneapolis, MN: Fortress Press, 1995.

McCarroll, Pamela. *Waiting at the Foot of the Cross: Toward a Theology of Hope for Today.* Eugene, OR: Pickwick, 2014.

Moltmann, Jürgen. *The Trinity and the Kingdom: The Doctrine of God.* San Francisco, CA: Harper and Row, 1981.

Nouwen, Henry. *The Wounded Healer.* New York, Doubleday, 1979.

Weil, Simone. *Waiting for God.* London: Collins, 1951.

Chapter 9

The Relevance of the Theology of Douglas John Hall for the Cuban Context

Adolfo Ham

A person becomes a theologian by living, by dying, and by being damned, not by understanding, reading and speculating.

—Martin Luther

This chapter is the result of a seminar held in Matanzas which studied the relevance of the Theology of Douglas John Hall in the Cuban context.[1] Dr. Hall—Douglas—is an outstanding contextual theologian with a radical projection, concerned with "what end [theology] serves, and whom it serves." He asserts that "we shall become witnesses against our own nations and classes"[2]—and yet he is not an extremist, but is able to harmonize Barth and Tillich! He defines his theological project as follows:

> I should like to regard myself as a child and contemporary representative of this New World pilgrimage, returning at a point of crisis to the cultic roots of the vision that has inspired our corporate sojourn, and asking of that tradition what it may still hold for such a critical context as ours.[3]

In the aftermath of the commemoration of the 500th anniversary of Luther's Reformation, it is significant that Hall remains a staunch defender of the Protestant Reformation, and especially of the "Protestant Principle" as it was enunciated by Paul Tillich: "nothing relative can become absolute!" In the words of Tillich himself, "Christianity is final only in so far as it has the power of criticizing and transforming each of its historical manifestations, and just this power is the Protestant Principle."[4] In keeping with this principle, Hall is always questioning himself, and asking What is Protestantism? "In short," he writes as he contemplates the malaise of the present moment, "everything seems to conspire to reduce the centrality of that 'Protestant core' to a shadow of its former self."[5]

I have been very much impressed by Hall's militant idea of theology, and of theological work, especially since we often substitute ideology for theology. For me a brilliant elaboration of this theology is his trilogy, *Christian Theology in a North American Context*, on which I will concentrate. In the volumes' prefaces Hall states that he wrote the trilogy because "North America is the last stronghold of Western Christendom," it is the end of the Constantinian era, it is a "post-Christian era," and yet, he thinks, we have not questioned our model of the church—pointing to the "incapacity of the churches to confront the deeper malaise." In the last resort, Hall says, the church is experiencing "a crisis of thinking."

Hall declares that the three volumes have a dual purpose. The first is to offer "a critical and constructive theological perspective from which the mainline Protestant churches, experiencing varying degrees of self-doubt, may be encouraged to rethink and renew life and mission"; the second is "to provide a basic introduction to the rudiments of Christianity, and an introduction of foundational teachings of the tradition."[6] He adds:

> It is easy to criticize empirical Christianity; the more difficult—and more urgent—task confronting serious Christians today is to present viable alternatives to the ecclesiastical status quo. I have been deeply critical of the churches although I have always done so as one who believes that there are possibilities for change and for faithfulness that are being missed by Christian institutions in their present forms. Here, however, I wish to be entirely responsible as a *church theologian*.[7]

Hall believes that the theology that is called for has to be prophetic theology: "The social, political and cultural realities that we have to resist are certainly less obvious than those celebrated in the sacred history of resistance, but they may be more insidious for all that."[8] If I were to try to characterize Hall's theology, I would certainly say that it is "prophetic theology," in which the two basic elements are, as he stipulates, (a) a constructive critique of society and culture, and (b) "sacred resistance."

In his first volume, *Thinking the Faith*, Hall argues that "only a thinking faith can survive, only a thinking faith can help the world survive!"

> The faith can be *thought*—that is, such reflection can become in the strict sense *theology*—only if, in the process of remembering all that precedes and excludes "us," we are simultaneously brought into a more articulate awareness of ourselves, our own identity, our "situation in life": Who am I? Who are we? What

do we bring to this struggle to understand? Why do we feel it to be necessary to do this? What is at stake for us? What are we afraid of? What do we hope for? This alone is an arduous task. Perhaps it is impossible. Certainly it is never finished. Nevertheless, it is absolutely indispensable to Christian theology. Without this, one ends with mere doctrine.[9]

In the preface to his second volume, *Professing the Faith*, Hall asks, "if we have no coherent basis of faith's profession, how shall we confess the faith?" Here he is referring to "mainline Protestantism" as "the stained glass dimension of 'main line culture.'" But arriving at a coherent understanding of what we profess, he argues,

> will only happen, if we stop being demoralized by our reduced status vis-à-vis power and learn enough about what the Christian faith really means to enable us to disengage ourselves from the dominant culture also at the level of what we believe and profess. . . . Dying to Christendom, we could become the church. . . . We confess the faith when, through this process of contemplating our world in the light of that whole heritage of mediation, we are thrust into an active engagement with that which threatens the life of our world.[10]

Hall carries this project forward in his third volume, *Confessing the Faith*, in which he argues that "the confession of belief is by no means irrelevant to the reality" to which it attests:

> For until this reality is received and appropriated, it has not yet attained its own internal aim and fullness. . . . Confessing the faith is the quintessentially *contextual* task of the disciple community. . . . In its thinking of the faith, the disciple community has known from the first that it could not abide in the house of thought, that it would have to go out into the marketplace and *perform* the thought. . . . No community of Christians ever arrives at the place of *confession* apart from an ongoing and disciplined struggle to comprehend the whole substance of what Christians *profess*."[11]

Hall's presentation of his theology has several notable themes:

1. What is most important for me is Hall's realistic description of the North American context, and then the critical analysis of the situation of the Church in North America. "North American society is a success oriented society," Hall observes, and goes on to say that "the malaise of modernity is the legacy of a Promethean optimism which did not take into account the limits of human power and the ubiquity and subtlety of evil."[12] The

situation of the Church in Canada, Hall points out, has changed; it now finds itself set in a pluralistic, post-Constantinian society, in a post-modern era. "The role of religion in our midst," Hall says, "(especially of truncated versions of the Christian religion), is by no means unambiguously laudatory . . . from the perspective of classical forms both of Protestant and Catholic thought";[13] indeed, "Protestantism in North America is an amalgamation of Protestantism and Americanism," for "to know the context is to participate in it":[14] "the form of faith's self-understanding is always determined by the historical configuration in which the community of faith belief finds itself."[15] What North America needs, then, "a *metanoia*, . . . a revolution of spirit and hope deep enough to turn it from the blind pursuit of oblivion towards the sincere and intelligent quest for peace."[16]

Surprisingly enough, Hall also speaks of the dangers of contextuality—of being "too uncritically" influenced "by dominant social trends simply setting the agenda for the churches," which might too easily "accommodate to main cultural trends."[17] "The obvious antidote to a contextualism which ends in what we might term localism—beyond the hope that it might become more genuinely contextual—is an ecumenical praxis theology which keeps building and repairing bridges between peoples amid worlds."[18] (Hall might have added "inter-religious" dialogue and relations, but at that time that issue was not so obvious.) "A contextual theology inevitably moves toward political and pastoral theology, that is toward praxis; it is therefore limited, incomplete, in many places inadequate, sometimes misleading, biased, and so on."[19]

2. Hall applies the *theologia crucis* of Luther to his theological work. Hall's theology, then, rests in this spirit of integrative suffering, and resists the commonly accepted, accommodating theology that prevails in North America's success-oriented society. "Theology done in the spirit of this [the *theologia crucis*] tradition is bound to be a contextual theology."[20] Hall writes: "A theology which looks for God's solidarity with a broken creation and aims to participate in God's healing of that creation *must* involve itself in the specifics of its society's problematique."[21]
3. The concept of faith, as we can see by the titles of the trilogy, is a key notion in Hall's work. For Hall, faith is always a category of relationship—a fundamental trust (*fiducia*), as Luther defined it (*Vertrauen*): love in understanding, faith in the God who is love. "Faith is the grace-given courage to engage that world," Hall writes; Theology is a disciplined reflection and commentary upon faith's engagement. Theology therefore *is* contextual, and that by definition."[22] Very important for him is "confessing the faith" (the title of his third volume): "Confession of

faith occurs when the church is sufficiently identified with the world's doubt and despair and evil that the world, in its turn, is made curious about the church's persistent belief, hope, and message of deliverance from evil."[23] "We confess the faith when through this process of contemplating our world, in the light of that whole heritage of meditation we are thrust into active engagement with that which threatens the life of our world."[24] Given all this, "profession and confession is a process, recurrent and reciprocal."[25] Indeed, Hall writes, "Confession implies the kind of intelligent participation in one's culture."[26]

4. And here we come to another key concept in Hall's theology: that of discipleship. Hall asserts very strongly that "it is not just a question of correct doctrine; it is a matter of discipleship." Facing so many expressions of fundamentalism in today's Protestantism, it is very important that orthodoxy not be the main criterion, but rather "discipleship." This is why Dietrich Bonhoeffer is always present in Hall's theology—the Bonhoeffer of *The Cost of Discipleship*, and of course of his own life and witness! Again, Hall says, "It is not a question of correct doctrine; it is a matter of discipleship!" And he praises the Barmen Confession, which by the way happens to be also part of our Book of Confessions (i.e., of the Iglesia Presbiteriana-Reformada en Cuba). It's inclusion in the formal confessions of our church is why I was asked by the *Ecumenical Review* for an article that would expounding upon the reason for our adoption of this foreign German Confession. Hall daringly lays out its relevance:

> [I]f one probes a little beneath the surface of our life, as we have tried to do in this trilogy, one discovers crisis that in the long run may be more decisive for the future than those that occasioned the confession of Barmen. And even where such crisis are held in abeyance by affluence, or costume, or inertia, or the vigilance of the few, the disciple community is obliged by its world commitment to mold its confession in response to them.[27]

5. A fourth key theme in Hall's work is the concept of God. Hall speaks of the political co-optation of the Christian doctrine: "A religion designed to serve the purposes of empire cannot present the spectacle of a God whose kenotic long-suffering detracts from 'his' majesty, a less than absolute deity, a deity torn between impartial judgment and unwarranted mercy, a deity who stoops to our weakness, and actually becomes weak for our sake. Such is not the blueprint for a God designed for empire, any empire."[28] Further, Hall argues that

> the dominant theology of Christendom has suffered from a too consistent application of the power principle to the godhead: that this theology not only fails to represent the biblical testimony to God but also contains inherent contradictions and inadequacies; and that these latter become

conspicuous and intolerable when the historical conditions that gave rise to such an image of God are replaced by conditions incompatible with the conclusion that the world is governed by a God of power and glory.[29]

"God defines love, not love God," Hall goes on to say, "for in our context the sentimentalization of divinity under the impact of cheap romanticism has inflicted upon the Christian faith a 'monism of love' (Kitamori) that renders such Christianity simplistic and untrue to the experience of the honest."[30]

6. Hall's work also has much to say on the theme of theological anthropology:

> What biblical faith demands that we ask, however, is whether humanity is ever well served by such images [i.e., those that have been dominant] of deity and humanity. For a sense of purpose—indeed, for the very existence of community—human collectivities need to achieve some measure of regulation *vis-à-vis* their environment: but do we really need to consider ourselves lords and masters of nature? Infinitely higher than other forms of life? Capable of unlimited achievements of which the advances of the past are only tokens? Veritable demigods, in fact? Is our need for security and meaning so insatiable that we can be satisfied with nothing less than absolute control and the elimination of every negating factor? Must chance be done away with entirely? On the contrary, do not such visions usually function destructively in the end? Of Western Christian civilization in its North American expression, which is perhaps its purest, least diluted form, must it now be asked: who can attain unto it? Having fashioned an "Almighty Father" who could both symbolize and hallow our pretensions to almighty sonship, have we not put ourselves in the way of being weighed in balances of our own devising, and found wanting? Who can measure up this theo-anthropology? What of those who could never even pretend to do so: the sons who were weak, afraid, "feminine"? the mentally and physically handicapped sons? the black, red, and yellow sons on the edges of our proud white societies? Above all, what of the daughters?[31]

Hall declines to "deprecate" those attributes of humanity that have in the past predominated, even allowing that "they may be considered admirable, even noble." But he calls attention "to the underlying assumption upon which this entire approach to the question—What is truly human?—depends":

> It is that the essence of human being is to be located in qualities of being for which we have a special aptitude, if they are not inherent in our very makeup. It is also presupposed that these qualities may be diminished by other, negating qualities or propensities. Authentic humanity, it is assumed, is achieved through

the displacement of negative qualities by the cultivation and enhancement of positive qualities of being.[32]

7. Finally, Hall's work is much concerned with the theme of *ecclesiology*. In *Thinking the Faith*, Hall offers "Guidelines for Discerning the Times," in which he gives four types of criteria to judge the authenticity of his discernment of the North American context. These criteria take the form of questions: (1) Who are *the victims* of our society? (2) How is our society perceived and depicted by its own *most reflective members*? (3) How do the pursuits and values of our society compare with images of the human in *our authoritative sources*? (4) Within the *corporate dialogue* of the disciple community, what emerges as the problematic of our culture?"[33] I will respond to these in relationship to the Cuban situation a little later on.

In the preface to the revised edition of *Lighten Our Darkness: Towards an Indigenous Theology of the Cross*, Hall makes the following comments:

> However much one empathizes with this worldly sorrow [i.e., of not having realized the American dream], the Christian does not indulge it, he or she tries instead to place it within a larger context—the context, namely, of that *divine* sorrow whose companionship prevents all human suffering from becoming morbid self-pity, and whose presence can make of our despair the genesis of new and better hope. More pathetic than failure itself is the incapacity of humankind, unaided by grace, for the honest and open contemplation of failure. What is needed is some point of vantage from which it is possible to view our human wreckages without being debilitated by the experience.[34]

It seems to me that this is an excellent description of Hall's purpose in his theological program.

I would like to comment also on some of Hall's remarks in his book *God and the Nations*, specifically in the second part of the book, in Hall's "Response to R. R. Ruether":

> To use contemporary jargon, we are both *praxis*-oriented theologians, and we both try to think the faith *contextually*. . . . [W]e closely agree on such matters as the humiliation and demise of Christendom and the problems and possibilities that this great transition raises for the Christian future. . . . Only in one matter do I have some reservations. It has to do with R. R. Ruether's discussion of the Israeli-Palestinian conflict, especially with her discussion of "ethnocentrism and exclusivism versus universalism." Obviously she prefers a faith that accentuates

God's love for all peoples. "Is God a God of one people? Or is a God of all nations, who creates and loves all peoples and wishes to bring them all into redemption?"

One must agree with the spirit of these questions. But the question beneath the questions is always *how* the love of God for "all" has to be effected. Christians as well as Jews have answered that the implementation of the universal *agape* of God necessarily entails particularity. Particularity is always a "scandal," but it is also the only way of getting to the universal.[35]

I am sorry that I do not agree with my good friend Douglas because "particularity" always entails segregation, *apartheid*.

MY RESPONSE TO DOUGLAS HALL

Hall's "Authenticity" and the Cuban Church

As noted above, Hall gives four criteria to judge the authenticity of his discernment of the North American context. I would now like to consider the relevance of these four criteria to our Cuban situation.

(1) *"Who are the victims of our society?"* After a revolution do we still have victims? My simple answer is that "no revolution is the realization of the Kingdom of God": obviously there are victims, conscious (those that would suffer from the political change, such as those who lost property, those very few people who died in the struggle, those who had to go into exile, etc.) or unconscious (unintended). I will say more later on.

(2) *"How is our society perceived and depicted by its own most reflective members?"* To quote Julio César Guanche in a recent publication:

> The author senses a deep dissociation between the political discourse and the ideological-cultural practice within socialism in Cuba, whose worst expression is the ideology which is presented as an infallible governmental program. Its dissociation is part of a democratic deficit: the insufficiency of the public debate about the ideological definition of the process.[36]

We have had more public discussions on this area, and as the internet develops there are more tweets and more comments via other social networks.

(3) *"How do the pursuits and values of our society compare with images of the human in our authoritative sources?"* This is a difficult question. I will refer to the precious book of Cintio Vitier, *Ese sol del mundo moral* (several editions), in which he presents a kind of "apostolic succession" in our history of all the founders of our nation around the idea

of "justice." Are we there? Pluralism, tolerance, subtle racism, left-over gender issues: back to Guanche.

(4) *"Within the corporate dialogue of the disciple community, what emerges as the problematic of our culture?"* What is problematic in our culture? How can we define Cuban culture? First, I will try to define Cuban culture, referring to two classical answers. The first is the famous dictum of Fernando Ortiz:

> It has been said repeatedly that Cuba is a melting pot of human elements. Such comparison may be applied to our land as with the rest of the American nations. But perhaps we could present another more precise metaphor, more comprehensive and more appropriate for the Cuban audience ... a better Cuban simile, a Cuban metaphor, which we will understand better and with more details: Cuba is an *ajiaco* ("dish made of different boiled meats and vegetables"). (Or, in Spanish: "Se ha dicho repetidamente que Cuba es un crisol de elementos humanos. Tal comparación se aplica a nuestra patria como a las demás naciones de América. Pero acaso puede presentarse otra metáfora más precisa, más comprensiva y más apropiada para un auditorio cubano, ya que en Cuba no hay fundiciones de crisoles, fuera de las modestísimas de algunos artesanos. Hagamos mejor un símil cubano, un cubanismo metafórico, y nos entenderemos mejor, más pronto y con más detalles. Cuba es un *ajiaco*.")[37]

The second classical answer is articulated by the Cuban philosopher and essayist Jorge Mañach: "A country can be said to be self-conscious when it is in solidarity with its memories and aspirations, when it has not only accumulated common experiences, but has a common idea of them and is founded on one sole collective will, a unique sense of its own destiny."

In 1986, the Cuban Roman Catholic Church had an important gathering, the *Encuentro Nacional Eclesial Cubano* (ENEC), in which, among other issues of Cuban life, they faced Cuban culture and gave some guidance for the pastoral work of the Church:

The following realities demand deeper thought and investigation:

- The more characteristic traits of our national identity.
- The principal qualities, signs and language of the emerging Cuban culture.
- A vital and prophetical synthesis between Christian humanism and Marxist anthropology, between the legitimate autonomy of science, arts and their relation with the Christian faith.
- [A further goal is to] [s]timulate the artistic creativity of people: musicians, sculptors, painters, writers with a Christian breath.[38]

The Barmen Confession and the Cuban Church

In his theology Douglas Hall refers many times to the importance of the church living *in status confessionis*, presenting the Barmen Confession (1934) as a good paradigm about how to confess the Faith in our world. Since Barmen is part of our Book of Confessions, adopted in a Synod in 1977, I was asked by the *Ecumenical Review* in an issue dedicated to the seventy-fifth anniversary of the Barmen Confession (March 2009) about the significance of Barmen for us. Some of the ideas I shared were these:

> Our socialist state does not present the same heretical challenge as Nazism, and yet because of the euphoria of the beginnings of the revolutionary process we should have adopted a more prophetic attitude towards the revolution than we did. In the very beginnings of the process, because of blind anti-communism, we ourselves restricted our criticisms, and found later on, that any government required this critical exchange with the people. But the declaration did help us:

(a) To obey the Gospel in a more radical way. In a Socialist society with its staunch secular drive, values have been neglected. Some of the old evils of society have come back in more subtle forms, such as consumer habit in the population, free love with the decomposition of the family, lack of honesty in the administration of the people's goods, and so on.
(b) To see the need for the renewal of the church.
(c) To offer to our people "a free and grateful service."
(d) To discern between patriotism/nationalism and blind obedience to the state.
(e) Having the conviction that the state cannot fulfill the vocation of the church.
(f) And that the church cannot fulfill either the vocation of the state.
(g) To affirm the freedom of the church.[39]

I will add: we have not taken Barmen seriously enough! And I question myself, really, do the churches anywhere take seriously their confessions of faith? As Hall says, "Confession of the faith certainly entails the correction also of doctrinal, ethical, and other 'errors' within the Church."[40]

The Nature of Mission in the Cuban Church

How then are we to define the mission of the churches in Cuba today? I stated in 1998 for a meeting on Missions held in Cuba that

> There is not a prefabricated paradigm for mission. It will be emerging as we are in the process of accomplishing the mission. There are, for sure some premises

such as the inter-relation between (1) mission and people, (2) mission and national and regional history, (3) mission and culture, and (4) mission and society. We cannot do missions in Cuba behind the back of the people, and more so now when there is the danger for some people of not participating in the benefits of the social revolution. But we cannot do mission either forgetting our history. For instance, precisely in this year 1998 we commemorate the centennial of the fall of the Spanish empire and the beginnings of the American empire! We cannot forget either that in 1992 we commemorated the arrival of Christopher Columbus and of "Christianity" in our lands, as we cannot ignore 1959 as the triumph of the Cuban revolution.

Dr. Hall is to be congratulated because in all his published work we can breathe the spirit of the OT prophets and those, often forgotten, in the history of the church. As someone coming from Latin America, I would say it is a good piece of a Theology of Liberation, and the merit is greater coming from North America!

NOTES

1. This paper was originally presented at "*Jornada Teológica* 2017," a theological symposium held at the Evangelical Theological Seminary (S.E.T.) in Matanzas, Cuba (February 20–22, 2017). Dr. Ham opened his presentation with these words: "Let me express first my gratitude to God for this opportunity, secondly to our seminary in Matanzas and our colleagues in Knox for this exercise I had been desiring for some time: that we study together the relevance of the theology of Prof. Hall, and of course, my privilege on being the presenter on the Cuban side, but sorry that he is not present."

2. Hall, *Thinking the Faith*, vol. 1 of *Christian Theology in a North American Context* (Minneapolis, MN: Augsburg, 1989; paperback reprint: Minneapolis, MN: Fortress Press, 1991), 136.

3. Hall, *Thinking the Faith*, 45.

4. Paul Tillich, *The Protestant Era*, Chicago, IL: University of Chicago Press, 1948. xviii.

5. Hall, *Confessing the Faith*, vol. 3 of *Christian Theology in a North American Context* (Minneapolis, MN: Fortress Press, 1996), 239.

6. Hall, *Confessing the Faith*, 21.

7. Hall, *Confessing the Faith*, 21.

8. Hall, *Confessing the Faith*, 334.

9. Hall, *Thinking the Faith*, 14.

10. Hall, *Professing the Faith*, vol. 2 of *Christian Theology in a North American Context* (Minneapolis, MN: Fortress Press, 1993), ix–x, 2.

11. Hall, *Confessing the Faith*, 8, 10, and 11.

12. Hall, *Thinking the Faith*, 37.
13. Hall, *Thinking the Faith*, 55.
14. Hall, *Thinking the Faith*, 81.
15. Hall, *Thinking the Faith*, 84.
16. Hall, *Thinking the Faith*, 38.
17. Hall, *Thinking the Faith*, 114.
18. Hall, *Thinking the Faith*, 125.
19. Hall, *Confessing the Faith*, 161.
20. Hall, *Thinking the Faith*, 29.
21. Hall, *Thinking the Faith*, 39.
22. Hall, *Thinking the Faith*, 74.
23. Hall, *Thinking the Faith*, 107.
24. Hall, *Professing the Faith*, 2.
25. Hall, *Thinking the Faith*, 58.
26. Hall, *Thinking the Faith*, 84.
27. Hall, *Confessing the Faith*, 347.
28. Hall, *Professing the Faith*, 106.
29. Hall, *Professing the Faith*, 125.
30. Hall, *Professing the Faith*, 154.
31. Hall, *Professing the Faith*, 264.
32. Hall, *Professing the Faith*, 280–81.
33. Hall, *Thinking the Faith*, Section 5.3, 134.
34. Hall, *Lighten Our Darkness: Toward an Indigenous Theology of the Cross* (Revised Edition. Lima, OH: Academic Renewal, 2001), xvii.
35. Hall, and R. R. Ruether, *God and the Nations* (Minneapolis, MN: Fortress Press, 1995), 107.
36. *La verdad no se ensaya* (La Habana: Caminos, 2016), 12.
37. Fernando Ortiz, "On *ajiaco*," in S. Susi Sarfati, ed., *Fernando Ortiz: Acercamiento a su Obra* (La Habana: Fundación Fernando Ortiz, 2019), 16–18.
38. Encuentro Nacional Eclesial Cubano (La Habana: Conferencia Episcopal de Cuba, 1987). For Enseñanzas fundamentales de nuestra historia eclesial, see 47ff; for Encuentro entre fe y cultura, 133ff; for Pastoral de Conjunto, 213ff; for Iglesia dialogante, 246ff.
39. Adolfo Ham, "The Barmen Declaration in Cuba," *The Ecumenical Review* (March 2009).
40. Hall, *Confessing the Faith*, 38.

WORKS CITED

Encuentro Nacional Eclesial Cubano. La Habana: Conferencia Episcopal de Cuba, 1987.
Hall, Douglas John. *Confessing the Faith*. Vol. 3, *Christian Theology in a North American Context*. Minneapolis, MN: Fortress Press, 1996.
———. *The End of Christendom and the Future of Christianity*. Eugene, OR: Wipf and Stock, 1997.

———. *Lighten Our Darkness*, Revised Edition. Lima, OH: Academic Renewal, 2001.

———. *Professing the Faith*. Vol. 2, *Christian Theology in a North American Context*. Minneapolis, MN: Fortress Press, 1993.

———. *Thinking the Faith*. Vol. 1, *Christian Theology in a North American Context*. Minneapolis, MN: Augsburg, 1989; paperback reprint: Minneapolis, MN: Fortress Press, 1991.

———. *Why Christian? For Those on the Edge of Faith*. Minneapolis, MN: Fortress Press, 1998.

Hall, Douglas John, and R. R. Ruether. *God and the Nations*. Minneapolis, MN: Fortress Press, 1995.

Ham, Adolfo. "The Barmen Declaration in Cuba." *The Ecumenical Review* 61, no. 1 (March 2009): 92–97.

Ortiz, Fernando. "On *ajiaco*." In S. Susi Sarfati, ed., *Fernando Ortiz: Acercamiento a su Obra*, 16–18. La Habana: Fundación Fernando Ortiz, 2019.

Tillich, Paul. *The Protestant Era*. Chicago, IL: University of Chicago Press, 1948.

Chapter 10

ReWilding the Gospel

Douglas John Hall and Post-Christendom Religious Dialogue

Gary A. Gaudin

We begin with a word of explanation about this chapter's title. The language of "reWilding" is borrowed from conservation biology, in which it is used to describe the goal of restoring natural processes and natural species to an area that had been rendered, by human action, "unnatural."[1] In this chapter "reWilding" becomes my preferred metaphor for recovering the gospel lived and proclaimed by Jesus. Unlike some metaphors of this task, such as "excavating," "reWilding" retains within it a reminder that we seek here not the lifeless shards of a broken past but the organic roots of the present. Our recovery will take place through a series of theological insights offered by Douglas John Hall to the contemporary Christian community, "a theologian who cares for the churches."[2] Each of these insights will be framed as a call to remember.

REMEMBERING WHAT HISTORIC CHRISTIANITY CONTRIBUTED TO AUSCHWITZ

Hall has consistently taught and written of the tradition of Jesus with respect, utterly convinced of both its continuing vitality as a witness to the Divine and of its ongoing significance for the Church. Students of his "History of Christian Thought" seminars were introduced to the insights of Buber, Heschel, Wiesel, Fackenheim, and many others as Hall laid the foundation for a central insight in which he describes Judaism as "*that* religious tradition which, in a way that is surely full of the deepest mystery, has never been willing to let the Christians assimilate it, has never allowed them to forget their indebtedness to it, has never left them alone to rule the Western soul: Israel."[3] Indeed, Hall avers that "after Auschwitz the question of our relation to Judaism (and therefore to all other religious traditions as well) is no longer a merely theoretical question. It is a question of the most existential and painful sort."[4] We therefore arrive at the first invitation to remember in our quest to reWild the Gospel: the existential and painful remembrance of the historic church's contribution to the Holocaust:

> It is not possible for thinking Christians today to reflect on Auschwitz and the holocaust of Judaism without asking themselves: What was wrong with our story that it gave the possibility of such a "final solution"? To have produced (perhaps even to have *demanded*) these victims, must there not have been something dreadfully wrong with that story? We should not crawl out from underneath this problem by answering that there may indeed have been something wrong with *the German version* of the Christian story. No! It is not so easy as that. The Jews have been made victims in every Christian country in the world. What was wrong with our story is wrong at the heart of it; it does not belong to one or two interpretations only. Perhaps the defect is there already in the New Testament. Perhaps already there one can find the seeds of a story of Christian success that could only become convincing if those people over whom the triumph at the heart of that success was won are themselves pushed aside, thrown into disgrace. What is the "final solution" of the Nazis final in relation to? The answer, alas, is that it is final in relation to a long series of attempts, on the part of a civilization inspired by the Christian success story, to eliminate any symbol of failure. And the Jews, throughout the centuries after Christ, were the most consistent symbol of that failure.[5]

Hall has repeatedly added his voice to a long list of theologians and exegetes decrying the abiding suspicion of Jews and Judaism which entered the Church's preaching, teaching, and theology very early on its historic trajectory as "preparing the ground for something like Auschwitz."[6] Centuries of this "teaching of contempt" (Isaac) helped lay the foundations of National Socialist ideology so well, in fact, that opposition to it from within the church was minimal, leading Hall to assert, "[i]f it is indeed our theology that has contributed so significantly to the social atmosphere favorable to such an unspeakable event, then this represents a crisis of *theology* and not only of the church or of Western 'Christian' civilization. It calls for a rethinking of *our belief* along lines that may be more agonizing than most Christians have yet envisaged."[7]

Almost forty years of pastoral leadership leads me to the conviction that this particular call to remember may well be the most difficult for many in the post-Christendom era. Decades of diminishment within a culture that no longer values religion as a partner in the social fabric, decades of reduced numbers in the pews and on the balance sheets, decades of seeing younger generations staying away in ever greater waves from the institutional church, have greatly reduced the church's capacity for addressing the painful memories of the past. Often the almost immediate reaction to speaking of the historic church's contribution to the Holocaust is personal and defensive. It can easily be heard as a call to express personal remorse, guilt for the anti-Judaism of the historic church. This call to remembrance is *not* such a call. It *is* a call to acknowledge that the church has, in its dominant tradition and under some of its greatest leaders, teachers, theologians, reformers, and councils, *simply been wrong* in its assessment of Jews, Judaism, and, therefore, of Jesus. To be sure, there has always been "a thin tradition" of those within the historic Church who taught respect for the tradition which claimed Jesus, who sought out practitioners of Judaism from whom to learn,[8] but their impact on the dominant tradition has been relatively insignificant. This call to remembrance is a call to acknowledge the historic church's corporate responsibility for shaping a culture that proved so welcoming of Nazi ideology. It is, further, a call to take such steps as to ensure, moving forward, that the gap between the church's gospel and Jesus' Gospel is closed.

REMEMBERING WHAT HISTORIC CHRISTIANITY HAS FORGOTTEN

Aiding and abetting the "teaching of contempt" in the heart of the historic tradition's version of the Gospel has been what Hall terms the move from relational to substantial ontologies. Hall grounds this insight in the witness of the Hebrew scriptures, that the Divine is always seeking to

> be *with us:* present to us, alongside us, beside us, face-to-face with us. This is by no means only a claim of the newer Testament.
>
> Neither, however, does it translate at once into the dogma that in Jesus we have, purely and simply, God in physical form. That is to leap over the boundary between Athens and Jerusalem. It is to substitute for the relational ontology of Jerusalem the substantialism of classical and modern thought. It is not the same thing at all to say, "In Jesus faith encounters the very presence of God—Emmanuel" as it is to say, "Jesus is God." The first statement has to do with communion, communication, relationship; and it combines a christological with a soteriological approach to the first and initiatory problem of Trinitarian thought. That is, it makes the christological claim serve the soteriological claim. The end of the matter is not that "God was in Christ" but rather (as the text itself says) "God was in Christ reconciling."[9]

That the church has been, and perhaps continues to be, only too willing to leap over the boundary between Athens and Jerusalem—to set up permanent camp in Athens—is traced, at least in part, to the primacy Athens gives to rationality in its discourse:

> But the rationality honored by Athens can only be attained by humans who overcome what, for biblical faith, is inextricably part of their essential humanity—their physicality, their capacity for emotion, their will to love what is other . . . , their urge to beget progeny, their joy in food, dance, laughter—life. From the vantage point of Jerusalem, Athens only affirms humanity at the expense of human creaturehood.
>
> It must therefore be considered a foregone conclusion that in the world of Hellenistic discourse the humanity of Jesus could not be greatly emphasized; or, to state it otherwise, one is not surprised that Jesus' humanity was acknowledged only in a formulary way. In a Hebraic context, on the other hand, it is by no means unusual that the human could be the bearer of transcendent purpose. In fact it is assumed that the normal medium of the divine would be the human; and while such human media would have to be in some way exceptional—as Abraham, David, Miriam, Jeremiah, and the Mary of the Magnificat are exceptional—it would be by no means expected of them that they should no longer manifest the admixture of positive and negative attributes that constitutes, for Jerusalem, actual human life.[10]

Indeed, Hall goes on to note the prominence given in the Hebrew scriptures to the drunkenness of Noah, the laughter with which Sarah greets the promise of childbirth, and the lustfulness of David, concluding "it seems mandatory, with this tradition, that the human emissaries of the divine should not only be human but very human. Only such credibly human beings could be received by the community of Israel as bearers of transcendent purpose."[11]

While the early church remained geographically rooted in and around Jerusalem and the Galilee, and theologically rooted in Hebraic thought, the credible humanity of Jesus (still discernible within the Synoptic traditions)[12] continued to be valued. When the early church expanded beyond the Gospel's homeland, however, the credible humanity of Jesus receded (was pushed?) into the background as the church's leaders and theologians entered into dialogue with the dominant philosophical traditions of the day.

The credible humanity of Jesus did not, to be sure, totally recede into the background. As the historic tradition of the church became ever more enamored of Athens, it yet required of its followers a formal acknowledgement of Jesus' humanity—but a humanity that pays little heed to Jesus as

> a particular human being, a Jewish man living and dying under specific, unrepeatable historical conditions. It seems to me that we must at last be prepared

to acknowledge, as Christians, that this Jewish human being called Jesus was almost wholly superseded, in evolving Christendom, by the theoretically human but really divine Christ. We would do well to add to this acknowledgement that it is therefore not surprising that those who were defeated in the process of the formalization of Christology were those who remembered what historic Christianity has always forgotten—that Jesus Christ was a Jew.[13]

The legacy of that forgetting is writ large in many of the great creeds of the Church, developed long after the church had accepted Athens as its model for theological discourse, and even longer after the testimony of the early Christian communities, which

> already in its biblical witness felt that it had to maintain two things in its testimony to Jesus as the Christ: *first*, that he was certainly a fully human being . . . and *second*, that in and through his humanity faith knows itself to be met by the ultimate—by very God. The Gospels and epistles of the newer Testament maintain this in one way, largely under the form of . . . relational ontology; but as soon as the Christian movement entered the Greco-Roman world, it had to translate this into the ontological terms prevalent in that world, which were not relational but substantialistic.
>
> Unfortunately, the church has never overcome its captivation to that substantialistic ontology—partly because it was that ontology that informed from start to finish the great conciliar decisions regarding the godhead and the doctrine of Christ's person, and these still remain definitive. Still today we are fighting in the churches over the extent to which the substances of humanity and divinity are to be seen in this person, which dominates, which is "the real Christ," how the two natures come together in one person, and so on.[14]

As Hall frames it, then, the credible humanity of Jesus is essential to the saving work of the Holy One. How else are we to understand the Incarnation, then, but as the Divine's commitment to humanity, to the humanity expressed by the individuality of each of us? If the credible humanity of Jesus can be set aside to achieve theological goals, does that not also require the diminishment of all human individuality? Here the call to remember is simply a call to embrace the particularity of Jesus on the way to acknowledging that all human particularity is important to the Holy One in a way far beyond our understanding and redolent of a mystery lying at the heart of Creation.

REMEMBERING EARLY CHURCH ROOTS

Our quest to reWild the Gospel proclaimed by Jesus, in other words to take the Jewishness of Jesus with utter seriousness,[15] now leads us to re-read the texts of the Newer Testament with the goals of being aware of any interpretation that contributes to an anti-Jewish and/or anti-Semitic polemic, or that continues the estrangement of the church's understanding of the Gospel from its Hebraic roots. Where the historic church eventually chose to "define" Jesus in his relationship to the Divine in terms of substantialistic ontology, the early church chose to bear witness to its experiences with the Divine in and through Jesus, creating "a certain necessary flexibility in doctrine . . . that must be expected, allowed, and even celebrated."[16] Hall goes on to delineate the importance of that flexibility:

> For faith in its Christian sense is engendered in people through their encounter with the Spirit of this person Jesus. And, as in all meeting between person and person, each individual brings to this encounter—the genesis of Christian faith—experiences, characteristics, foibles, problems, needs, hopes, anxieties, and so forth that are unique to that person. It is natural therefore that different feelings and articulations of the meaning of the person Jesus will occur. They have occurred from the very beginning. The four Gospels and the epistles of Paul already testify to this diversity. Paul's picture of the Christ is not that of John; Mark's witness to the Christ differs from Luke's; and so on. The differences do not (at least in my opinion) add up to gross inconsistencies or contradictions; on the contrary, I think these various testimonies serve to give us a quite well-integrated picture of the one at the centre of this story. The witnesses that were *glaringly* different (such as those that did not take the flesh-and-blood reality of Jesus seriously) were excluded from the canon precisely because of their conspicuous divergence from the witnesses that had gained authenticity in the church.
>
> All that is true. But there are, all the same, real differences already in the biblical testimony to the Christ, and there could be no alternative to such an outcome so long as the New Testament tended to insist, as it does with great consistency, that it is the person Jesus who stands at the center of the faith it professes. . . . Only if Christianity were to define itself propositionally, by basing itself on specific truth claims that can be articulated in precise and unchangeable language, could it avoid the flexibility of doctrine.[17]

Perhaps it was in response to the Newer Testament's inability to offer a clear answer to the question "Who is Jesus?" and to the tradition's growing dependence on substantialistic ontology that the historic church lost, or chose to set aside, its tradition of doctrinal flexibility. It came to understand its role as that of Truth-Possessor. It abandoned the humility that permitted different experiences of the Divine-human relationship to coexist, and in so doing gave up its capacity to accept, explore, perhaps even revel in the truth expressed by Martin Buber: "God is infinitely more than merely God."[18] In the diversity expressed with the texts of the Newer Testament we catch a glimpse of the insight to which Buber was pointing. In the move from Jerusalem to Athens, that appreciation of diverse viewpoints for the Divine-human relationship was gradually submerged under the weight of the truth claims made by the historic church, which came to think of its language as the expression of the definitive Truth about the Divine, rather than a very human metaphor attempting to grasp the ungraspable. How was it that the church's great councils—some centuries after the writings of the Newer Testament simply pointed to a variety of encounters with the Divine through Jesus—decided on and adopted as normative definitive language for the Divine and for the Christ to which all followers in the Way must adhere?

In remembering the early church roots, we may well be confronted by the most challenging of the tasks before the Church in its reWilding of the Gospel for the post-Christendom era: to surrender its dogmatic insistence that its understanding of the Divine-human relationship is Truth for all humanity. As Hall writes: "When it comes to *religious* truth, however, we are still terribly immodest. For the most part we are at one with the perpetrators of the Inquisition. Though we are too humane to execute the heretics of other religious persuasions, the same mentality informs our hearts: we know we are right! This conviction lies behind our efforts in world mission. Everyone must know the truth, and we possess it. We are the truth's curators and teachers."[19]

We have traced, under Hall's guidance, a trajectory of remembrance fashioned by the historic church as curator, teacher, and possessor of truth. It has taken the church from a diversity of encounters founded in the relationship of God through the Jesus of history to an almost complete sundering of the church from its Hebraic roots; from a tradition centered on the credible humanity of the Jewish Jesus to a tradition utterly focused on the dogma of the Christ; from an awareness that the truth about the Divine-human relationship can be expressed in many ways to a dependence on creedal formulations to express a Truth that the Divine has given the church as its unique possession. Other traditions were simply wrong. Salvation, as understood by the church, was only, *could* only be, available within the church. Those who rejected the church rejected salvation. As a result, this trajectory, over the centuries, contributed "to a climate of opinion that eventually led to the railway platform at Buchenwald."[20]

The call for a reWilding of the Gospel is nothing more—and certainly nothing less—than a call for the church to recover its humility when in conversation with the Other, whether that Other is a member of a different ecclesial community or a completely separate religious tradition. It is a call for the church to surrender its claim to possess, curate, and teach the Truth on the Holy One's behalf: "Only a revised understanding of who we are in relation to 'the truth' can bring about the kind of modesty that is prerequisite to genuine dialogue. We have to know that we, too, are *searchers* after 'the truth', and to lose every trace of the former arrogance of those who 'possess' it."[21]

Laying the groundwork for Auschwitz took at least two thousand years. ReWilding the Gospel in the post-Christendom era will require significant and ongoing commitments from denominational leaders, from ecumenical councils, from congregational leaders and parishioners alike as we together own the responsibility to shape the tradition that claims us. Hall writes,

> What is called for here is enormously complex, and it will require several generations of careful scholarship and profound spiritual reflection to meet the challenge. It is not simply a matter of discovering, as Christians, our lack of Christian caritas with respect to the Jews. It is a matter of becoming exposed to the essential, i.e., theological, roots of our centuries-long ambiguity about the Jews. The problem lies not so much in our deeds of violence or our doctrinal narrowness and neglect as it does in the positive affirmations of our theology, especially our Christology. We could not have presented the Christ in the way that we have, through centuries, presented him; we could not have worked out our ecclesiologies in the way that we have worked them out, and lived them; we could not have devised the sorts of eschatologies that we have in fact devised, without it all preparing the ground for something like . . . Auschwitz.[22]

IMPLICATIONS OF TAKING THE JEWISHNESS OF JESUS WITH UTTER SERIOUSNESS

Our comments here are divided into two sections: the theological and the liturgical. The latter must be given consideration, as the vast majority of those who gather for Christian community on Sundays do not choose to read theology. Their theological understandings are framed within the weekly (and increasingly less frequent than that) liturgical celebrations.

We begin where traditions of Jerusalem must always begin—with the absolute unity of the Divine as expressed in the central affirmation of the Jewish tradition: "Hear, O Israel: The LORD our God is one LORD; and you shall love the LORD your God with all your heart, and with all your soul, and with all your might" (Deut. 6:4–5, RSV). Mark's Jesus accepts that central affirmation as key to his own proclamation: "And one of the scribes came up and heard them disputing with one another, and seeing that he answered them well, asked him, "Which commandment is the first of all?' Jesus answered, 'The first is, "Hear, O Israel: The Lord our God, the Lord is one; and you shall love the Lord your God with all your heart, and with all your soul, and with all your mind, and with all your strength"'" (Mark 12:28–30, RSV).[23]

Heeding the call to enter into a deeper theological humility in the post-Christendom era, then, we start with the unity of the Holy One, upon which the traditions of Jerusalem agree. For all Christians involved in inter-religious dialogue, it can be quite challenging to assert that the unity of the Divine is central, while laying so much of our theological stress upon Trinitarian thought and language. Perhaps in the reWilding of the Gospel we can recover the Newer Testament conviction that our words do not capture the essence of the Divine so much as capture the human experience of the Holy One? To be sure, all language about the Divine is metaphorical, but the Church has, over the centuries, invested some of that metaphorical language with special standing as Truth. Thus God *is* Father, Son, and Holy Spirit, not simply God is experienced *as* Father, Son, and Holy Spirit. Yet the scriptural traditions of the church also use many other metaphors for the Divine-human encounter, providing a largely untapped and rich resource for the church's consideration. Beyond the scriptures, we might consider the 99 Names of the Islamic tradition. If, following Buber, we celebrate the God who is infinitely more than merely God, perhaps the post-Christendom era will usher in a new, deeper, broader understanding within the church of the infinite human experience of God. Such an understanding would leave us free to explore other metaphors for the Divine, taking us beyond the artificial boundaries set by the church. Many of our denominations, for example, participate in a baptismal agreement ensuring that all those baptized within our traditions have their baptisms recognized and affirmed should they choose to join a different communion—as long as the baptisms are in the traditional formula of "Father, Son, and Holy Spirit." We do not propose to put those agreements at risk, but we do propose that we shape the liturgy around the baptismal sacrament so as to ensure that all participants understand that Christians worship the Holy *One*. So we might speak of baptizing "into the family of the Holy One, whom we name as Father, Son, and Holy Spirit." Then we could add other metaphors, so that the richness of the tradition might be experienced and celebrated as we talk about the Divine: "Welcome, child of the living God, the One who creates, redeems, and sustains us now and always."

Accepting that the unity of the Divine is absolutely central to the traditions of Jerusalem, the simplistic language of "Jesus is God" or "Jesus is Divine" must be considered suspect. The substantialistic ontology of the past led the historic church to conclude that only a Divine Messiah could redeem the people, and that the credible humanity of Jesus was therefore a hindrance within the church. Yet within the Hebraic tradition, Hall argues, the redeeming work of the Holy One is always reliant on credible human beings—frail, faulty, and fickle. This insight leads to a series of questions which the post-Christendom church must address: "Does Jesus really need to be Divine to redeem?" "Since we now accept that all our language of the Divine is metaphor,—that is, that it expresses only a part of the Truth—can we let go of the fiction that we can pursue Christology from below as well as from above?" "How far can we push the gap between 'the Jesus of history' and 'the Christ of the Church's faith'?" As Hall has demonstrated, however, while "the Christ of the Church's faith" is a figure rich in Divinity, it lacks in credible humanity. Lacking in credible humanity, this figure cannot simply be declared by the church as the long-awaited Messiah of the Hebraic tradition. As part of its commitment to post-Christendom inter-religious dialogue, has the time not come to refocus our dialogue on the early church's witness to the Divine-human encounter in and through "the Jesus of history"? As well as to listen with respect to the voice of the Others as they describe their Divine-human encounters?

While there have been significant gains in Christian self-understanding in the past seventy years, one struggles to find those gains expressed during the one time each week when most Christians are gathered: the celebration of the liturgy. Heeding the call to reWild the Gospel, and to do so with humility, what might we name as some of the most significant implications for the faithful remnant still gathering in the church's pews?

First, as worship is planned and led the first and only goal is to worship the Holy One. The unity of the Divine is central to all Christian worship. The community does not gather to worship Jesus, or the Holy Spirit. It gathers to worship the One who has drawn close to humanity in Jesus. It gathers to worship the One whose Spirit enlivens our witness. The church does not gather to worship the way we worship—the hymns we sing, the traditions which claim us, the liturgical calendar; it gathers to worship the One in whom we live and move and have our being. It does not gather to worship our buildings or our pews or our bottom line; it gathers to worship the One who calls us into community to care for one another, for our neighbors, and our creation. The language of our liturgies must reflect the primacy of the One whom Jesus worshipped and called "Abba."

Second, as worship is planned and led, attention must be paid to the entire biblical witness. This has been one of the gifts to the church of the lectionary. For most of the year, worshippers are met with texts from the Hebrew scriptures, the Psalms, the Epistles and the Gospels. As each is considered, the Jewishness of the tradition which claimed Jesus, of Jesus, of the apostles, and of the earliest Christian communities must be brought to the forefront. The traditional Christian practice of interpreting Hebrew scriptures as predictive of the Gospel must be discontinued. Rather, the texts of the Older Testament must be valued in their own right for the foundation they lay for the Gospel. Indeed, every opportunity to connect the church's liturgy with its Jewish roots must be highlighted.

Third, since the connections between the Jewish roots of the church's liturgy are well-established, there should be very little difficulty in drawing attention to the Jewish foundations of Easter, Pentecost, and Advent on a regular basis. In addition, liturgical leaders could consider adding two extra moments to the church's calendar: on the Sundays closest to and preceding *Yom HaShoah* (Day of Holocaust Remembrance) in the spring and *Kristallnacht* (Night of Broken Glass) in the fall. Neither of these needs to see the entire liturgy built around it to be taken seriously in a Christian context. Educational notes could be printed in the bulletin, specific prayers could be added to the existing liturgy, guest speakers can be invited to say a few words, and, yes, occasionally an entire liturgy could be developed to heed the call to remembrance. Resources to that end are readily available on the internet.

Fourth, use could be made of the local congregation's media opportunities to celebrate the special moments of the Other faith communities in the local area. On websites, other social media platforms, exterior sign boards, we can celebrate with our neighbors their special moments. That requires knowing what those moments are, and that requires building relationships with the Other, but we are perhaps in a better position to appreciate just how important this call to remembrance is if the church is to participate more fully in the Holy One's mending of the world.

The task before us is huge. It does involve some agonizing discussions and decisions on the part of the church and of local Christian communities. We may well have to discern how some of the church's most cherished traditions have been used to harm or diminish the Other. We may have to learn how to lessen the grip with which our traditions—theological and liturgical—hold us. We may well have to develop significantly different vocabularies for the Holy One and for the Divine-human encounter. We may have to invest generations in the development of new hymns and statements of faith. We may have to learn how to say "I do not know" rather than "this is what the Church teaches, this is the Truth you must accept."

We are not alone as we face this task. We have colleagues in ministry with whom we can discuss all manner of things theological and liturgical. We have the leaders of any number of other faith communities who face many of the same questions we face. And we have teachers like Douglas John Hall to guide us.

NOTES

1. Conservationist and activist Dave Foreman, founder of *Earth First!*, is credited with coining the term in the late 1980s. It was further refined by Michael Soulé and Reed Noss in "Rewilding and Biodiversity: Complementary Goals for Continental Conservation," *Wild Earth* 8, no. 3 (Fall 1998): 19–28.

2. Douglas John Hall, *The Reality of the Gospel and the Unreality of the Churches* (Philadelphia, PA: Westminster, 1975), 9.

3. Douglas John Hall, *Thinking the Faith: Christian Theology in a North American Context* (Minneapolis, MN: Augsburg, 1989; paperback reprint: Minneapolis, MN: Fortress Press, 1991), 210.
4. Douglas John Hall, *Has the Church a Future?* (Philadelphia: Westminster, 1980), 99.
5. *Has the Church a Future?*, 45–46.
6. *Thinking the Faith*, 211.
7. *Thinking the Faith*, 212.
8. Here we must list Hall among them.
9. Douglas John Hall, *Professing the Faith: Christian Theology in a North American Context* (Minneapolis, MN: Fortress Press, 1993), 161; 2 Cor. 5:19, RSV.
10. *Professing the Faith*, 450–51.
11. *Professing the Faith*, 451.
12. *Professing the Faith*, 451.
13. *Professing the Faith*.
14. Douglas John Hall, *The Cross in Our Context: Jesus and the Suffering World* (Minneapolis, MN: Fortress Press, 2003), 125.
15. Douglas John Hall, *Imaging God: Dominion as Stewardship* (Grand Rapids, MI: Eerdmans, 1986), 188.
16. *The Cross in Our Context*, 115.
17. *The Cross in Our Context*, 114–15.
18. As cited in *Has the Church a Future?*, 95.
19. *Has the Church a Future?*, 99.
20. *Imaging God*, 190.
21. *Has the Church a Future?*, 107.
22. *Thinking the Faith*, 211.
23. See also Matthew 22:34–40, Luke 10:25–28.

WORKS CITED

Hall, Douglas John. *The Cross in Our Context: Jesus and the Suffering World.* Minneapolis, MN: Fortress Press, 2003.

———. *Has the Church a Future?* Philadelphia, PA: Westminster, 1980.

Hall, Douglas John. *Imaging God: Dominion as Stewardship.* Grand Rapids, MI: Eerdmans, 1986.

———. *Professing the Faith: Christian Theology in a North American Context.* Minneapolis, MN: Fortress Press, 1993.

———. *The Reality of the Gospel and the Unreality of the Churches.* Philadelphia, PA: Westminster, 1975.

———. *Thinking the Faith: Christian Theology in a North American Context.* Minneapolis, MN: Augsburg, 1989; paperback reprint: Minneapolis, MN: Fortress Press, 1991.

Isaac, Jules. *The Teaching of Contempt: Christian Roots of Anti-Semitism.* Trans. H. Weaver. New York: Holt, Rinehart and Winston, 1964.

Soulé, Michael and Reed Noss. "Rewilding and Biodiversity: Complementary Goals for Continental Conservation." *Wild Earth* 8, no. 3 (Fall 1998): 19–28.

Chapter 11

The Memory of Divine Pathos
Heschel, Hall, and the Hebrew Bible
Patricia G. Kirkpatrick

Abraham Heschel once wrote that "Echoed in almost every prophetic statement divine pathos is the central category of the prophetic understanding of God."[1] For Hall, this was a valuable insight as it links the Theology of the Cross to what is arguably the core of the biblical tradition. Furthermore, it makes plain that the Theology of the Cross was not invented by Saint Paul and Luther, but is instead, the faithful transmission of the prophetic tradition of "divine pathos" to the interpretation of the Cross of Christ.[2] It is precisely this prophetic voice that seems to have been lost to us in the twenty-first century.

GOD SUFFERING WITH US

From the outset of the Hebrew Bible, we are presented with the portrayal of God who is not shy of admitting His failures regarding His created order. True, the majesty of Genesis 1 is such as to portray a God in control: all he need do is speak, and the created order comes to be. Moreover, all is well and good in the created order. Nevertheless, Genesis 2 seems to contradict the position immediately, and so we are tossed into a seemingly endless round of reading about God in control and then not so much so.

As the story progresses, we come to that moment in Genesis where we are faced with a God who recognizes that things have become so horribly wrong in his creation that he "repents" of his having created. He is in so much despair as a result of his actions that he determines to destroy every human save one and his family (along with specimens of each of the animals), as having had no part in the destructive forces of violence that now control the creation:

Yahweh regretted that he had made humanity on the earth. It pained his heart. Yahweh said, "I shall wipe out the earthling [humanity] that I created from the face of the ground, from humanity to animals to moving things to birds in the heavens, because I regret that I made them."[3]

This same God, so the storyteller recounts, determines that after the destruction he will never again destroy the world, and to that end places a bow in the sky to remind him, so that he does not destroy his creation again.

God's retributive actions from that moment on may result in disaster for certain humans but never again will he sacrifice the entire creation. He will call Israel into the wilderness to find there a place to woo her back, to lure her back into the right covenantal relationship (Hosea 2), but he will never again utterly destroy His creation. Finally, out of a deep conviction of Judah's sin, he will leave the Temple (Ezekiel 10). He may not destroy his creation, but he will utterly remove himself, never again to return until the end of time at the coming of the Messiah—or, for Christians, the moment signified by Jesus' entrance into the Temple. We know this drama so well. We relive it repeatedly through the Christian liturgical year even though it is not one that suits the tenor of our hubris.

It is the Bible's refusal to sacrifice God's independence from his creation that marks all of this as a unique tale of Divine pathos on the one hand and human greed on the other—a tale that seems so out of place, given its Ancient Near Eastern context. The gods and goddesses of the Ancient Near East, whatever else they might have been, were never so involved with humans as to grieve for and after them, much less to want to be with them, by them, and for them.

It is the Divine pathos that makes this story so unique. Thus, it is strange when we hear in church history about the church's tendency to support a God who more resembles an absolute ruler: unmoving, unchanging, non-suffering.

Mindful of the admonition coming from the Council of Chalcedon in 485 CE stating that "the synod deposes from the priesthood those who dare to say that the Godhead of the only-begotten is passible,"[4] as a biblical exegete I nevertheless need to say a few words on this matter.

Apart from Luther, Calvin and Reformed theology generally assumed Divine impassability. So the Westminster Confession of faith explicitly asserts that God is "without body, parts, or passions, immutable." Indeed, today one can find certain evangelical theologians who would maintain the same, arguing that it was Jesus' human nature and not the Divine nature that suffered. That, in certain circles, is still a heresy.

I have no intentions, however, of taking on the whole of the Christian tradition in the next few pages and will not deal with the arguments of those who maintain the necessity of the impassability of God. I will not argue that this

Greek notion that emotions or pain are unfit for deity is quite alien to biblical thought, for it quite plainly is not.

Instead, my task is relatively simple and straightforward. It is to situate Douglas John Hall's Theology of the Cross in that very well worn trajectory that understands such a theology to emanate out of the prophetic tradition of the Hebrew Bible, which Christians know as the Old Testament, or as Hall calls it, the Older Testament, and to do so through the theology of Abraham Heschel. Indeed it is to Heschel that Hall himself turns as the one who has best expressed the divine pathos for the post-Holocaust generation.

Inevitably, a notion of God that maintains such an impassability must provide for how this same God can love.

For Heschel, of course, the essence of the God of the Hebrew Bible is that God takes the people of his covenantal love, that is his *"hesed,"* his steadfast loving kindness, and suffers because of their actions. For Heschel, God "indwells" in the Israelites so that he even goes with them into Babylonian exile: he leaves his Temple and feels their sorrowful plight. It is precisely this capacity to feel for the other in vulnerable love that is part of what it means to be God.

If it is thought that God does not suffer for various theological grounds, I would argue that we will have to rewrite the Bible—something that biblical scholars from time to time suggest happens when theologians do not pay close enough attention to the biblical text and context. Such is not the case, however, with Hall.[5]

It is Hall's refusal to lose sight of the Christian tradition's Hebraic roots that compels him to interact with such intellectuals as Abraham Heschel, themselves steeped in the Hebrew Bible.

And it is Heschel's theological position that allows him to speak of God's involvement with humanity's pain and suffering, and to do so because of the witness of the Hebrew prophets. It will be Heschel's sensibilities in presenting these same that will allow the direct connection with the prophetic aspects of the Jesus tradition.

The Hebrew Bible's prophetic witness provides Hall with the vehicle to trace the antecedents of the theology of the Cross to the pathos of God in the Hebrew prophets. God's nature is relational; God's covenant with Israel is relational in that it is upheld by God's *hesed*, God's steadfast loving kindness. Therefore one cannot speak of God apart from the relational.

HESCHEL AND DIVINE PATHOS

In both *Man Is Not Alone* and *God in Search of Man*, Heschel explores the notion of Divine Pathos. Both titles express in themselves Heschel's understanding of how the Bible portrays God. So "Man is not alone" indicates that the experience of being human is not one of lonely solitude; rather, something greater exists, a power greater than ourselves that is not aloof and distant from ourselves. No hidden God is this. Heschel, perhaps echoing Rudolph Otto, invites us to *feel* what the human recognition of God that he describe is like:

> A tremor seizes our limbs; our nerves are struck, quiver like strings; our whole being bursts into shudders. But then a cry, wrested from our very core, fills the world around us, as if a mountain were suddenly about to place itself in front of us. It is one word: GOD. Not an emotion, a stir within us, but a power, a marvel beyond us, tearing the world apart. The word that means more than universe, more than eternity, holy, holy, holy . . . He to whom our life can be the spelling of an answer.[6]

The essence of this moment is the realization that we are not alone. It is this moment when we understand God searching after his earthling in Genesis 2 as the God whose essence is only known in relationship. Heschel refers to this as "the summary of Jewish theology."

In *God in Search of Man*, Heschel writes that the essence of Divine Pathos in all its forms is that it reveals the extreme pertinence of man to God, His world-directedness, attentiveness, and concern. God "looks at" the world and is affected by what happens in it; man is the object of His care and judgment.[7]

Which is not to say that Heschel ignores the matter of Divine silence. God's silence, Heschel argues, is as a result of human sinfulness. God is not silent in the face of the atrocities of the Holocaust; rather, he is silenced by human actions.[8] So whatever else the silence is, it is *not* part of the essence of God's relationship with humans. According to Heschel,

> [w]e have trifled with the name of God. We have taken ideas in vain, preached and eluded Him, praised and defied Him. Now we reap the fruits of failure. Through centuries His voice cried in the wilderness. How skillfully it was trapped and imprisoned in the temples! How thoroughly distorted! Now we behold how it gradually withdraws, abandoning one people after another, departing from their souls, despising their wisdom.[9]

HESCHEL AND THE PROPHETS

The dynamic relationship between God and the human is what Heschel speaks of as *pathos*. The prophet, for Heschel, is not only a hearer of God's logos, a speaker of God's word; the prophet is also always one who can feel

God's emotions and thus God's pathos, which he enters into as he speaks. If this articulation of the role of the prophet begins to sound somewhat like a mystical language, I think it is. The prophet enters into the pathos of God precisely at the moment he is needed to convey blessing and condemnation.[10] Fundamentally, this is the prophetic consciousness of God. The one who created the human in His image has chosen to make the human "a consort, a partner, a factor in the life of God."[11]

This God who is forever seeking out the human to repair and redeem is the God of whom Heschel speaks in relational terms, the God who allows humans to presume a dialogical relationship with the divine.

DOUGLAS JOHN HALL AND THE HEBREW BIBLE

It is the God of the Hebraic tradition that Hall turns to when he suggests that Christianity's Greek tradition has covered over or sidelined that aspect of God most needed in the post-Christendom period. In a 1999 lecture, Hall asks simply, How in this North American context do we proclaim the One whom the Biblical tradition understands as the Redeemer?[12]

Hall quotes Tillich, who writes:

> Christianity is what it is through the affirmation that Jesus of Nazareth, who has been called "the Christ," is the Christ, namely, he who brings the new state of things, the New Being. Whenever the assertion that Jesus is the Christ is maintained, there is the Christian message; wherever this assertion is denied, the Christian message is not affirmed. Christianity was born, not with the birth of the man who is called Jesus, but in the moment in which one of his followers was driven to say to him, "Thou art the Christ." And Christianity will live as long as there are people who repeat this assertion.[13]

Hall then asks, "How, in our present context, shall we say this, represent this, live this,

> without seeming to endorse the kind of christomonism (Dorothee Sölle called it "Christofascism"!) that inevitably ends in religious triumphalism and exclusivity?"[14] His answer is to seek out a foundational theology—a doctrine of God—that is informed by a Judaic sense of the dialectic of divine distance and proximity, otherness and sameness, transcendence and immanence.

Hall puts the matter most succinctly when he states,

> The question that is put to Christians today where our Christology is concerned is whether we can return our thought and the ethical consequences of our thought concerning Jesus the Christ to the ontological matrix in which it

was originally enfolded—namely, the relational ontology of the tradition of Jerusalem; and thus overcome this obdurate temptation, neither biblical nor contemporary, of regarding the one at the centre of our confession as the bearer of "substances" that are as incomprehensible as they are incompatible. I know that the decisions of the ecumenical councils with regard to Christ's person were sincerely meant to translate the received testimony of the primitive Church into the more universal, established, and highly nuanced philosophic language of the period. But it is a language that is, like all language, more than language; and it is a language that is as foreign to us today as it would have been to the disciples of Jesus themselves.[15]

By and into this twenty-first century, Christianity has become a plethora of thought systems. Some of these are in direct opposition to one another. Some still struggle for authenticity as they seek to rid themselves of the confines of colonial theological perspectives. Some have abandoned all pretense of sacred discourse and prefer instead to witness in solidarity with secular movements that look askance at religious institutions. The Canadian context is home to many of the perspectives. In Quebec, the secularity of its institutions, along with the deep skepticism of all authority, particularly religious authority, born out of the church's betrayal of its mission many times over, has meant that the church's voice has been all but silenced. And perhaps this is how it should remain, at least for a while.

CONCLUSIONS

However we define our mortality, the prophetic witness spends a great deal of its time reminding us that there are boundaries that we ought not to cross if the integrity of our covenantal relationship with God is to be preserved. The prophets of the biblical period were, of course, many of them, concerned with how it was that Israel had overstepped her limitations and had now entered a path of self-destruction. Almost without exception the limits overstepped had to do with Israel's refusal to take her mortality seriously, or, as the story of the Tower of Babel points out, with her hubris in wanting to become immortal. This refusal to take seriously mortal limits is indeed the story of the entire Bible, which has yet to conclude. The prophetic call is a call to the Cross, which reminds us that our mortal boundaries do not bind God and that God's grace is global in reach.

Perhaps the most challenging aspect of managing limits is the issue of joy. This is a strange notion to introduce here, for so many biblical prophets seem unable to speak of joy, given their messages of condemnation, except as it is projected into the eschatological future. Yet we would do each prophet a disservice were I not to point out that the joy that comes from faith is what the prophets are capable of responding to, as they take on the task of being a mouthpiece of God's *shalom*. As one theological writer has put it, "The difference between real joy and mere pleasure is that joy is the taste of suffering transformed. Moreover, it is precisely this transformation that allows us, rightly, to speak of the Eucharist as a celebration."[16] When the biblical prophets spoke of a transformation that would occur in the heart and that would be a new covenant (Jeremiah 31:31), they were speaking of a time when those who sought *shalom* would look not only within the tribe of Jacob; instead, God's *shalom*—God's salvation—would reach to the ends of the earth (Isaiah 49:6). There is nothing in this prophecy to suggest that everyone would become members of the tribe of Jacob, one unified global Jacob tribe, but rather salvation would embrace diverse peoples. The question of *shalom* for the prophets of today is as difficult to articulate as it was in the days of Deutero-Isaiah, especially for those whose "global village" is nothing but a mask for a tribalism that refuses unity in diversity.

I do not think it too much a generalization to say that all spiritualities are grounded in the individual's willingness to seek and to understand an ultimate reality that undergirds his or her being. What the prophets remind us of is that, having found this ultimate reality, we are obligated to push beyond the boundaries of our own personal spirituality to recognize that the well-being of the entire created order is our responsibility. "Our mandate is for a justice and peace which is global," one which is reliant on our abilities to read the signs of the times and not be afraid to pronounce God's *shalom*.[17] This will not mean, however, that we find the one paradigm to which everyone must submit, but instead, as is the case with the event of Pentecost, that there must be a mutuality that recognizes the diversity in the reception of the revelation. As Simon Barrow has put it, with regards to Pentecost:

> Chaos, conflict, contract, control: these are all that difference can lead to when it is bereft of genuinely loving connectivity. In the taxonomy of the Holy Spirit, however, there is a new possibility abroad. Our differences need not cancel each other out. Instead, they hold the potential to become part of that endless interplay of voluntary, proximate relationship we call *communion*. Freedom thus proves the condition for love (compassionate attention to the other, as to ourselves) and vice versa.[18]

The quotation from the book of Joel in the Book of Acts ("I shall pour out my Spirit upon all flesh . . ." [Acts 2:17]) underlines the fact that the time of prophecy is now, that those to whom the gift has been given are those daughters and sons prepared to take the diversity of the global village seriously, and to seek a *shalom* that unites our diversities: a *shalom* that can withstand the forces of totalitarianism and tribalism whatever their form, be they political, ecclesiastical, or spiritual; a shalom that takes seriously that God is the God of all creation, one who is reconciling the world to himself in Christ (2 Corinthians 5:19), who in all ways, is the embodiment of *hesed*. Have we still the will power to embody this *hesed*, and have we the strength to forswear the systems of meritocracies that define so many of our institutional values?

Finally, I leave you with a reflection from Douglas Hall, which challenges us to question the ideological framework of so many of our churches:

> [O]ur churches do not need managers, they need thinkers! They need people whose knowledge of the Scriptures, traditions, and contemporary Christian scholarship is more deeply developed than has been required of clergy in the past. They need teachers, resident theologians, teaching elders, rabbis: learned persons who can prevent the faith from being reduced to platitudes and ethical truisms and pious reflections of the regnant "values." . . . Ours is a time for prophetic ministry, not for "pastoral directors." We have been so busy producing pastors—and, for the most part, pastors who are more "director" than "pastor"—that the entire prophetic and sapiential (wisdom) side of ministry has been vitiated.[19]

NOTES

1. Abraham J. Heschel, *Between God and Man: An Interpretation of Judaism* (New York: Free Press Paperbacks, 1959; rpt. Simon and Schuster, 1997), 116.

2. Douglas John Hall, *Thinking the Faith: Christian Theology in a North American Context* (Minneapolis, MN: Augsburg, 1989; paperback reprint: Minneapolis, MN: Fortress Press, 1991), 22–33.

3. John Goldingay, *The First Testament: A New Translation* (Westport, IL: InterVarsity Press, Kindle Edition, 2018); Genesis 6:6–7.

4. John Goldingay, *The First Testament: A New Translation* (Westport, IL: InterVarsity Press, Kindle Edition, 2018); Genesis 6:6–7.

5. Interestingly, when I was conducting some research for this book I came across a PhD thesis that had its roots in Hall's mentoring, one written by Asakawa Toru called "Kitamori Kazo: Theologian of the Pain of God" (2003). It is in Kazo's theology that we find the following phrase: "The 'pain' of God reflects his will to love the object of his wrath. . . . We conclude from this that God's pain was fitting for him. 'To be fitting' means to be necessary to his essence. The pain of God is part of his essence! This part of God's Essence is the wonder. God's essence corresponds to his eternity. The Bible reveals that the pain of God belongs to his *eternal being*." *Theology of the Pain of God: The First Original Theology from Japan*, trans. 1958, 5th ed. (Rpt. Eugene, OR: Wipf and Stock, June 10, 2005), 45. At the same time,

Kazo comments, "The most urgent business before the church and theology today is the recovery of wonder, the pronouncement of the gospel afresh in order to make this wonder vivid again" (44).

6. Abraham Joshua Heschel, *Man Is Not Alone: A Philosophy of Religion* (New York: Noonday, 1991), 78.

7. Abraham Joshua Heschel, *The Prophets*, vol. 2 (New York: Harper Torchbooks, 1969), 263.

8. Heschel, *Man Is Not Alone*, 152.

9. Heschel, *Man Is Not Alone*, 1991, 152.

10. Heschel, *Man Is Not Alone*, 1969, 25–26.

11. Heschel, *Man Is Not Alone*, 1969, 292; italics mine.

12. "Confessing Christ in a Post-Christendom Context," address, Atlanta, GA, 1999 Covenant Conference, Network of Presbyterians, November 6, 1999; rpt. *Religion Online*, http://www.religion-online.org/author/douglas-john-hall/.

13. Paul Tillich, *Systematic Theology*, vol. 2 (Chicago, IL: University of Chicago Press, 1957), 97.

14. Hall, "Confessing Christ in a Post-Christendom Context."

15. Hall, "Confessing Christ."

16. Giles Fraser: "Try Being Transformed by Joy," *Church Times* (July 25, 2008), http://www.churchtimes.co.uk/content.asp?id=60740.

17. Patricia G. Kirkpatrick, "The Biblical Prophets and Global Spirituality," *The Way Supplement*, 10.

18. Simon Barrow, "Hearing Hope through the Babble," *Ekklesia* (May 27, 2008), http://www.ekklesia.co.uk.

19. Douglas John Hall, *Confessing the Faith: Christian Theology in a North American Context* (Minneapolis, MN: Fortress Press, 1998), 195–96.

WORKS CITED

Barrow, S. "Hearing Hope through the Babble." *Ekklesia*, May 27, 2008. http://www.ekklesia.co.uk.

Fraser, Giles. "Try Being Transformed by Joy." *Church Times*, July 25, 2008. http://www.churchtimes.co.uk/content.asp?id=60740.

Goldingay, John. *The First Testament: A New Translation*. Westmount, IL: InterVarsity Press; Kindle Edition, 2018.

Hall, Douglas John. *Thinking the Faith: Christian Theology in a North American Context*. Minneapolis, MN: Augsburg, 1989; paperback reprint: Minneapolis, MN: Fortress Press, 1991.

———. *Confessing the Faith: Christian Theology in a North American* Context. Minneapolis, MN: Fortress Press, 1998.

———. "Confessing Christ in a Post Christendom Context." Address; Atlanta, GA: 1999 Covenant Conference, Network of Presbyterians, November 6, 1999. Rpt. *Religion Online*, http://www.religion-online.org/author/douglas-john-hall/.

Heschel, Abraham Joshua. *Between God and Man: An Interpretation of Judaism.* New York: Free Press Paperbacks, 1959; rpt. Simon and Schuster, 1997.

———. *The Prophets.* New York: Perennial, 2001.

———. *Man Is Not Alone: A Philosophy of Religion.* New York: Noonday, 1991.

Kitamori, Kazoh. *Theology of the Pain of God: The First Original Theology from Japan.* Trans. 1958; 5th ed. 1965. Reprint, Eugene, OR: Wipf and Stock, June 10, 2005.

Kirkpatrick Patricia G. "The Biblical Prophets and Global Spirituality." *The Way Supplement*, 60–70. http://www.theway.org.uk/article.php.

Stevenson, J., ed. *Creeds, Councils and Controversies.* London: SPCK, 1966.

Tillich, Paul. *Systematic Theology*, Vol. 2. Chicago: University of Chicago Press, 1957.

Chapter 12

The Gospel of Irresolution

Thinking along with Douglas John Hall About Cross Theology, Illness, and Not Yet Resurrection

Deanna A. Thompson

Raised a Lutheran and with a degree in religion from a Lutheran College, I came to graduate school seeking new horizons. But after several years of wide-ranging theological study and a deepening commitment to feminist thought, I came across Douglas John Hall's work on an indigenous North America theology of the cross. Through Hall's work I began to see a way to integrate my growing feminist theological orientation with my Lutheran inheritance. I resonated with Hall's approach to Luther's theology of the cross as a "usable past"[1] to help us better understand and approach the present. Witnessing Hall's application of this "thin line of tradition"[2] for a North American Christian context helped me envision a horizon for an emerging feminist theology of the cross.

My first book laid out how key insights from Luther's theology of the cross could be seen as usable for a twenty-first-century feminist theology.[3] While my feminist self strongly concurred with Dorothee Sölle's insistence that Reformation thinkers like Luther "*strengthened* theology's sadistic accents,"[4] which must be critiqued and discarded, I also agreed with Hall's claim that Luther was a deeply contextual theologian[5] whose cross-centered approach provided an unflinchingly realistic look at human suffering and life before God, a context that offered some surprising resonance with several key feminist insights.

In December 2008, as I was speaking and writing on issues related to a feminist theology of the cross, life was derailed by a stage IV breast cancer diagnosis. The landscape of my life became virtually unrecognizable as I went from a healthy, active forty-two-year-old wife, mother, daughter, sister, professor, neighbor, and friend, to a virtual invalid with a life and family in crisis and a lousy prognosis for the future.

By the time I was diagnosed with metastatic breast cancer, the cancer had spread from breast to bones, fracturing two vertebrae and camping out in my pelvis and hips. While family and friends immediately sought out statistics on my prognosis, it took being weaned off oxycodone before it occurred to me to hunt down those numerical predictors of my future: the statistics that said that five years out, 80 percent of people who have what I have are dead.

But months of intense treatment reduced the pain enough for me to remove the fentanyl patch on my arm and begin physical therapy. After becoming thoroughly overwhelmed by the incurable status of my cancerous life and fearing the end was near, I went into remission—a lovely, disorienting, state of being.

And yet, in the past ten years I have lost and found remission again. And again. And while any day with remission is better than any day without it, I've experienced first-hand how the dominant Christian death-to-new-life storyline isn't quite able to hold the frayed edges of life with cancer. Perhaps not surprisingly, this ongoing relationship with incurable cancer has led me more deeply into my identity as a theologian of the cross.

Over the course of my decade of living with cancer, I've become aware of how the "official optimism"[6] of North America also very much applies to the context of illness. In the cancer world, there's an emphasis on telling stories of life with cancer that aim toward resolution. Everyone knows getting cancer is lousy—it's serious and can and does kill way too many people. But the language we tend to use to talk about it often promotes a secularized version of a theology of glory—we fight cancer with the goal of "winning" and defeating the disease. If you "lose," the goal is to go down "fighting valiantly."

How cancer actually works in the body, however, is more complicated than the dominant stories about cancer often reveal. Author John Green's popular book, *A Fault in Our Stars*, offers a window into the challenge of using such resolute language to describe what it's like to have cancer. One of the teenage protagonists living with cancer, Augustus Waters, asks, "What am I at war with? My cancer. And what is my cancer? My cancer is me. The tumors are made of me just as surely as my brain and my heart are made of me."[7]

It becomes vital to speak out, as Hall has taught us, against theologies of glory and the ways they can impose meaning on situations of suffering that defy tidy explanations. Fellow theologian and cancer-traveler Kate Bowler recounts how her husband pressed their neighbor for more details when she suggested that everything—even Bowler's stage IV cancer in her early thirties—happens for a reason. Confronted with a demand to flesh out this claim, the neighbor is rendered speechless. Bowler reflects on the challenges for her neighbor's theology: "She wanted some kind of order behind this chaos.

Because the opposite of [being blessed by God] is leaving a husband and toddler behind, and people can't quite let themselves say it: 'Wow. That's awful.' There has to be a reason, because without one we are left as helpless and possibly unlucky as everyone else."[8] In the face of a seemingly inexplicable cancer diagnosis, many turn to theologies and theodicies that impose meaning where meaning is notoriously hard to find.

Living in the Land of the Ill has reinforced for me Hall's claim that the cross remains the authentic representation of our human situation.[9] Suffering is built into our bodies, into the created order.[10] And if our theologies are to matter, they must attend to the myriad forms of suffering that dominate our world.

Recently I've been introduced to new research on trauma and its relationship to illness, and I'm finding it a useful conversation partner in formulating a cross-centered theology of illness. While researchers have been tracking for some time how trauma affects those who've endured war, or who've experienced sexual violence or forced migration, recent research has turned to how being diagnosed with a serious or chronic illness also produces trauma. This trauma lens is helpful not just in understanding my and others' illnesses but also in thinking more critically about our investment in contemporary theologies of glory that strive to make sense of sickness by putting it in a framework of resolution.

Trauma is described by theologian Shelly Rambo as "the suffering that remains."[11] There's an event—war, sexual assault, a cancer diagnosis—and those who continue to live beyond the awfulness experience a suffering that remains. But because trauma is most often "an invisible wound," it's not easily seen from the outside and often difficult to detect.

In *God and Human Suffering*, Hall proposes the central question: "How can one at the same time acquire sufficient honesty about what needs to be faced, and sufficient hope that facing it would make a difference, to engage in altering the course of our present world towards life and not death?"[12] This question remains vital for any theology of the cross, and I've discovered that trauma studies provide us with some necessary honesty about the kinds of suffering faced by those who are seriously ill.

In my most recent book, I use the insights of illness-related trauma to describe the suffering that accompanies those who are seriously ill.[13] Then, in a Hallian way, I explore spaces in the biblical story that don't flinch from the forms of suffering most familiar to those who are ill. Like Hall, I argue that the biblical story is one that avoids triumphalism and instead deals in stripped down, real hope, the kind of hope that meets those who are ill in the complicated, irresolute spaces where they live.

I start where many have gone before: the Book of Psalms. The Hebrew name of the book translates as "Book of Praises." It's worth noting that out of the 150 psalms, sixty of them—that's 40 percent—are lament psalms. Tempted by pressure to embrace optimistic forms of faith, Christians don't talk about this enough, that almost half of the psalms in the "Book of Praises" are about grief, trauma, desolation, and being undone by the sufferings of this world.

One psalm that deserves more attention, particularly by theologians of the cross, is Psalm 88, perhaps the most irresolute of all psalms. The psalmist's "soul is full of troubles" (v. 3), buried under the weight of isolation brought on by psychic, spiritual, and emotional distress. "But I, O Lord, cry out to you; in the morning my prayer comes before you. O Lord, why do you cast me off? Why do you hide your face from me?" (vv. 13–14). The psalmist cries out, and God seems silent. The psalm ends irresolutely, with darkness as the pray-er's only companion.

Theologian Kathryn Greene-McCreight meditates on this psalm in the context of her own experience with life-threatening mental illness. While living with diseases like cancer differs from living with mental illness, there are important moments of overlap, commonalities that become more apparent when this psalm is read as a psalm about someone who is seriously ill. Greene-McCreight's important insight about being ill is appropriate for those living with cancer as well: "Sick people are not necessarily weak," she writes. "I am ashamed to admit I did not already know this. Sick people are afflicted."[14] To be ill is to be afflicted not only physically but also with the disintegration of previously held theological frameworks, and even, as this psalm profoundly attests, by the acute experience of the absence of God.

Even though experiences of the absence of God fill the prayers of the psalms and are so ubiquitous that Jesus himself cannot avoid them, this particular kind of affliction often fails to get the pastoral and theological attention it deserves. Pastoral theologian Piet Zuidgeest's work with those who are grieving leads him to call for a retrieval of religious experiences of God's absence and their reintegration into Christian theology and practice. Zuidgeest rightly indicates that biblical testimony of humans' relationship to God illustrates that the experience of God's absence is much more than a momentary phenomenon; rather, God's "presence is in the nature of absence."[15]

This insight leads a theologian of the cross to the actual story of the cross and Jesus' anguished cry, "My God, my God, why have you forsaken me?" It is this moment in the biblical story perhaps more than any other in which "the God who guarantees meaning," as Hall puts it, is expelled from the picture. Poet Christian Wiman zeros in on this cry of Jesus' from the cross as the place that addresses his own trauma and suffering from cancer. Wiman suggests that the terror of death—and of Christ's death in particular—burst the bounds of judgment of sin, moving beyond, into "blankness, meaninglessness."[16]

While most contemporary first-world Christians tend to be preoccupied with seeing Jesus as an example to follow, what is most "moving" and most "durable" about Jesus for Wiman are the disruptive, disturbing moments of god-forsakenness. It is precisely the sense of meaninglessness that issues from Jesus' cry that orients Wiman's understanding of himself as a Christian. He insists that Christians can and should learn from atheists about the absence of God. "If you haven't ever experienced God's absence," Wiman insists, "you haven't been paying attention."[17] The radical nature of Christian faith comes in committing oneself to the crucified God.

It is in this irresolvable moment of Christ's god-forsakenness that we catch a glimpse of a *more* to life than these experiences of suffering and forsakenness produced by the cancer. Christ's suffering and death confirm that human love can reach right into the heart of death. But the Christian affirmation that Christ is also God means that it is not merely human love that touches death. This excess, this *more* of sharing our experiences of suffering and anomie, is the source of Wiman's faith in God, whom he names our "bright abyss."[18]

Wiman's encounter with Jesus' cry of god-forsakenness allows him to imagine that he is not simply a victim of cancer, that his story doesn't end in isolation, overcome by the solitary nature of his pain. Instead his story of suffering from cancer is held within the story of God's experiences of bodily suffering in the person of Jesus. Because of Jesus' story, Wiman is able to imagine *more* to his own story as well. He provides a compelling portrait of a theologian of the cross in the context of illness.

Being a theologian of the cross in the context of chronic illness leads me to pay more attention to spaces and places of irresolution in the biblical story, even as I take comfort in knowing that resurrection is how the story ends. My journey with cancer helps me see more clearly that even when the biblical story gets to the chapter of resurrection, irresolution persists. The gospel of Luke tells of the women who go to the tomb and find no body, only men in dazzling clothes who tell them, "He is not here, but has risen" (Luke 24:5). An irresolute resolution persists when disciples make their way from Jerusalem to Emmaus and are joined by the risen Christ, whom they do not recognize until he breaks bread with them. And just as the story moves toward resolution in their recognition of him as the Risen Lord, he vanishes from their sight (vv. 28–31), and again, leaves us with a sense of irresolution.

Lectionaries claim this story as an Easter story. Yet as pastor and fellow cancer traveler Jason Micheli insists, it could just as easily be understood as a Good Friday text.[19] To claim it as an Easter story, however, reinforces a claim often made by Hall: that resurrection is a chapter within a theology of the cross. The Lukan story reinforces how difficult it can be to identify resurrection, how fleeting and elusive the experience of resurrection often is. Even as Jesus Christ lives, dies, and lives again, his presence is also, often, experienced as an absence. In Christ's resurrection we glimpse a foretaste of the feast to come—a time of promised resolution, when our lives return to God and participate in God's eternal communion. But for now, cross remains the dominant reality. Most of us live in spaces of not-yet-resurrection, where we hope for—but are not always able to glimpse—that new age.

So what does all this mean for how we are to live? Hall argues that for Apostle Paul, a *theologia crucis* inevitably leads to an *ecclesia crucis*.[20] As not-yet-resurrection realities persist in our present age, the church continues to be called to make room for those undone by such sufferings, even as it continues to proclaim a more expansive story of a God whose own life—and whose intention for our lives—is bigger than any of the pain, even when that pain seems totalizing. Church as a space for the undone is a space where meaning is not necessarily restored, but where there's room for trauma and all that illness brings with it.

Luther counseled Christians on the importance of the sacrament of baptism, stressing that it is not something that occurs just once, only to be remembered as a past event. Rather the divine grace imparted through the sacrament persists in the here and now as well as into the future, actively renewing Christian life on a daily basis through the power of the Spirit. Riffing off of Paul's image in Galatians that all who are baptized are clothed in Christ (3:27), Luther imagines baptism as a "daily dress" for Christian lives.[21] Even as the power of sin continues to be a daily reality, so too the power of baptism continues to call Christians back to putting on Christ and conforming to his life.

Jason Micheli's own journey with the suffering caused by cancer has led him to reflect more deeply on what it means to conform not only to the life of Christ but also, specifically, to his death. "Therefore we have been buried with him by baptism into death, so that, just as Christ was raised from the dead by the glory of the Father, so we too might walk in newness of life" (Romans 6:3–4). Facing his own mortality and being opened up in new ways to the suffering of others, Micheli has come to see his walk with cancer as a form of Christian vocation. "The manner in which we're sick, the way we handle our sufferings, how we die . . . all of it are ways we live out, live up to, our baptism."[22]

Living out and up to our baptism in sickness and in health, in our caring for one another, in our living in the face of death, and in our dying—this is the vocation of the body of Christ.

But it can be incredibly challenging to bring one's very sick body to church. Especially when bodies are in the throes of chemotherapy or other treatments, it is often physically too difficult to make it to church for worship or other communal events. The pain and other physical unpleasantries from cancer and treatment often prevent those who are seriously ill from being able to attend anything other than the necessary medical appointments, especially during the worst times of the illness.

After being diagnosed with a rare form of cancer, Pastor JoAnn Post was forced to take a leave of absence from her ministerial work at her church. But as her treatment progressed, she deeply missed Sunday morning worship. Knowing how hard it might be to worship at her home congregation, Post attended worship at a neighboring church. Even in a church where she was known by some rather than all, Post still became overwhelmed by the mixture of worship and embraces she received from people who knew and cared for her. She fled before the service ended. "It was too much, this love."[23]

This sudden leave-taking of worship unnerved Post. As a pastor she'd had a life-long enthusiasm for worship and has often been confused and a little affronted when members of the congregation who were dealing with serious sadness stay away. Why wouldn't they seek out the body of Christ, a community committed to bearing one another's burdens, especially during the worst of times?

She admits that being undone by cancer offered an explanation. "I was suddenly and unwillingly vulnerable. . . . The familiar warmth and welcome of worship was disarming enough that I allowed the walls of imagined control to relax. And in that unguarded moment of vulnerability, the truth of my situation rushed in."[24] The truth of being undone by cancer, the truth of having little control over the experience of being undone, the truth that being vulnerable, even with those who love you dearly, can be more than we can bear.

If the church is going to be a space for those who reside deep within the Land of the Ill, the community needs to acknowledge that sometimes, it's just not possible for those who are really sick to be physically present in the communal gatherings of the church. At the same time, it's worth considering how communities of faith might form themselves into communities spacious enough to hold the vulnerable bodies and spirits of those undone by illness and other awfulness.

One of the realities for those who live with trauma is the way they can become stuck because they cannot integrate the traumatic experience(s) and aftermath into their lives. The ongoing reality of post-traumatic stress interrupts and obstructs the ability to find words to capture and organize thoughts on what it means to be undone. In his book, *The Body Keeps the Score*, trauma researcher Bessel van der Kolk recounts the capacity of art, music, and communal rituals and rhythms to help circumvent the challenges of finding words appropriate to articulating the trauma. Such rituals and nonverbal expressions of emotion are often able to facilitate integration—physical, psychic, emotional, spiritual—of the suffering that remains into the lives of those who have been traumatized. Recovery, van der Kolk has witnessed time and again, is facilitated through practices that involve the body renegotiating its relationship to embodied responses to trauma.[25]

This means that communal worship can be an important occasion for encouraging expressions of trauma to be re-formed, of offering opportunities for body-selves to be ushered into ritual spaces where trauma might be able to become more integrated. We know that one of the things religious rituals can do is reinforce a sense of coherence, meaning, and order in times when chaos and disorder run high. Such rituals invite our body-selves into practices that can make room for expressions of trauma.

Unfortunately, expressions of lament tend to be relatively rare in many contemporary forms of worship. Lectionaries have excised the rawest expressions of grief or complaint in their psalm selections. Churches that do not follow a lectionary often choose psalms of thanksgiving or particular verses of trust from lament psalms while casting aside the verses of anguish. Many contemporary hymnals overflow with songs of praise while songs of lament can be difficult to find.

"Particularly since my diagnosis, I feel this [lack of lament in worship] as a stinging loss," writes theologian Todd Billings.[26] Participating in worship while living with advanced-stage cancer has heightened Billings' awareness of the confidence Christians tend to have in petitioning God for help in difficult times or in rejoicing over answered prayers. At the same time he has also become keenly aware of how many in his community simply do not know how to be with others when they're undone by sorrow.

Praying the psalms and other prayers of lament corporately during worship has the opportunity to enact something that cannot be done when one prays alone. The embodied experience of participating in a community of believers that prays prayers of lament out loud, together, not only helps incarnate experiences of loss and grief, but also enables such incarnation to offer strength to counter the persistent threats of disorder, chaos, and meaninglessness.[27] The community's embodiment of lament forms not just individual body-selves but also corporate bodies into bodies practiced in giving voice to their and others' sadness, grief, anger, complaint, agony, and hope before God. By performing such practices, the community rebuts the dehumanizing effects of serious illness and breaks through the debilitating isolation that can be constant partners during the worst of being sick. And when our sorrow and anguish are acknowledged and borne with others, we can become unstuck, and able to move, as the psalmist often does, toward healing and hope.

While it is vital, as Hall insists, that theologies of the cross live in spaces of unrealized eschatology,[28] the longer I sit in chemo rooms the more convinced I am that our indigenous, contextual theologies need to dare to talk more about a future life with God to those whose bodies are undone by illness. The biblical vision of recreation is one where God makes all things new

(Revelation 21:5). But what exactly might this mean for our diseased bodies? Tellers of the Christian story have consistently rejected attempts to envision life with God in fully spiritual, disembodied terms. Just what bodies might look like in life beyond this one remains a mystery.

But if we look again at the depiction of Christ's resurrection body, we realize that it was not simply a resuscitation of his earthly body, for the gospels repeatedly testify to how those closest to Christ in life before his crucifixion could not immediately recognize his resurrected body. In his letter to the Corinthians, Paul describes the resurrected body as a spiritual body, imperishable and from heaven (1 Corinthians 15:42–49). So the resurrected body is different from the body we have now, but it remains a body, one made to be in communion with God. And while our resurrected bodies are not simply our earthly bodies resuscitated, theologian David Jenson points out that if we look to Christ's resurrection for signs of what our own resurrection might be like, we also see that something about Christ's individuality was preserved in resurrection, for eventually those who knew and loved him were able to recognize him in his resurrected state.[29]

Part of that continuity between Christ pre- and post-resurrection is the way his resurrected body continues to bear the wounds of crucifixion. These wounds on Christ's resurrected body suggest that resurrection doesn't erase the scars that we accumulate during our lives. But even as bodies may still bear the wounds of this life, the book of Revelation's image of the New Jerusalem suggests that our wounds will no longer cause suffering.

To claim with Paul, then, that Christ will come again is more than simply saying yes to the claim that he will descend from the heavens at some future point. To encourage one another with realistic hope means embracing the idea (the truth?) that while this life requires much room to grieve our losses, traumas, and sorrows, the promised future Parousia can be glimpsed and experienced in the here and now. And if the second coming recalls the first, Jenson notes, "we should also expect Christ to appear in unexpected and neglected spaces."[30]

Friend and fellow metastatic breast cancer traveler, Camille Scheel, found a way to talk about her hope in God's promised future amid the trials of cancer. Here's what she said:

> As an Episcopalian, I bow to the cross as it passes, which makes me imagine what it will be like the first time I experience the Lord in heaven; I imagine needing to bow and cover my eyes to the light. It's wonderful to think of a place that is all love, light, and peace. Feasting on the sensual nature of this world now makes me feel as if I'm choosing between two delicious meals and I can't decide which is better. That being said, I won't give up this world easily.[31]

Even when lives are limited by illness and the trauma and isolation that can accompany it, the promise of the Parousia is that humans are created not only for relationship with God and others in the here and now, but for relationship with God and others in life beyond this one: that the love that binds them to God and one another is a love that persists, even in the face of death.

The vocabulary of hope offered by biblical faith opens up avenues for contemporary theologians of the cross to proclaim a realistic hope that leaves space for the ambiguity and the indefinite loss that is integral to living with life-threatening illness. The image of promised resurrection does not offer resolution to *anomic* situations (situations that are unstructured, unordered and often don't make sense). Nevertheless, the image of a promised life with others and with Christ helps reframe the power of the trauma and suffering and diminishment and death.

This image of hope helps those who are ill envision that being entombed by disease is not the end of the story of our embodied lives—that our stories of lives dominated by loss of health are encompassed by a larger story of hope in the *more* of life, increasingly often the *more* life in this world, as well as life in the beyond. I remain indebted to Douglas John Hall for helping so many of us see the potential for this "thin line of tradition" to speak to situations of being undone by the sufferings of this life, and to offer hope even in the midst of situations where hope it so hard to find.

NOTES

1. Douglas John Hall, "The Theology of the Cross: A Usable Past," in *Encounters with Martin Luther: New Directions for Critical Studies*, eds., Kirsi Stjerna and Brooks Schramm (Louisville, KY: Westminster John Knox, 2016), 74.

2. Hall, "The Theology of the Cross: A Usable Past," 75.

3. See Deanna A. Thompson, *Crossing the Divide: Luther, Feminism, and the Cross* (Minneapolis, MN: Fortress Press, 2004).

4. Dorothee Sölle, *Suffering*, trans. Everett R. Kalin (Philadelphia, PA: Fortress Press, 1973), 22, as quoted in Douglas John Hall, *God and Human Suffering: An Exercise in a Theology of the Cross*, (Minneapolis, MN: Fortress Press, Reprint Edition, 1987), 76.

5. Hall, "The Theology of the Cross: A Usable Past," 80.

6. Douglas John Hall, *Lighten Our Darkness: Toward an Indigenous Theology of the Cross* (Louisville, KY: Westminster, 1976), 40.

7. John Green, *The Fault in Our Stars* (New York: Dutton Books, 2012), 216.

8. Kate Bowler, "Death, Prosperity Gospel, and Me," *New York Times*, February 13, 2016, https://www.nytimes.com/2016/02/14/opinion/sunday/death-the-prosperity-gospel-and-me.html.

9. Hall, *Lighten Our Darkness*, 123.

10. Hall, *God and Human Suffering*, 55.
11. Shelly Rambo, *Spirit and Trauma: A Theology of Remaining* (Louisville, KY: Westminster John Knox, 2010), 15.
12. Douglas John Hall, *God and Human Suffering*, 47.
13. See Deanna A. Thompson, *Glimpsing Resurrection: Cancer, Trauma, and Ministry* (Louisville, KY: Westminster John Knox, 2018).
14. Kathryn Greene-McCreight, *Darkness Is My Only Companion: A Christian Response to Mental Illness* (Grand Rapids, MI: Brazos, 2015), 162.
15. Piet Zuidgeest, *The Absence of God: Exploring the Christian Tradition in a Situation of Mourning* (Boston, MA: Brill, 2001), 133.
16. Christian Wiman, *My Bright Abyss: Meditation of a Modern Believer* (New York: Farrar, Straus and Giroux, 2014), 106–7.
17. Christian Wiman, speaking in "A Poet and a Theologian Discuss Incurable Cancer—Christian Wiman and Todd Billings," Western Theological Seminary's James I. Cook Endowment in Christianity & Literature and the Osterhaven Lecture Series, March 31, 2015, accessed February 20, 2017, http://jtoddbillings.com/2015/03/penetratingly-honest-and-expansively-hopeful/.
18. Wiman, *My Bright Abyss*.
19. Jason Micheli, *Cancer Is Funny: Keeping Faith in Stage-Serious Chemo* (Minneapolis, MN: Fortress Press, 2016), 150.
20. Hall, *God and Human Suffering*, 143–44.
21. See Martin Luther's *Large Catechism*, paragraphs 83–84, accessed June 29, 2017, http://bookofconcord.org/lc-6-baptism.php.
22. Micheli, *Cancer Is Funny*, 161.
23. JoAnn A. Post, *Songs in My Head: A Cancer Spiritual* (Eugene, OR: Wipf and Stock, 2015), 12.
24. Post, *Songs in My Head*, 13.
25. Bessel van der Kolk, *The Body Keeps the Score: Brain, Mind, and Body in the Healing of Trauma* (New York: Penguin, 2015); see especially chapters 14, 18, and 20.
26. J. Todd Billings, *Rejoicing in Lament: Wrestling with Incurable Cancer and Life in Christ* (Ada, MI: Brazos, 2015), 40.
27. Kathleen Billman and Daniel Migliore, *Rachel's Cry: Prayer of Lament and Rebirth of Hope* (Eugene, OR: Wipf and Stock, 2007), 137.
28. Hall, "The Theology of the Cross: A Usable Past," 81.
29. David Jenson, *Living Hope: The Future and Christian Faith* (Louisville, KY: Westminster John Knox, 2010), 33.
30. Jenson, *Living Hope*, 41.
31. Camille Scheel, *Camp Chemo: Postcards Home from Metastatic Breast Cancer* (Edina, MN: Beaver's Pond Press, 2015), 246.

WORKS CITED

Billings, J. Todd. *Rejoicing in Lament: Wrestling with Incurable Cancer and Life in Christ*. Ada, MI: Brazos, 2015.

Billman, Kathleen, and Daniel Migliore. *Rachel's Cry: Prayer of Lament and Rebirth of Hope*. Eugene, OR: Wipf and Stock, 2007.

Bowler, Kate. "Death, Prosperity Gospel, and Me," *New York Times*, February 13, 2016, https://www.nytimes.com/2016/02/14/opinion/sunday/death-the-prosperity-gospel-and-me.html.

Green, John. *The Fault in Our Stars*. New York: Dutton Books, 2012.

Greene-McCreight, Kathryn. *Darkness Is My Only Companion: A Christian Response to Mental Illness*. Grand Rapids, MI: Brazos, 2015.

Hall, Douglas John. *God and Human Suffering: An Exercise in a Theology of the Cross*. Minneapolis, MN: Fortress Press, Reprint Edition, 1987.

———. *Lighten Our Darkness: Toward an Indigenous Theology of the Cross*. Louisville, KY: Westminster, 1976.

———. "The Theology of the Cross: A Usable Past," in *Encounters with Martin Luther: New Directions for Critical Studies*. Edited by Kirsi Stjerna and Brooks Schramm. Louisville, KY: Westminster John Knox, 2016.

Jenson, David. *Living Hope: The Future and Christian Faith*. Louisville, KY: Westminster John Knox, 2010.

Luther, Martin. *Large Catechism*. Accessed June 29, 2017. http://bookofconcord.org/lc-6-baptism.php.

Micheli, Jason. *Cancer Is Funny: Keeping Faith in Stage-Serious Chemo*. Minneapolis, MN: Fortress Press, 2016.

Post, JoAnn A. *Songs in My Head: A Cancer Spiritual*. Eugene, OR: Wipf and Stock Publishers, 2015.

Rambo, Shelly. *Spirit and Trauma: A Theology of Remaining*. Louisville, KY: Westminster John Knox, 2010.

Scheel, Camille. *Camp Chemo: Postcards Home from Metastatic Breast Cancer*. Edina, MN: Beaver's Pond Press, 2015.

Thompson, Deanna A. *Crossing the Divide: Luther, Feminism, and the Cross*. Minneapolis, MN: Fortress Press, 2004.

———. *Glimpsing Resurrection: Cancer, Trauma, and Ministry*. Louisville, KY: Westminster John Knox, 2018.

Wiman, Christian. *My Bright Abyss: Meditation of a Modern Believer*. New York: Farrar, Straus and Giroux, 2014.

Van der Kolk, Bessel. *The Body Keeps the Score: Brain, Mind, and Body in the Healing of Trauma*. New York: Penguin, 2015.

Zuidgeest, Piet. *The Absence of God: Exploring the Christian Tradition in a Situation of Mourning*. Boston, MA: Brill, 2001.

Afterword

Christian Theology after Christendom—Three Essentials

Douglas John Hall

INTRODUCTORY

We have heard many excellent and moving statements concerning the implications of a theology that engages its worldly context with both critical awareness and compassion.[1] In this afterword, as a way of expressing my sincere gratitude for all that I have received here, I should like to add my contribution to the basic theme of our gathering, *Christian Theology after Christendom.*

Since I have published a good deal about all this, I felt that it would be appropriate on this occasion to approach the subject in a somewhat more autobiographical manner, or at least to draw upon aspects of my own theological history. To that end, I have chosen three emblematic themes, with three specific biblical texts—themes and texts that have been important in my own spiritual and intellectual struggle and which, I believe, suggest significant directions for the Christian movement at this time of radical change—this metamorphosis—in the form of the church. First, I wish to speak about the role of critical theology in fashioning the *koinonia* as a "zone of truth."[2]

CRITICAL THEOLOGY AS "ZONE OF TRUTH"

At the age of twenty, I left my home in "the garden of Canada" (Oxford County in Southwestern Ontario) to go to the Royal Conservatory of Music in nearby Toronto in order to pursue my great ambition. The only conspicuous gift that nature had bestowed on me was what I was told was an exceptional aptitude for music; so I intended to undertake advanced studies in composition and piano with a view to perfecting that gift. It was the year 1948, just three years after World War II had finally ended. Toronto's population was then only about 650,000, but it was still a big city for a village and small-town boy. Although I was surrounded by a sympathetic community of support in my pursuit of my high ambition, still, the tentativeness of it, combined with personal loneliness, prompted in my youthful psyche an upsurge of the great questions that had been pursuing me for a long time. Who was I, really, to imagine such a career? Did I have any genuine talent? Was the future possible—as a musician? As a human being?

One night, sitting alone in my small room on Tennis Crescent off Broadview Avenue, I recalled an old man of our village who, quietly listening to our enthusiastic youthful opinions and plans, would sometimes interject with a certain sage authority, the phrase, "Vanity of vanities, all is vanity." The good folk of my congregation had given me, at my departure, a beautiful, India-paper edition of the King James Version of the Bible. With my old sage's cautionary voice sounding in my mind, I picked up this book and read for the first time the Old Testament document—called somewhat ironically by Christians "Ecclesiastes"—the source of this *vanitas vanitatum, et omnia vanitas*:

> *Vanity of vanities,* saith the Preacher, *all is vanity* [emptiness, futility]. *What profit hath a man of all his labour which he taketh under the sun? One generation passeth away, and another generation cometh. . . . The sun also ariseth, and the sun goeth down. . .*
>
> *. . . he hath set 'olam in their heart, so that no man can find out the work that God maketh from beginning to end . . . .*

This document, which only barely made it into the canon of scripture, became—that night—my personal entrée into the House of the Interpreter, or at least the foyer of that great and ancient House. Qoheleth seemed to verbalize my own existential condition—my nascent skepticism, my vulnerability, my *'Olam*. With his relentless examination of the foibles, failures, and false hopes of the human odyssey, this "Preacher" forced me to face head-on my own muted anxieties—yes, *but in an odd way Qoheleth's imperative also came through to me as a sort of permission*—a *holy* permission to enter the deep, inhibited places of the soul openly, freely, courageously. I think I knew already then that Qoheleth's message could not contain the whole "story": the little document was only part, after all, of a large and weighty collection—the Bible! Yet I sensed even then that whatever else the Holy Book might have to say to me, it would have to pass through the dark valley of this austere assessment of human prospects. Probably, indeed, one would have to return to that analysis regularly if one were to avoid simplistic ideas and the fond illusions of one's "sunny days." Ecclesiastes, Job, Lamentations, and many of the Psalms stand, I think, as guardian angels against religious presumption and spiritualistic humbug! I am very glad that I encountered those cautionary angels early in my adult life.

Years later—in 1956—after I had been led by other helpers in the House of Interpretation to pursue a vocation (Christian ministry!) that, at twenty, I had by no means entertained, I discovered that many others had also been taught by Qoheleth. Among these were the two professors under whose guidance I undertook my dissertation for the degree, Master of Divinity—in those years at Union Seminary in New York a major and demanding piece of work. My dissertation was of course on *Ecclesiastes*, for throughout the previous seven years of undergraduate and graduate study, I had never lost sight of my stern old mentor. Samuel Terrien, the Old Testament scholar who directed my thesis, believed that Qoheleth was a quite conscious commentary on Genesis 3—the Fall. My other advisor, Reinhold Niebuhr, saw a parallel between Qoheleth's analysis of humanity's driven, frustrated quest for meaning and Friedrich Nietzsche's theory of time's eternal return, his cyclical view of history.

And now, after a long life of seeking to understand what I believe, I return to the pews beneath the pulpit of "the Preacher." Qoheleth teaches us, I think, to know ourselves as mortals before we give ourselves to ideologies and systems of belief that too soon seduce us and tranquilize our restless minds. He wants us to be searching still. We are programmed, surely, to search for meaning: that's what *'olam* signifies. But Qoheleth insists that that search can be trustworthy only when it begins with some profound experience of privation, some new and (likely) distressing sense of the enormity of life and of one's appalling lack of the wherewithal for living. Tillich called it "the shock of non-being." Only when we have begun to recognize the boundless depths of our need, the inadequacy of our understanding, the presumption and naivety of our habitual ways, are we in a position to ask for greater wisdom, greater courage, greater trust. Only when we have come face-to-face with our own *im*possibility are we able to open ourselves to God's possibility for us.

Theological thought and discourse can help to create in the *koinonia* a zone of truth only when it conveys an invitation and permission consciously and intentionally to enter those depths—to become *thinking* persons. We need such a push, such permission and exhortation, because our natural tendency is to avoid precisely those depths. We repress the truth, even the truth that shouts at us daily in the media, because truth is never merely affirmative and pleasurable; there is always pain or sorrow or judgment in it. So, while we allow ourselves to consider the little truths that are necessary to ordinary existence, our watchful minds almost automatically reject the great truths of our condition—our vulnerability, our guilt, our covert anxiety about tomorrow, above all our mortality. Most of the great social issues that loom on our near horizon today are the consequences of truth's constraint. We have built a civilization on the illusion of human mastery; therefore every reality that does not readily submit to our control is relegated to that great submerged iceberg of *unknowing*, the subconscious, where it wreaks infinitely more havoc than it ever could have done had we confronted it openly. So here we are, threatened by multifarious challenges to planetary existence, yet witnessing the buffoonery of the elected leader of the most powerful empire in recorded history announcing (in his July 4th address) that the United States would endure "forever and ever." (I don't think that he added "Amen," but I'm sure many of his "evangelical *base*" did so!).

It's called repression.

This, then, is the challenge to Christian theology. Does our faith, at its core, give us the courage openly to contemplate the negations that, as humans, we fearfully suspect? Does it give us the boldness to explore hope despite the despair we feel in our unguarded moments? Does it allow us to affirm our mortality, our death, without capitulating to "the *sting* of death"?

This leads me to the second of my three emblematic themes and texts.

THEOLOGY OF THE CROSS

We preach Christ crucified, unto the [reputedly religious] a stumbling-block, unto the [reputedly wise] foolishness, but unto them which are called, both religious and wise, the power of God and the wisdom of God, because the foolishness of God is wiser than [human beings] and the weakness of God is stronger than [human beings]. (1 Corinthians 1:23–24)

It was the year 1960. After seven years in the New York City, I was sent by my denomination to the town of Blind River at the top of Lake Huron. Rhoda's Nova Scotia relatives (we had just been married) told their friends that we were going to Blind Alley! It took me quite a while to realize that I should smile at people on the main street of that wonderful little town; if you did that in New York you might be arrested!

Of course, no theology can speak directly to the human condition—the condition of the "impossible creature" (Becker). Theology is to the gospel and to faith only what musicology is to music. It can help you to hear the music a little better. The theology of the cross, which I learned from Paul and Luther and Kierkegaard and Reinhold Niebuhr and a whole host of helpers in the House of Interpretation, is not understood very well in our English-speaking lands. We think it's about the doctrine of atonement, if we get that far. No, said Jürgen Moltmann (and behind him a whole host of others, including Bonhoeffer), no, the *theologia crucis* is "the key signature" in which the music of faith is played.[3] The resurrection, said Ernst Käsemann, "is a chapter in the theology of the cross." In the English-speaking world, including most Christians of that world, we like our stories to have straightforwardly happy endings. Dickens takes one through some harrowing scenes in nineteenth-century industrializing England, but his heroes always come out on top. Even E. M. Forster, whom I love, couldn't bear to have his homosexual hero, Maurice, face Oscar Wilde's wretched ending, so he caused Maurice and his gamekeeper lover to go off to some never-never land where early twentieth century gay men could live happily ever after.

Luther, the least understood of the Reformers in Anglo-Saxon lands, insisted that the Gospel was about a crucified man—and behind him a crucified God: against the background of officially rejected patripassionism he dared to speak of *Der gekreuzigte Gott*. God's manner of "happy endings," he believed, is hidden in and beneath the dust and tumult of life. *Deus revelatus* is *Deus absconditus*. God's victory is *concealed* in its revealing:

> As it is, we do not see everything in subjection to that glorious being [*ha 'Adam*], a little lower than the angels. We see Jesus, who for a little while was made lower than the angels, crowned with glory and honour because of the suffering of death, so that by the grace of God he might taste death for everyone. (Hebrews 2:8–9)

We see Jesus!

It is unfortunate in the extreme that liberal and moderate Protestantism in our time, fearful lest the *particularity* of this name should seem to exclude someone, has been trying for some decades to soft-pedal this particularity, thus leaving Jesus to those who crucify him again by reducing him to sentimentality or some orthodoxy of the Right! A close friend of mine, one of the most thoughtful Moderators our denomination has ever had, laments that he hears this name very seldom now, even in church. And he is right: it *is* lamentable, not only because this name represents the very core and cornerstone of Christian faith, but because it represents our one and only chance, as Christians, to illumine and confront and comfort citizens of a global civilization that may soon find itself without a globe (have you read David Wallace-Wells' *The Uninhabitable Earth*). Whether we agree with the "extreme" environmentalists or not, it is pretty well obvious by now that the future we are speaking about is going to be a rough one, one way or another. We need this name, not just to give life to our rapidly dwindling churches, but to contribute to our contemporaries the only kind of hope that *we*, Christians, can give them, which St Paul calls "hope against hope" (Romans 4:18, 8:24, etc.).

But we shall only be able to do this if we can free this name from its centuries of use and misuse, from its captivation by cultural Establishments, and above all from bad theologies, some of them so hoary that they can seem eternal! *Theologia gloriae* Luther calls them. Theologies of glory, triumphant answers to human questions insufficiently pondered, or not pondered at all! The *Christology* of these triumphant answers always turns Jesus, straightaway or after a little "seeming" suffering, into God, thus trashing the whole idea of "incarnation": But for the School of Antioch, said the great Orthodox theologian, Father George Florovsky, the early church would have lost altogether the confession of Jesus' full humanity. North American fundamentalist orthodoxy unfortunately did not know about the School of Antioch, so it announces twenty-four/seven, in the line of T. T. Shields, simply "Jesus is God."[4]

Soteriologically, rescuing Jesus from the toils of bad theology is even more daunting; for, at least in the Christian West, the significance of Jesus' work, of the cross, is almost inextricably bound up with the so-called Latin theory of the atonement, as stated in classical form by Anselm of Canterbury. Jesus is presented as God's answer to His own problem: How can He, who is so transcendently holy, accept a creature so besmirched by sin and guilt? Jesus, the only unblemished human being, brought into being for the very purpose, is the perfect sacrificial answer.

But not to *our* question, we who languish in a different Slough of Despond—and not, I suspect, to the greatly magnified version of our question that will confront the generations of our grandchildren, who may not be able to any longer ignore global warming, or racial injustice, or economic disparity, or the war-mongering Right, and so on! *Our* question is not how we can wash away our guilt and sin, but how we can find *meaning* in a world that, from the sciences to the arts, seems to deny any such possibility. *Our* question (and as far as one can see it will only become more ubiquitous in the decades ahead) is not how to assuage the anxiety of guilt and condemnation, but how to live with the anxiety of emptiness and meaninglessness (unapologetically, I use the categories of my teacher, Paul Tillich, not because he said them but because I have found them to be true).[5] Jesus as God's sacrificial lamb, slain to blot out our sin, may have seemed real to medieval men and women—partly, let us recognize, because the whole apparatus of the church was designed to make them feel that way: *that* Jesus does not speak to our epoch. Most of us don't get so far as guilt; we're preoccupied trying to find out whether life has any possible purpose. "What are people for?" asks Kurt Vonnegut. So does Wendell Berry.[6] So do most of our own young! Qoheleth's question. "What profit hath a man (or a woman!) for all their labour which they take under the sun?"

"We would see Jesus," said some curious outsiders to the disciples. Perhaps our contemporary outsiders, who are the majority, would be more curious too if we could present Jesus as one not unlike them, tempted like unto them—yet—a human being who did not repress the nothingness, the Nihil, the abyss over which creaturely existence is strung; a man of sorrows and acquainted with grief; a human being courageous enough to confront the Nihil, the darkness, the apparent oblivion of death. If the churches could learn to spend as much energy and imagination addressing the reality of our mortality as they have spent on sin and guilt, their sermons might be more gladly heard.

The incarnation is not just about the *birth* of the humble, holy representative—no this dear child in the manger has to go all the way to Golgotha, not, I think, to atone for our wickedness so much as to participate in our ontological impossibility. The God Jesus represents is the One who knows our frame and remembers that we are dust—just, in fact, as our Maker made us, knowing full well the awesome risk. Jesus shows up again and again in the gospels as one of profound compassion—seeing the people as sheep without a shepherd. "Jesus wept": that one little statement, describing what Jesus felt and did at the tomb of his young friend, says, almost, everything. And that isn't because "compassion" is a good thing, something we should all have; it's because that is the character of the God Jesus represents—the Creator God whose *pathos* is in part the consequence of his awareness of the dangers implicit in the creation of such a "thinking animal"—perhaps, as Elie Wiesel often wonders, even God's self-reproach for having underestimated the suffering that such a being would have to endure.

The theology of the cross is not a novel thing, devised by a few Christians who noticed that the Jesus of the New Testament spends more time identifying with suffering and confused people than he does in railing out at their wickedness, hypocrisy, and lust. The source of this theology lies in the God-consciousness of the prophets of Israel, as the Jewish theologian Abraham Heschel helped some of us to understand. "Prophecy," wrote Heschel, "consists in the inspired communication of divine attitudes to the prophetic consciousness. . . . The divine *pathos* is the ground tone of all these attitudes. . . . It is echoed in almost every prophetic statement."[7] "God *is concerned about the world and shares its fate. Indeed, this is the essence of God's moral nature: His willingness to be intimately involved in the history of man.*"[8] Between the pathos of the God of Israel and the *passio Christi* of the Gospels there is a direct line of continuity. And if I had another lifetime I would spend part of it exploring this question: *If Christians in their formative periods had followed the* prophetic *traditions of Israel instead of developing their soteriological theologies along the lines of Israel's sacerdotal and juridical* conventions, combined with the ontology of Athens, *what difference might that have made in the picture of Jesus that they presented to the world? What difference could it still make?* Might it, among other things, help to heal the gap between Christianity, that "grafted on branch," and the tree onto which it was grafted (Romans 11)—might it help the child return, after its ambitious prodigality in the world, to the home of the Abrahamic parent, who in the meantime has suffered dearly for the estrangement and lostness of this child, might willingly come out to meet the prodigal on the road?

But now to the final essential and text, which will concern the nature and mission of the church.

THE SUFFERING OF THE CHURCH

And here I shall presage my intention by citing one of the many New Testament texts that could be used in this connection—1 Peter 4:12–17:

> Beloved, do not be surprised at the fiery ordeal which comes upon you to prove you, as though something strange were happening to you. But rejoice in so far as you share Christ's sufferings. . . . For the time has come for judgement to begin with the household of Christ.

Due partly to the influence of Dietrich Bonhoeffer, who had wandered in those cloisters and classrooms of Union Seminary a few years before me, I chose in 1957 to write my dissertation for the degree of Doctor of Theology on the topic, *The Suffering of the Church: A Doctrinal Study of an Aspect of the Nature and Destiny of the Christian Church.*

There is more about the suffering of the church in the New Testament, you know, than about any other single aspect of ecclesiology. The Nicaean theologians decreed that the identifying marks of the true church were four: unity, holiness, catholicity, and apostolicity. And these *notae ecclesiae* should never, I think, be ignored. *But*, said Martin Luther, the only *indispensable* mark of the church, without which all the others mean nothing, is that it is the bearer of the holy cross—that is, that it suffers with Christ in and with and for the life of the beloved world. That, of course, is the basic meaning of the church's suffering, namely, that it is a matter of "continuous baptism" into the suffering of the Christ—*our* participation in *His* participation in creaturely existence. This is certainly a *mystical* conception of the church, as Pope Pius XII insisted in his encyclical *Mystici corporis Christi,* promulgated in the midst of World War II. But it is not so mysterious as to locate the life of the "Body of Christ" completely outside this problematic and dangerous world, as the famous encyclical tends to do. To the contrary, it is a matter of being sent more explicitly *into* the world, indeed of being refused a way out—like Saint Peter of legend, sent back into Rome as he fled along the Appian Way, back into burning Rome to "suffer with Christ." As Bonhoeffer insisted in his last letters from prison, the ongoing

Afterword

identification of the disciple community with the crucified One means that the church has to become more "worldly," not less; more involved in the life of this beautiful, threatened planet and civilization, less merely "religious." In being denied a sacerdotal existence, the church learns to *image God* in its loving stewardship of God's creation. In that "incarnational" immersion in the world, the church quite naturally suffers. It does not seek suffering; it seeks to follow its Head—to make discipleship of Christ real, authentic, not merely rhetorical. Therefore, given the nature of historical existence, it suffers.

Does this suffering also include the present decline and decimation of Christendom—the closing of one church after another, the empty, cathedral-sized churches of this city, the termination of seminaries once filled with eager young priests and candidates for ministry, the demotion of faculties to schools? Certainly none of that, which is for the most part a quiet, incremental decrease, would seem to warrant the description of "fiery ordeal"! Yet, as I have observed (and been dismayed by) the "disestablishment" of Christendom over the decades, it does often seem a kind of slow burning. Maybe the conflagration of Notre-Dame-de-Paris should be seen as a dramatic metaphor for this two- or three-century winding-down of imperial Christianity. We are being harrowed, sifted, weighed in the balances. We had grown presumptuous, smug, bored—and boring! We thought our continuation and replenishment would go on, world without end, each generation obediently filing into the pews left by their departing elders. We refused to notice the incongruity of our once well-oiled ecclesiastical systems with the life of the crucified one. We rejected any thought of our historical humiliation. "The real humiliation of the church," said the Dutch theologian and chaplain to the old Queen Wilhemina, Albert van den Heuvel, "is its refusal to be humiliated."[9]

When I first began to notice these changes in the social status of the churches—it was in 1962, when I began my principalship of St. Paul's College in the new University of Waterloo, just at the dramatic onset of the countercultural and student revolutions—I picked up a small book, ostensibly on account of the name of its famous author (but I suspect Providence had something to do with it!), a book that greatly helped me to interpret the vast changes that were occurring to the churches. If there were time, I would read the entire book to you here and now, but instead I shall only quote a sentence or two. Only then shall I reveal the name of their author:

> The Christendom of the Middle Ages and after, pleasant and individualistic petty-bourgeois Christendom is going to disappear with ever-increasing speed. For the causes which have brought about this process in the West are still at work and have not yet had their full effect.

> If we live in the *diaspora,* then the office-job type of pastor will have one future to die out.
>
> Let us get away from the tyranny of statistics. For the next hundred years they are always going to be against us. . . . One real conversion in a great city is something more splendid than the spectacle of a whole remote village going to the sacraments.
>
> Why should we not today alter to our use, quite humbly and dispassionately, a saying of St. Augustine's: "Many whom God has the church does not have, and many whom the Church has God does not have." Why, in our defeatism, which springs from a muddled feeling of pity for mankind, do we forget that it is not truth but a heresy that there is no grace outside the Church?[10]

These are not the words of a radical liberal firebrand; they are words of Karl Rahner, thought by many (including myself!) to be the greatest Roman Catholic theologian of the epoch. He lived in the same beautiful city (Muenster in Westphalia) as I did when I wrote my first major book, *Lighten Our Darkness: Towards an Indigenous Theology of the Cross.* Professor Rahner was ill then, but I heard him speak, and with everyone else I marveled at his erudition—and his humility. Along with Bonhoeffer, Reinhold Niebuhr, and others, Rahner helped to give me the impetus to try to face, decipher, and make something meaningful, in my own North American context, out of this humiliation of churches that refused to notice their humiliation, let alone accept it and give it some positive Christian direction.

The *critical* theological aspect of the suffering that the church today and tomorrow has to undergo is simply that it will have to *unlearn* Christendom; and that is hard and will be ever harder, for after sixteen centuries of establishment in the West we are all more or less programmed to "think big." But in his references to his disciple-community Jesus Christ always used metaphors of smallness—little things that could do important work for small things: salt, yeast, the light of a small city on a hill. He spoke of his followers as a "little flock." So the *constructive* theological aspect of the ecclesiology that the future church must seek to comprehend is (to state it in its simplest form) to discover again the possibilities of smallness. In 1973 I attended a large ecumenical conference in France, one of whose guest speakers was E. F. Schumacher, the author of a book famous among ecologists: *Small is Beautiful.* The task of theology in the future church is to show Christians that small can be beautiful—and faithful, and ethically provocative!

That, of course, will involve suffering, for the world to which the disciple community is called to "return" today is "burning," as it was when Peter was turned back. It is a world filled with horrendous and multifarious suffering for billions of earth's inhabitants. The future is always unknown, but surely there are already enough "knowns" for us to realize the high probability that in the decades, perhaps centuries, that are ahead—are already upon us—this global suffering will increase exponentially. Will the planet indeed become "uninhabitable"?; or (as James Lovelock believes), while the planet survives, will the human species self-destruct? How as Christians should one read such prospects? At any rate, we should all hearken to a statement of Martin Buber that warns against complacency: "He . . . who today knows nothing other to say than 'See there, it grows lighter!'—he leads into error."[11] Will the churches of the future be able to suffer in, with, and for such a world as the great seers of our age now speak of openly, daily? Will Christians manifest, besides the passion to fix what can be fixed, the spiritual depth and courage to face what can't be fixed—and help others to do so?

CONCLUSION

I must conclude; and what better way to end this little review of my professional life than to refer to this very event that has brought us all together. It would be impossible, I think, to conceive a more glorious way of recognizing the effective completion of one's work as a theologian. I began this work as a student at the University of Western Ontario and Huron College almost exactly seventy year ago, full of curiosity and a sense of my own ignorance! I will not say that I have completed that work. I suspect it never ends. Nor does one become master of it!

Two Latin phrases express, in their strange and suggestive juxtaposition, the dilemma of the theologian: Anselm of Canterbury set down for all time the thing that gives impetus to the theologian, namely the burning need to *comprehend* what faith believes: *Fides querenens intellectum.* Faith, if it is truly faith and not merely spiritual froth, plunges one headlong into a tenacious quest for understanding. The other statement that ought always to accompany Anselm's was penned by his earlier and more commanding forebear, Augustine of Hippo. *Si comprehendis, non est Deus.* If you think you comprehend, it's not God!

Only those who go a little way into the quest for understanding can imagine that theology provides answers to all questions. Some answers, it is true, are available to those who seek diligently. But always, beneath the answers, there is the great silence that has no other explanation than that of a Presence transcending all explanations. That Presence accepts all questions, but answers none definitively. And yet, now and again (and for those moments the theologian lives) there falls across one's path a bright ray of a thought so compelling that it fills the empty spaces of the mind and wonderfully consoles the sorrowing heart. One knows then, the silence notwithstanding, that one has brushed shoulders with the truth that passes, but does not scorn, understanding—truth that is *one* in a way that neither paradox nor contradiction may impede. And that, of course, is where theology in the deepest sense begins. That is also why it will never end.

NOTES

1. For the McGill-Emmanuel College Colloquium, November 1–3, 2019.
2. I am borrowing this term from the late Charles Davis.
3. Jürgen Moltmann, *The Crucified God: The Cross as the Foundation and Criticism of Christian Theology*, trans. by R. A. Wilson and John Bowden (London: S.C.M. Press, 1974), 72.
4. See, e.g. the doctoral dissertation of Mark Parent, completed for McGill University, under my direction.
5. See Tillich's *The Courage to Be* (New Haven, CT: Yale University Press, 1952).
6. See the book of that title: Wendell Berry, *What Are People For?* (1990; rpt. Berkeley, CA: Counterpoint, 2010).
7. Hall, Douglas John, *Thinking the Faith: Christian Theology in a North American Context* (Minneapolis, MN: Augsburg, 1989; paperback reprint: Minneapolis, MN: Fortress Press, 1991), 26.
8. Heschel, quoted in Hall, *Thinking the Faith*, 223–24 [italics added]. See Michael Chester, *Divine Pathos and Being Human: The Theology of Abraham Joshua Heschel* (London and Portland, OR: Valentine Mitchell, 2005).
9. Albert van den Heuvel. *The Humiliation of the Church* (Philadelphia, PA: Westminster Press, 1966).
10. Karl Rahner, S. J., *Mission and Grace: Essays in Pastoral Theology* (London, Melbourne, New York: Sheed and Ward, 1963), 25–26.
11. Martin Buber, *The Philosophy of Martin Buber*, ed. P. A. Schilpp and Maurice Friedman (La Salle, IL: Open Court, 1967), 716; quoted by Emil Fackenheim, *God's Presence in History* (New York: New York University Press, 1970), 61.

WORKS CITED

Berry, Wendell. *What Are People For?* 1990; rpt. Berkeley, CA: Counterpoint, 2010.

Buber, Martin. *The Philosophy of Martin Buber*. Edited by P. A. Schilpp and Maurice Friedman. La Salle: Open Court, 1967. Quoted also by Emil Fackenheim. *God's Presence in History*. New York: New York University Press, 1970.

Chester, Michael. *Divine Pathos and Being Human: The Theology of Abraham Joshua Heschel*. London and Portland, OR: Valentine Mitchell, 2005.

Hall, Douglas John. *Thinking the Faith: Christian Theology in a North American Context*. Minneapolis, MN: Augsburg, 1989; paperback reprint: Minneapolis, MN: Fortress Press, 1991.

Moltmann, Jürgen. *The Crucified God: The Cross as the Foundation and Criticism of Christian Theology*. Translated by R. A. Wilson and John Bowden. London: S.C.M. Press, 1974.

Rahner, Karl S. J. *Mission and Grace: Essays in Pastoral Theology*. London, Melbourne, New York: Sheed and Ward, 1963.

Tillich, Paul. *The Courage to Be*. New Haven, CT: Yale University Press, 1952.

van den Heuvel, Albert. *The Humiliation of the Church*. Philadelphia, PA: Westminster Press, 1966.

Bibliography

"Accounting for Hope." *Journal for Preachers*, Vol. 24, No. 4, Pentecost, 2001.
"Am Wendepunkt: Wird die christliche Religion ihre Adoleszenz ueberwinden?" *Die Theologie auf dem Weg in das dritte Jahrtausend -Festschrift fuer Juergen Moltmann zum 70. Geburtstag.* Edited by Carmen Krieg, Thomas Kucharz, and Miroslav Volf. Gueter5loh: Chr. Kaiser Verlagshaus, 1996.
"An Absurd Ambition." *Sharing the Practice*, Vol. XX, No. 3, Summer, 1997.
An Awkward Church. Theology and Worship Committee, Presbyterian Church (USA), 1993.
"Barmen: Lesson in Theology." *Toronto Journal of Theology*, Vol. L, No. 2, Fall, 1985.
"Beyond Cynicism and Credulity: On the Meaning of Christian Hope." *Princeton Seminary Bulletin*, Vol. VI, No. 3, New Series, 1985.
"Bound and Free: On Being a Christian Theologian." *Theology Today*, Vol. 59, No. 3, October, 2002.
Bound and Free: A Theologian's Journey. Minneapolis, MN: Fortress Press, 2005.
The Canada Crisis: A Christian Perspective. Toronto: Anglican Book Centre, 1980.
"Canada: Separate Stairways." *ARC*, Vol. 5, No. 2, Spring, 1978.
"The Canadian Context." *Hope for the World: Mission in a Global Context.* Louisville: Westminster John Knox Press, 2001.
"Christian Faithfulness on a Polluted Planet." *Signs of the Times: Resources for Social Faith.* Toronto: United Church of Canada, 1984.
"Christian Mission in a Post-Christendom World." *The Ecumenist*, Vol. 38, No. 2, Spring, 2001.
Christian Mission: The Stewardship of Life in the Kingdom of Death. New York City: Friendship Press, 1985.
"Christian Theology in a North American Context." *Kirisutokyo Kenkyu: Studies in the Christian Religion.* Kyoto, Japan, Vol. LI, No. 1, December, 1989.
"Christliche Theologie und interdisziplinaere Wissenschaft." *Siegner Hochschule Blaetter.* Heft 1, Jahrgang 4, Juni, 1981.

"Claiming the Vision for a Transformed Church." *Small Church Newsletter of the MSR Center for Rural Ministry*, Vol. 7, No. 2, June, 1996.

"Commencement Address: Wartburg Theological Seminary, Dubuque, Iowa—May 19, 2013." *Currents in Theology and Mission*, Vol. 40, No. 4, pp. 274–277.

"The Condemnation of Modernism and the Survival of Catholic Theology." *The Twentieth Century: A Theological Overview*. Edited by Gregory Baum. Ottawa: Novalis, 1999.

"Confessing Christ in a Post-Christendom Context." *The Ecumenical Review*, Vol. 52, No. 3, July, 2000.

"Confessing Christ in the Religiously Pluralistic Context." *Many Voices, One God: Being Faithful in a Pluralistic World-Essays in Honor of Shirley Guthrie*. Edited by Walter Brueggemann and George W. Stroup. Louisville: Westminster John Knox Press, 1998.

"Confessing Faith on the Edge of Empire: A Response to the Proposed 2005 'Statement of Faith.'" *Touchstone*, Vol. 23, pp. 7–21, September, 2005.

Confessing the Faith: Christian Theology in a North American Context. Minneapolis, MN: Fortress Press, 1996.

A Covenant Challenge to Our Broken World. Edited by Allen O. Miller. Atlanta: Darby Printing Company, 1982.

"Creation in Crisis." *Dianoia: A Liberal Arts Interdisciplinary Journal*, Vol. 2, No. 2, Spring, 1992.

"The Cross and Contemporary Culture." *Reinhold Niebuhr: And the Issues of Our Time*. Edited by Richard Harries. London and Oxford: Mowbray, 1986.

The Cross in Our Context: Jesus and the Suffering World. Minneapolis, MN: Fortress Press. 2003.

"Despair as the Spiritual Condition of Humankind at the Outset of the Twenty-First Century." *Journal For Preachers*, Vol. Xxv, No. I, Advent, 2001.

"Die Vielgestaltigkeit christlichen Zeugnisses im Spannungsfeld zwischen Wortgebundenheit und Contextbezug." *Oekumenische Erschleissung Martin Luthers*. Edited by Peter Manns and Harding Meyer. Paderborn und Frankfurt am Main: Verla Bonifatius u. Verlag Otto Lembeck, 1982.

"Discovering Gospel for the Here and Now." *The Living Pulpit*, Vol. 11, No. 1, January–March, 2002.

"The Diversity of Christian Witnessing in the Tension Between Word and Relation to the Context." *Luther's Ecumenical Significance*. Edited by Carter Lindberg and Harry McSorley. Philadelphia: Fortress Press, 1984.

Ecclesia Crucis: Church of the Cross. Chicago: Chicago Community Renewal Society and St. Paul's Church, 1980.

"Ecclesia Crucis: The Disciple Community and the Future of the Church in North America." *Theology and the Practice of Responsibility: Essays on Dietrich Bonhoeffer*. Edited by Wayne W. Floyd Jr. and Charles Marsh. New York: Union Seminary Quarterly Review, Vol. 46, Nos. 1–4, 1992.

"Ecclesia Crucis: The Theologic of Christian Awkwardness." *Church: Between Gospel and Culture*. Edited by George R. Hunsberger and Craig Van Gelder. Grand Rapids: William B. Eerdmans Publishing Company, 1996.

"Ecumenism: Twenty-First Century Possibilities." *Ecumenical People, Programs, Papers: Institute for Ecumenical and Cultural Research*. Collegeville, MN, May, 2002.

"Ein Anderes Bild von Christus." *Theologie der Gegenwart*. Muenster, Germany: 23 Jg., 1980/81.

The End of Christendom and the Future of Christianity. Harrisburg: Trinity Press International, 1995.

Etre image de Dieu. Translated by Louis Vaillancourt. Paris: Les Editions du Cerf; Montreal: Bellarmin, 1998.

"For and Against a Theology of Liberation." *ARC*, Vol. Xii, No. 2, Spring, 1980.

For Such a Time as This, Esther 4:14. Princeton, NJ: Institute for Youth Ministry, Princeton Theological Seminary, 2006.

"From Faith Majority to Faith Community." *The Observer*, Vol. 64, No. 10, New Series, May, 2001.

The Future of the Church: Where Are We Headed? Toronto: United Church Publishing House, 1989.

The Future of Religion in Canada. Sackville: The Ebbut Lecture, Mount Allison University, 1988.

"A Generalization on the Theological Situation of Protestantism in Quebec." *Theological Education in the 80's*, Fall, 1978.

God and Human Suffering: An Exercise in the Theology of the Cross. Minneapolis, MN: Augsburg, 1986.

"The Great War and the Theologians." The Twentieth Century: A Theological Overview. Edited by Gregory Baum. Maryknoll: Orbis Books, 1999.

Has the Church a Future? Philadelphia: Westminster Press, 1980.

Hope Against Hope: Towards an Indigenous Theology of the Cross. Geneva: World Student Christian Federation, 1972.

Imaging God: Dominion as Stewardship. Grand Rapids: Wm. B. Eerdmans Publishing Company, 1986.

"Interview." *The Future of Religion: Interviews with Christians on the Brink*. Edited by Bob Harvey. Ottawa: Novalis, 2001.

"Introduction." *More than Survival: Towards a Theology of Nation*. Don Mills: Canec Publishing & Supply House, 1980.

"Introduction" and "The Integrity of Creation: Biblical and Theological Background of the Term." *Reintegrating God's Creation: A Paper for Discussion*. Edited with James Lovelock, et al. Geneva: World Council of Churches, Church and Society Document No. 3, September, 1987.

"Introduction: The Scheme of Our Study: The Method of Correlation" and "Developing a Critical Theology." *A Covenant Challenge to Our Broken World*. Edited by Alen O. Miller. Atlanta: Darby, 1982.

"The Ironies of Reinhold Niebuhr." *Reinhold Niebuhr Revisited: Engagements with an American Original*. Edited by Daniel F. Rice. Mich: W.B. Eerdmans Pub. Co, 2009.

"JPIC: The Message and the Mission." *Ecumenical Review*. Geneva: World Council of Churches, Vol. 41, No. 4, October, 1989.

"Keeping the Church Together in a Pluralistic World." *Open Hands*, Vol. 16, No. 2, Fall, 2000.

Lighten Our Darkness: Toward an Indigenous Theology of the Cross. Philadelphia: The Westminster Press, 1976.

"Luther and the Peace Movement." *The Ecumenist*, Vol. 22, No. 4, May–June, 1984.

"Luther's Theology of the Cross." *Consensus: A Canadian Lutheran Journal of Theology*, Vol. 15, No. 2, 1989.

"Man and Nature in the Modern West: A Revolution of Images." *Man and Nature on the Prairies*. Edited by Richard Allen. Regina: Canadian Plains Research Centre, 1976.

The Messenger: Friendship, Faith and Finding One's Way. Eugene: Cascade Books, 2011.

Mission as a Function of Stewardship. Toronto: United Church of Canada, 1980.

"Mission as a Function of Stewardship." *Spotlighting Stewardship*. Edited by M. J. Parr. Toronto: Canec, 1981.

"The Modest Science: Christian Theology, the University, and the Church." Birks Lectures, 1995. *ARC*, Vol. 24, 1996.

"Moving Beyond the Haze of Christendom." *The Gospel and Our Culture*, Vol. 14, No. 1, March, 2002.

"The New Theology." *Canada and Its Future*. Toronto: Annual Report, Board of Evangelism and Social Service, United Church of Canada, 1967.

"New Way of Being Christian." *Christian Thought in the Twenty-First Century: Agenda for the Future*. Edited by Douglas H. Shantz and Tinu Ruparell. Eugene, OR: Cascade Books, 2012. "On Being the Church After Christendom." *In Essentials Unity: Reflections on the Nature and Purpose of the Church-Essays in Honor of Frederick R. Tros*. Edited by M. Douglas Meeks and Robert D. Mutton. Minneapolis: Kirk House Publishers, 2001.

"On Being the Church in English Montreal." *The Ecumenist*, Vol. 15, No. 6, September/October, 1977.

"On Being the Church in Quebec Today." *ARC*, Vol. 5, No. 1, Autumn, 1977.

"On Being Stewards." *Journal for Preachers*, Vol. XI, No. 1, Advent, 1987.

"On Contextuality in Christian Theology." *Toronto Journal of Theology*, Vol. 1, No. 1, Spring, 1985.

"Our New Challenge: Speak Hope from the Wilderness." *The Observer*, Vol. 63, No. 6, New Series, January, 2000.

"Peace Needs Women." *Faith that Transforms: Essays in Honor of Gregory Baum*. Edited by Mary Jo Leddy, Mary Ann Hinsdale, and Gregory Baum. New York: Paulist Press, 1987.

"The Post-Christendom Church in Rural Communities." *Word and World: Theology for Christian Ministry*, Vol. 20, No. 2, Spring, 2000.

"Preaching Lenten Discipline at the Start of a New Millennium." *Journal for Preachers*, Vol. 23, No. 2, Lent, 2000.

"Le Prix de la Grace: Dietrich Bonhoeffer." *La Vie Chretienne*, January/February, 1981.

Professing the Faith: Christian Theology in a North American Context. Minneapolis, MN: Fortress Press, 1993.
"La Question Nationale." *The Chelsea Journal,* Vol. 5, No. I, January/February, 1979.
The Reality of the Gospel and the Unreality of the Churches. Philadelphia: Westminster Press, 1975.
"Recasting the Mould: *Honest to God* in North America." *Honest to God.* 40th Anniversary Edition. Edited by John A. T. Robinson. Louisville: Westminster John Knox Press, 2002.
"Reconciling Memories." *Theology in Service of the Church: Essays in Honor of Joseph D. Small.* Edited by Charles Wiley, et al. Louisville: Geneva Press, 2008.
"Reflections on the Theme: Reclaiming the Text." *Journal for Preachers,* Vol. Xxiv, No. 1, Advent, 2000.
"Reinhold Niebuhr: An American Theologian." *Journal of Theology for Southern Africa,* No. 79, June, 1992.
Reinhold Niebuhr (1892–1971): A Centenary Appraisal. Edited by Gary A. Gaudin. Atlanta: Scholars Press, 1994.
"Religion and Empire: Triumph or Trap?" *Alternatives: An Alternative Lifestyle Newsletter,* Vol. 13, No. 3, Fall, 1987.
Remembered Voices: Reclaiming the Legacy of "Neo-Orthodoxy" Louisville: Westminster/John Knox Press, 1998.
"Rethinking Christ." *The Theological Roots of Christian Antisemitism.* Edited by Alan Davies. New York: Paulist Press, 1979.
"Saving Words: A Theological Response to the Twentieth-Century Crisis of Language." *Word and World: Theology for Christian Ministry,* Vol. 20, No. 1, Winter, 2000.
"The Significance of George Grant's Cultural Analysis." *George Grant in Process: Essays and Conversations.* Edited by Larry Schmidt. Toronto: House of Anansi, 1978.
"A Song from the Basement." *DCE Directions,* Fall, 1994.
"The Spirit to the Churches: Justice, Peace and the Integrity of Creation." *Minutes: Sixteenth General Synod, United Church of Christ.* Cleveland, June, 1987.
"The Spirit Speaks to Today's Churches." *Perspectives: A Journal of Reformed Thought,* Vol. 3, No. 5, May, 1988.
"The State of the Ark: Lessons from Seoul." *Between the Flood and the Rainbow.* Edited by D. Preman Niles. Geneva: World Council of Churches Publications, 1992.
The Steward: A Biblical Symbol Come of Age. New York City: Friendship Press, 1982.
"Stewardship as a Missional Discipline." *Journal for Preachers,* Vol. Xxii, No. 1, Advent, 1998.
The Stewardship of Life in the Kingdom of Death. Revised Edition. Grand Rapids: Wm. B. Eerdms Publishing Company, 1988.
"Telling the Story; Living the Story: Classical Protestantism's Tenets Threatened in Post-Christian World." *The Presbyterian Record,* Vol. 9, 2005.

"Theological Education as Character Formation?" *Theological Education*, Supplement 1, 1988.

"A Theological Proposal for the Church's Response to Its Context." *Currents in Theology and Mission*, Vol. 22, No. 6, December, 1995.

"Theological Reflections on Shusaku Endo's *Silence*." *Interpretation*, Vol. x:xxiii, No. 3, July, 1979.

"A Theological Response to the 20th Century Crisis of Language." *Yanjing Journal of Theology*, No. 2, 2001.

"Theology Between the Tradition and a Banana Peel: A Perspective on Theology for Christian Ministry." *Word and World*, Vol. X, No. 3, Summer, 1990.

"The Theology and Ethics of the Lord's Prayer." *The Lord's Prayer: Perspectives for Reclaiming Christian Prayer*. Edited by Daniel L. Migliore. Grand Rapids: William B. Eerdmans Publishing Company, 1993.

"The Theology and Ethics of the Lord's Prayer." *The 1991 Frederick Neuman Symposium on the Theological Interpretation of Scripture; The Princeton Seminary Bulletin*, Supplementary Issue No. 2, 1992.

"Theology Is an Earth Science." *Faith that Transforms: Essays in Honour of Gregory Baum*. New York/Mahwah: Paulist Press, 1987.

"The Theology of the Cross and Covenanting for World Peace: A North American Reflection." *Covenanting for Peace and Justice*. Edited by Choan-Seng Song. Geneva: World Alliance of Reformed Churches, 1989.

"The Theology of the Cross and the Quest for World Peace." *ARC*, Vol. Xiii, No. 1, Autumn, 1985.

"The Theology of Hope in an Officially Optimistic Society." *Religion in Life*, Vol. XL, No. 3, Autumn, 1976.

"Think, for the Night Is Coming." *The Living Pulpit*, Vol. 5, No. 3, September, 1996.

"Thinking Biblically About the Trinity." *The Living Pulpit*, Vol. 8, No. 2, April–June, 1999.

"Thinking the Faith in Canada." *Seeds*, 28 September, 1984.

Thinking the Faith: Christian Theology in a North American Context. Minneapolis, MN: Augsburg, 1989; paperback reprint: Minneapolis, MN: Fortress Press, 1991.

"Thinking the Faith on the North American College Campus." *Plumbline: A Journal of Ministry in Higher Education*, Summer, 1996.

This World Must Not Be Abandoned. Toronto: Church World Development & Relief, 1981.

"Three Theses on the Role of the Church in International Affairs." *Eglise et Systeme Mondial: The Church and World Systems*. Edited by Annemarie Jacomy-Milette, et al. Quebec: l'universite Laval, 1980.

"To Whom Shall We Go?" *No Other Foundation*, Vol. L, No. l, March, 1980.

"Towards a Theological Perspective on Human Sexuality." *Biblical and Theological Understanding of Sexuality and Family Life*. Toronto: Canadian Council of Churches, Faith and Order Commission, November, 1969.

"Towards an Indigenous Theology of the Cross." *A Christian Declaration of Human Rights*. Edited by Allen Miller. Grand Rapids: William B. Eerdmans Publishing Co., 1977.

"Towards an Indigenous Theology of the Cross." *Interpretation*, Bicentennial Edition, Vol. Xxx, No. 3, 1976.

"Towards an Indigenous Theology of the Cross." *Theology and Technology*. Edited by Carl Mitcham and Jim Grote. London: University Press of America, 1984.

"The United Church of Canada: A Drama in Three Acts." *Living the Experience: in the United Church of Canada, 1925–2000: Theological Digest and Outlook*, Vol. 15, Special Issue, 2000.

"*Usus Crucis*: The Use and Abuse of the Cross and the Practice of Resurrection." *Encounters with Luther: New Directions for Critical Studies*. Edited by Kirsi Irmeli Stjerna and Brooks Schramm. Louisville: Westminster John Knox Press, 2016.

"A View from the Edge of Empire: Prophetic Faith and the Crises of Our Time." *ARC*, Vol. 20, 1992.

Waiting for Gospel: An Appeal to the Dispirited Remnants of Protestant "Establishment." Eugene, OR: Cascade Books, 2012.

What Christianity Is Not: An Exercise in 'negative' Theology. Eugene, OR: Cascade Books, 2013.

"What Is Theology?" *Cross Currents*, Vol. 53, No. 2, Summer, 2003.

When You Pray: Thinking Your Way into God's World. Valley Forge: Judson Press, 1987.

"Who Tells the World's Story?" *Interpretation*, Vol. xxxvi, No. 1, January, 1982.

Why Christian? For Those on the Edge of Faith. Minneapolis, MN: Fortress Press, 1998.

"A World Unfolding." *The Observer*, Vol. 63, No. 3, New Series, October, 1999.

And David B. Lott. *Douglas John Hall: Collected Readings*. Minneapolis, MN: Fortress Press, 2013.

And Rosemary Radford Ruether. *God and the Nations*. Minneapolis, MN: Fortress Press, 1995.

Index

Note: Page numbers followed by "n" refer to notes.

Abba, 140
Acts 2:17, 149
agape, 88, 124
age of mobilization, 41n9
Anfechtung, 52
Anthropocene, 85, 88, 89, 91, 95;
    becoming human in, 95–96;
    reimaging theo-anthropology in,
    85–98
Apostle Paul, 105, 158
apostolic succession, 124
Auschwitz, 131–33, 138
authenticity, 61, 64, 112, 123, 124, 136,
    148

bad theologies, 170
Banting, Keith, 21
baptism, 139, 158
Barmen Confession, 121, 126
Barrow, Simon, 149
Barth, Karl, 105
*Believing Again: Doubt and Faith in a
    Secular Age,* 31
Berry, Thomas, 73
Berry, Wendell, 170

Bible, 73, 75, 77, 79, 106, 109, 110,
    144, 146
biblical prophets, 148, 149
biblical story, 155–57
Billings, Todd, 160
biodiversity, 71
biographical connections, 30–32
The Body Keeps the Score, 159
Bonhoeffer, Dietrich, 74, 79, 121, 172
Book of Confessions, 126
Book of Praises, 155, 156
*Bound and Free: A Theologian's
    Journey,* 3
Bowler, Kate, 154
Buber, Martin, 136, 175

Calder, Alexander, 9
Canada, 18, 21, 22, 30, 31, 45, 47, 49,
    51, 53, 57, 58, 60, 62, 64; contextual
    theology in, 45–55
Canada Crisis, 18, 52
*The Canada Crisis: A Christian
    Perspective,* 18, 52
Canadian Broadcasting Corporation, 15
cancer, 154, 156–59, 161

Caputo, John, 10
Cardinal, Harold, 48
Christendom, post-Christendom, xiii, xiv, xv, 4, 17, 18, 24, 35, 58, 65, 76, 78, 101–13, 131–41. *See also individual entries*
Christian ecological theology, 70, 80
Christian eschatology, 23
Christian faith, 77, 119, 122, 125, 136, 157, 169
Christianity, 3–6, 18, 73, 101, 117, 118, 122, 127, 147, 148
Christians, 9, 16–18, 63, 64, 118, 119, 123, 124, 135, 147, 157, 169, 171
Christian Theology in a North American Context, 6, 118
Christology, 140, 147
chronological approach, 2, 4
churches. once mainline church, 34, 46, 51, 53, 57, 59–61, 63, 65, 103, 111–13, 126, 137, 139, 172–74
church history, 144
church's liturgy, 140
climate change, 21, 22, 71, 73, 76, 79
climate crisis, 3, 8, 21, 22, 24, 69–71, 76–80, 90
Cold War, 18, 20, 74, 103
colonial, colonizing, colonize, xiii, xiv, xv, 18, 29, 46, 51, 57, 58, 59, 61, 63, 65, 66, 85, 148
Cone, James, 10
Confessing the Faith, 77, 80, 119
confession, 119, 121, 126, 148, 170
contemporary theologies, 7, 155
contextual theology, Canada, 45–55; contextual and covenant, 45–47; covenant, testament, and treaty, 49–51; cross, testament and theology, 51–53
conversational approaches, 8–11
1 Corinthians 1:25, 75
1 Corinthians 13, 42n16
1 Corinthians 15:42–49, 161
2 Corinthians 5:19, 150
The Cost of Discipleship, 121

courage, 63, 65, 90, 91, 95, 105, 167, 168, 175
covenant, 45–47, 49–51; theology, 46, 47; of works, 46
covert despair, 103, 104, 106, 108, 110, 112
credible humanity, 134, 135, 137, 139, 140
critical theology, 165
"Cross and Context: How My Mind Has Changed," 3
Cross and Cosmos: A Theology of Difficult Glory, 10
The Cross in Our Context, 88
cross pressure, 39–40
crucifixion, 61–63, 66, 161
cruciform love, 110–13
cruciform power, 106, 109, 110
Cuba, 121, 124–27
Cuban Church: "authenticity" and, 124–25; Barmen Confession and, 126; nature of mission in, 126–27
cultural anachronisms, 4
curators, 1, 2, 5, 7, 9, 137

darkness, 3–6, 9–11, 72–75, 88, 171, 174
death, 2, 39, 40, 52, 53, 74, 88–91, 94, 95, 157, 158, 162
de-colonial, de-colonize, de-colonizing, xiii, xiv, xv, 86, 88, 89, 91, 95
decontextual approaches, 6–8
despair, 17, 19, 53, 87, 90, 103–6, 108, 110, 112, 121, 123
discipleship, 8, 121, 173
dis-illusioned hope, 23–24
divine, 62, 64, 93, 94, 108, 109, 131, 133, 134, 136–40
divine-human relationship, 64, 66–67, 136, 137
divine pathos, 52, 88, 143–47, 149, 171; God suffering with us, 143–45; and Heschel, Abraham, 145–46; memory of, 143–51
dominant theological traditions, 75, 76

domination power, 105, 106, 108–12

early Church roots, 135–38
Ecclesiastes, 166
ecclesiology, 123
eco-anxiety, 90
ecological theology, 70, 72–75, 80
economic inequality, 17, 21, 23, 70
ecotherapy, 91, 92
Emmanuel. *See* Jesus Christ
Encuentro Nacional Eclesial Cubano (ENEC), 125
end of Christendom, 60
"The End of History?," 20
environmental crisis, 16, 85, 90, 92
epistles of Paul, 136
Ese sol del mundo moral, 124
ethic of authenticity, 41n11
evaluative approaches, 5–7
excarnation, 41n11
Ezekiel 10, 144

faith, 7, 17, 18, 29–42, 50, 75, 77, 79, 80, 90, 92, 102, 119–20, 123, 126
faith communities, 91, 141, 159
Father, Son, and Holy Spirit (God), 139
Father Almighty, 78, 122
A Fault in Our Stars, 154
Florovsky, George, 170
Foreman, Dave, 141n1
Forster, E. M., 169
Fox, Matthew, 73
fragilization, 29, 31, 33, 35–40; of belief, 36, 39
Fukuyama, Francis, 20

Gaia theory images, 89
Genesis 1, 143
Genesis 1:28, 73
Genesis 2, 143
Genesis 2–3, 89
gift of authenticity, 63–65
God and Human Suffering, 4, 5, 79, 155
God and the Nations, 123
God in Search of Man, 145, 146

God's *shalom*, 149
Golding, William, 89
Golgotha!, 88
goodness, 15, 20, 62–64, 86, 87, 102
goodness of creation, 61–63
gospel, 17, 60, 104, 131–33, 135–41, 168, 171; of irresolution, 153–62; rewilding, 131–42
Grant, George, 72
Green, John, 154
Greene-McCreight, Kathryn, 156

Hagen, Kenneth, 50
Haldimand Tract, 45
Hall, Anthony, 48
Hall, Douglas John, 1–3, 29, 64, 66, 85–88, 131, 165, 166, 168, 170, 172, 174; "authenticity" and Cuban Church, 124–25; Barmen Confession and Cuban Church, 126; becoming human, 89; being-with, ontology of communion, 107–9; contextual theology, elements, 16–19; doctrine of Western Christendom, 109–12; eco-theology of cross, 69–83; God and Church, 101–15; and Hebrew Bible, 147–48; journey to the cross, 88; redemption and, 106–7; relevance of theology, Cuban context, 117–28; rethinking God and Church, 109–12; theology, 16, 36, 38, 69, 70, 118, 120, 121; time and place, 102–4. *See also individual entries*
Hansen, James, 70
Hebrew Bible, 143, 145, 147–48
Hebrew scriptures, 140
Heidelberg Disputation, 52, 61, 86
Heschel, Abraham, 75, 143, 145; and Divine Pathos, 145–46; and prophets, 146–47
Hildebrant, Walter, 48
historic Christianity, 131–35
historic church, 133, 136, 137, 139
history of Christian thought, 109, 131

holocaust, 132
hope, 3, 15, 17, 19, 21, 23
hope against hope, 3
Hosea 2, 144
human beings, 10, 72, 73, 106, 111, 134, 168
human creature, 61, 86–89, 95, 108
humanity, 64, 65, 67, 69–73, 102, 103, 122, 134, 135, 137, 144
human life, 85–87, 89, 92, 134
human love, 157

illness, 153–55, 157–60, 162
illusions, 11, 15, 16, 19, 21, 23, 24, 87, 167, 168; post-cold war Global North, 19–22
Imaging God, 74
imago nominis, 86, 87
immanent frame, 37, 38; creatures, 37–39
incarnational theology, 93
Indian Residential Schools, 57–67
Israel, 47, 61, 132, 134, 138, 145, 148, 171

Jenson, David, 161
Jeremiah 31:31, 149
Jerusalem, 108, 133, 134, 137–39, 148, 157 161
Jesus Christ, 36, 39, 50, 75, 112, 131, 133–40, 147, 156–58, 161, 169–71
Jewishness, 138–41
Johnson, Lyndon, 22
Judaism, 131–33

Käsemann, Ernst, 169
Kavanaugh, Brett, 15
kenosis, 78, 93
kenotic theology, 94
Khashoggi, Jamal, 15
kingdom of death, 74, 79, 80, 89, 96
"Kitamori Kazo: Theologian of the Pain of God," 150n5
Klein, Naomi, 22–24, 71
Kolbert, Elizabeth, 71

Kristallnacht, 141
Kyoto Protocol, 22

lament, 88, 91, 160
Latin theory of the atonement, 170
laws of nature, 79
Letters and Papers from Prison, 74
liberal churches, 60
liberal democracies, 20, 21, 23
"The Life of Animals in Japanese Art," 2
lifework, 2, 6
Lighten Our Darkness, 4, 9, 72, 74
liturgy, 139–41
"Lose Your Illusions. It's an Ugly, Dystopian World," 15
Lovelock, James, 70, 89
Luke 24:5, 157
Lundin, Roger, 31
Luther, Martin, 39, 61, 66, 75, 92, 105, 120, 158, 170; theology, 50, 75, 76, 153

Macdonald, Neil, 15, 19
Mañach, Jorge, 125
Man Is Not Alone, 145
Mark 9, 39
market capitalism, 71
matter of faith, 77
McFague, Sallie, 86, 92–93; becoming human, 94; journey to the cross, 93–94
McKenna-McBride Commission, 58
methodism, 59
Micheli, Jason, 158
mitsein (being-with), 77, 88, 105, 107, 108, 113
Moltmann, Jürgen, 36, 105
monism of love, 122
Morrison, Bill, 10
mortality, 148, 158, 168, 171
Myles, John, 21
myth of Sisyphus, 87

neo-Niebuhrian, 69

Newer Testament, 136, 137
Newman, Barnett, 8
New York, 167, 168
Nguyen, Viet Thanh, 10
Niebuhr, Reinhold, 70, 105
North America, 9, 17, 18, 45, 46, 58–60, 86, 87, 104, 118–20
Noss, Reed, 141n1

officially optimistic society, 72–75
"The Older Brothers," 62
Older Testament, 140
ontology of communion, 107–9
optimism, 59, 70, 80, 103, 104
optimistic anthropology of liberalism, 77
Ortiz, Fernando, 125
Otto, Rudolph, 146

Parousia, 162
pastoral theology, 120
1 Peter 4:12–17, 172
Pihkala, Panu, 86, 90–91; becoming human, 91–92; journey to the cross, 91
political theology, 76
Pope Pius XII, 172
Post, Pastor JoAnn, 159
post-Christendom church, 111, 139
powers, 59, 78, 86–88, 101–12, 117, 146, 158; of death, 89, 91
Professing the Faith, 79, 119
prophetic theology, 118
prophets, 72, 146–49, 171
Protestantism, 117, 119
Protestant Principle, 117
Protestant Reformation, 117
providence of God, 76–80
Psalm 88, 156
Psalms, 87, 140, 155, 156, 160, 167

Qoheleth, 166, 167

Rahner, Karl, 174
Rambo, Shelly, 155

reappropriation, 39–40
redemptive power, 65
reductionism, 18
residential schools, 51, 60, 61, 65–67
resurrected body, 161
resurrection of Jesus Christ, 23
The Return of History: Conflict, Migration, and Geopolitics in the Twenty-First Century, 20
Rhineland Calvinists, 46
Romans 4:18, 8:24, 169
Romans 11, 172
Rothko, Mark, 8
Ruether, R. R., 123
Ryerson, Egerton, 59

sacrament, 50, 158, 174
salvation, 137
Sarpi, Paolo, 32
Scheel, Camille, 161
School of Antioch, 105, 170
Schumacher, E. F., 174
secular, 32–36
secular age, 30–33, 35, 37–40
A Secular Age, 31, 40n4
sense of place, 17
shalom, 149, 150
Shields, T. T., 170
sin of estrangement, 63–64
Sisyphus imitating Prometheus, 87
Sisyphus/Prometheus phenomena, 91
Sittler, Joseph, 108
Small is Beautiful, 174
socially constructed silence, 90
social necrophilia, 74
Sölle, Dorothee, 153
Soul, Michael, 141n1
State of the World 2010 report, 92
The Steward: A Biblical Symbol Come of Age, 74
stewardship, 4, 6–8, 74, 75, 79
The Stewardship of Life in the Kingdom of Death, 74, 79, 80
suffering, 155
suffering love, 108, 110

suffering of the church, 172–75
The Sympathizer, 10
systematic theology, 90

Taylor, Charles, 30, 31, 38
Terrien, Samuel, 167
testament, 47, 49–53, 75, 77, 79, 133, 135
thematic approach, 5–6
theologia crucis (theology of the cross), 36, 52, 61, 70, 75–76, 88, 101–15, 120, 158, 168–72; contemporary church and, 65–67; and gift of authenticity, 63–65; and goodness of creation, 61–63; residential schools and, 60–65; and sin of estrangement, 63–64; theological and faith posture, 75–76
theologia gloriae (theology of glory), x, xiv, 51, 75, 76, 86, 87, 88, 105, 154
theological liberalism, 59
theological tradition, 78, 101, 105
theological work, 4, 118, 120
theology of testament, 51
Theology of the Pain of God: The First Original Theology from Japan, 150n5
Thinking the Faith, 7, 75, 76, 118, 123
This Changes Everything: Capitalism vs. the Climate, 22
three secularities, 32; Secular 0 (S-zero), 32–33; Secular 1 (S1), 33–34; Secular 2 (S2), 34–35; Secular 3 (S3), 35–36
Thunberg, Greta, 21
Tillich, Paul, 117, 147, 170
Tintoretto, Jacopo, 1, 2
Toronto Journal of Theology, 70
Toru, Asakawa, 150n5
transformation, 95, 106, 111, 149
trauma, 38, 62, 155, 156, 158–62
TRC Calls to Action, 46, 51

"A Treatise on the New Testament, that is, the Holy Mass," 50
Treaty Elders of Saskatchewan, 48
truth, 45, 62, 65, 136, 137, 139–41, 159, 161, 167, 174–76
Truth and Reconciliation Commission (TRC), 45, 46, 51, 65
Turtle Island, 45, 47, 53

United Church, 31, 57, 59, 60, 63, 64
United Church of Canada, 57, 58, 60, 62
United Nations Environmental Program (UNEP), 22
United States, 11, 22, 30, 33, 34, 49, 74, 168

van den Heuvel, Albert, 173
van der Kolk, Bessel, 159
"Venus Syndrome," 70
Vitier, Cintio, 124
Vizenor, Gerald, 49
Vonnegut, Kurt, 170
vulnerability, 86, 88, 91, 95, 111, 112, 159, 166, 167

Waiting for Gospel, 4, 74
Warrior, Robert, 47
Waters, Augustus, 154
Welsh, Jennifer, 20, 21, 23, 24
What Christianity Is Not, 3
White, Lynn, 73
Wiesel, Elie, 171
wilderness, 89, 95, 144, 146
Williams, Dolores, 10
Wiman, Christian, 156, 157
worship, 39, 102, 105, 140, 158–60

Yom HaShoah, 141

zone of truth, 165–68
Zuidgeest, Piet, 156

About the Contributors

Harris Athanasiadis
Rev. Dr. Athanasiadis is a minister at Armour Heights Presbyterian Church in Toronto, Canada, and a sessional lecturer in theology at Knox College at the University of Toronto. He studied under the supervision of Dr. Hall during his BTh and PhD degrees. He is author of *George Grant and The Theology of the Cross* (University of Toronto Press, 2001), and other articles on theology of the cross.

Michael Bourgeois
Professor Bourgeois recently retired as associate professor of theology at Emmanuel College of Victoria University in the University of Toronto, where he taught historical, contextual, and constructive theologies. He is author of several articles and chapters, and most recently contributor and coeditor of *The Theology of the United Church of Canada* (McGill-Queen's, 2019).

Walter Brueggemann
Rev. Professor Brueggemann continues to frame an era on theology and the church. Professor emeritus in Old Testament, Columbia Theological Seminary, Decatur, GA, he is author of over one hundred books and innumerable articles and is known throughout the global community as someone who uses the lenses of literary and sociological analyses when interpreting the Bible. He is considered the most influential Old Testament scholar of his generation. He has written widely critiquing Empire and seeking out just ways of living together in peace with justice in North American church and society.

Gary Gaudin
Rev. Dr. Gaudin recently retired after forty years as "theologian-in-residence" (or pastor) in a number of different contexts across Canada. Under the guidance of Douglas John Hall, Gary completed his doctoral research on Hope in post-Shoah Jewish Theology and Its Implications for Jewish-Christian Dialogue.

Adolfo Ham
Professor Ham is professor emeritus at Matanzas Evangelical Seminary in Cuba. He has been a leader in Protestant liberation theology of Latin America and in the worldwide and Cuban church over the decades since the Cuban revolution. He is author of several books and articles and a close friend of Douglas John Hall.

Allen G. Jorgenson
Rev. Dr. Jorgenson is professor of systematic theology at Martin Luther University College in Waterloo, Ontario. He is ordained in the Evangelical Lutheran Church in Canada (ELCIC) and is author of several articles and books. His most recent works include "Theology, Immigration and First Nations Foundations" in *Strangers in this World: Reflections on Immigration*, eds. Allen G. Jorgenson, Alexander Y. Hwang, and Hussam Timani (Fortress Press, 2020).

David Lott
Mr. Lott served as an editor for many years with the Alban Institute and Fortress Press. Following this he edited both *Douglas John Hall: Collected Readings* (Fortress Press, 2013) and *Sallie McFague: Collected Readings* (Fortress Press, 2013). He has been involved in several key works of contemporary theology over the last decades.

Patricia G. Kirkpatrick
Rev. Professor Kirkpatrick is associate professor of Old Testament studies in the School of Religious Studies at McGill University. She is the author of *The Old Testament and Folklore Study* (Sheffield Academic Press, 1988) and the editor, with Timothy Goltz, of *The Function of Ancient Historiography in Biblical and Cognate Studies* (LHBOTS; Bloomsbury T. & T. Clark, 2008), and has written articles on facets of folklore and the Hebrew Bible in ecumenical dialogue. She is an ordained priest in the Anglican Church of Canada.

Pamela R. McCarroll
Rev. Professor McCarroll is associate professor of practical theology and director of the MPS at Emmanuel College of Victoria University in the University of Toronto. She is author of *At the End of Hope, the Beginning*

(Fortress Press, 2014) and *Waiting at the Foot of the Cross* (Pickwick, 2013), and is editor and author of several other books and articles. She is ordained as minister of Word and Sacrament in the Presbyterian Church in Canada.

Andrew Root
Professor Root is the Carrie Olson Baalson Professor of Youth and Family Ministry at Luther Seminary. He is the author of several books, including *Faith Formation in a Secular Age* (Baker, 2017), *The Pastor in a Secular Age* (Baker, 2019), and *Christopraxis: A Practical Theology of the Cross* (Fortress Press, 2014).

Deanna A. Thompson
Professor Thompson is director of the Lutheran Center for Faith, Values, and Community and Martin E. Marty Regents Chair in Religion and the Academy at St. Olaf College in Northfield, Minnesota. Prior to this she was at Hamline University for several years. She is author of several books, including *The Virtual Body of Christ in a Suffering World* (Abingdon, 2016) and most recently, *Glimpsing Resurrection: Cancer, Trauma, and Ministry* (Westminster John Knox, 2018).

Brian Thorpe
Rev. Dr. Thorpe is minister emeritus at Pacific Spirit United Church in Vancouver and a Sessional Lecturer at the Vancouver School of Theology. He was a student of Douglas John Hall at St. Andrew's College in Saskatoon and at McGill University in Montreal. For ten years, he worked as senior advisor for the United Church of Canada, helping to construct the church's response to the legacy of its involvement in the Indian Residential Schools system.

Harold Wells
Rev. Dr. Wells is an ordained minister of the United Church of Canada who served as minister of three pastoral charges in Ontario, and taught Theology in Lesotho (southern Africa). He is professor emeritus of systematic theology, Emmanuel College, University of Toronto, and is author of *The Christic Centre* (Orbis, 2004), as well as dozens of scholarly articles, chapters, and books.

Douglas John Hall
Professor Hall is a member of the Order of Canada, emeritus professor of theology at McGill University in Montreal, Quebec, and ordained in the United Church of Canada. Prior to joining the McGill Faculty of Religious Studies in 1975, he was MacDougald Professor of Systematic Theology at St.

Andrew's College in the University of Saskatchewan (1965–1975), Principal of St. Paul's College in the University of Waterloo (1962–1965), and minister of St. Andrew's Church in Blind River, Ontario (1960–1962).

Professor Hall was born in 1928 in Ingersoll, Ontario. He attended high school and business college in Woodstock, Ontario, and worked for four years in that city's daily newspaper. In 1948–1949, he studied composition and piano at the Royal Conservatory of Music in Toronto. He graduated (Bachelor of Arts) from the University of Western Ontario (London) in 1953. His graduate degrees are all from Union Theological Seminary in New York City: Master of Divinity (1956), Master of Sacred Theology (1957), and Doctor of Theology (1963).

Professor Hall continues to be one of the most influential theologians in the North American context in the last half century. The author of twenty-four published books, including a three-volume systematic theology (Fortress), and numerous articles, Hall lectured widely in the United States and Canada between 1974 and 2010. His books continue to be essential reading for those being formed for leadership and thought in once-mainline Protestantism. Professor Hall was Gastprofessor at the University of Siegen, Germany, in 1980; visiting scholar at Doshisha University in Kyoto, Japan, in 1989; professor of Theology at the Melanchthon Institute of Houston, Texas, in 1999; member of the Campbell Seminar on the Future of the Church at Columbia Seminary of Decatur, Georgia, in 2000; distinguished visiting professor at Trinity Lutheran Seminary, Columbus, Ohio, in 2001; Theologian-in-Residence, Church of the Crossroads in Honolulu, Hawaii, in 2003 (and after); and Theologian-in-Residence, International Protestant Church in Vienna, also in 2003.

Professor Hall has been an active participant in many international consultations, including the World Convocation of the World Council of Churches (WCC) in Seoul, South Korea (1990) and the UN AIDS theological symposium in Namibia (2003). He has served on the theological committees of the WCC and the World Alliance of Reformed Churches, the United Church of Canada, and The National Council of Churches USA, among others.

www.ingramcontent.com/pod-product-compliance
Lightning Source LLC
Chambersburg PA
CBHW070830300426
44111CB00014B/2510